LAND AND ENVIRONMENT

The Survival of the English Countryside

By the same author:

THE ENGLISH VILLAGE
DARTINGTON HALL (with W. B. Curry)
IN A LIBERAL TRADITION
FARMING THE LAND
EXPLORING PARISH CHURCHES
SOLDIER TRUE
SURGEON IN THE CRIMEA (ed.)

LAND AND ENVIRONMENT

The Survival of the English Countryside

by
VICTOR BONHAM-CARTER

RUTHERFORD • MADISON • TEANECK
FAIRLEIGH DICKINSON UNIVERSITY PRESS

137691

LAND AND ENVIRONMENT: THE SURVIVAL OF THE ENGLISH
COUNTRYSIDE. © Victor Bonham-Carter 1971. First
American edition published 1973 by Associated Uni-
versity Presses, Inc., Cranbury, New Jersey 08512

Library of Congress Catalogue Card Number: 72-3522

ISBN: 0-8386-1195-8
Printed in the United States of America

To

ROBERT WALLER

Acknowledgments

All sources of information, published or unpublished, are made clear in the Notes, if not in the text proper. I would like however to record my thanks for permission to make longer quotations from, or to use by way of reference, the following books:

Forestry in the English Landscape, by Roger O. Miles, Faber, 1967.
Farmer's Glory, by A. G. Street, Faber, 1932.
Problems of Rural Life, by C. S. Orwin, C.U.P., 1945.
Estate Villages, by M. A. Havinden in collaboration with D. S. Thornton and P. D. Wood, Lund Humphries for the University of Reading, 1966.
The Orators, Book II, 'Six Odes', IV by W. H. Auden, Faber, 1966.
'Land and Human Population', by Sir Joseph Hutchinson, C.M.G., Sc.D., F.R.S., *Advancement of Science*, Vol. 23 (September, 1966).
'Maximum Profit—Not Maximum Output', by H. G. C. Sexton, *Country Life*, 2nd July, 1970.
Modern Architecture and Rural Planning, by John Weller, Architectural Press, 1967.

I would like also to express my gratitude to my wife and all those kind friends who have endured my reading to them long passages from the manuscript, whether they liked it or not. Errors and terrors, if any, are of my making.

Victor Bonham-Carter
Spring 1971

East Anstey
North Devon

Contents

Illustrations

Key to acknowledgments

1 National Parks Commission
2 University of Reading, Museum of Rural Life
3 *Farmers Weekly*
4 Author
5 Crown copyright
6 Hereford City Library

7 Messrs Tayler and Green, Lowestoft, architects
8 Countryside Commission
9 British Insulated Callender's Cables Ltd
10 Soil Association
11 Richard Rushton, Dartington

Map

Introduction

This book is about the countryside of England; very little about other parts of the United Kingdom. In no sense is it a detailed guide to landscape, fauna, flora or villages: each of which is a subject in its own right, each with a bibliography as long as your arm. Nor does it contain a catalogue of Government departments, voluntary societies and Acts of Parliament, though I do mention many of these things as I go along. Environment comes into it of course, and there is a great deal about farming, since this concerns the primary use of the land. In essence the book is about man's attitude to the countryside, traced historically and told simply, right up to the present day. It looks forward as well as back.

I am not writing for experts but for people who, like myself, want to know what the experts say. There are many of us, and we are anxious. We are bewildered and disturbed by the radical changes that seem rapidly to be destroying the countryside: not only the rate at which towns and factories and motorways are eating up the land, but the way in which farmers are forcing husbandry into an industrial straitjacket. Economics and environment seem to be fighting each other to death. We are sorry too about the collapse of rural society. We regret the loss of hedges and hayricks, the rape of villages, and all the familiar features of country life we read about or used to know. We are told this is a sterile sentiment—mere sentimentality. We cannot mummify life anywhere, certainly not on the land; and for that reason preservation has become a dirty word. Instead we have a new word—conservation—which may be a quibble, but it is meant to convey a profounder understanding of what is at stake.

Much is now being written about the value of the surroundings in which we live. Ecology—the science of environment—is revealing its complexity and vulnerability: the forces and resources of Nature, how they interact, the danger that derives from disturbing their equilibrium. Pollution has become a bugbear, and none too soon. Beauty is being admitted here and there as an essential, not an extra. Yet as we begin to get a grasp, the problems proliferate. With a population rising to nearly seventy million by the year 2000, the majority living in England, and with urban development swallowing land at a rate equal to converting a county the size of Worcestershire into concrete every ten years—we have to ask ourselves the most urgent questions.

Will there be by the end of the century enough countryside to breathe in, live on, live off? Is the present trend so inflexible that we can do nothing about it? Are we going to freewheel to extinction? As this is literally a matter of life and death, it is difficult in the small hours sometimes not to panic, not to shrug the whole thing off on to the 'wonders' of science, or—if you are old enough—not to deaden thought by intoning the invocation, *après moi le déluge*, until you fall asleep again. With the arrival of breakfast and return of courage, you realise that facts must precede answers; and that means going back to the beginning. How has it all happened? I believe that history provides most of the clues, and that is how I am approaching the subject in this book.

Part One traces the civilisation of the English countryside up to and since the Industrial Revolution. It describes how in the nineteenth and twentieth centuries industry divorced farming (and other rural employments) from the national economy, hastened the separation of country life and town life, and undermined the marriage between man and his natural environment. It ends with the technical rehabilitation of the land during the Second World War, and refers to the preliminaries to post-war legislation.

Part Two outlines the approach to amenity, in its sense as a series of movements, mostly conducted by townspeople, to protect the countryside for the sake of its wild life, its beauty, and its opportunities for leisure: merging with early essays in the control of land use. Amenity is defined as 'the enhancement of life through the agency of environment'. It is a tale mainly of isolated attempts at repairing the damage done by industrialism: and is extended by an account of the formative years of the Dartington Hall Estate in Devon, a comprehensive experiment in re-marriage between town and country—hence its relevance here.

Part Three considers what has been happening to the countryman's countryside since the Second World War: particularly the industrialisation of farming, the expansion of forestry, the place of rural industries, and the reaction of village life to modern pressures and mobility, and it tries to look a little into the future. It also reflects briefly upon the concern for conservation, and the demand for land—for work, living and leisure—by a growing population that threatens to engulf our capacity to contain it.

The Postscript is not an afterthought, but a commentary on some of the significant events that occurred between manuscript and proof.

The Appendix, written by Robert Waller of The Soil Association, is entitled 'The Organic Answer' and speaks for itself.

Although my aim is to tell the story from the inside, from the countryside *outwards*, I believe that the way forward lies in the integration of townside and countryside: not the imposition of one civilisation upon the other, nor progressive suburbanisation which passes for both but is neither. Since we are predominantly a nation of townsmen, it is difficult to resist the urban attitude which seeps daily into the consciousness, if it is not more crudely put over. While paying lip service to rural life, at heart the townsman is inclined to regard the countryside in one of two ways: either as raw material for urban use, be it a building site or a holiday playground; or as a museum where the *status quo* must be preserved, and kept free from urban influences. Both views, though diametrically opposed, represent the two sides of the same coin.

Integration is something very different. First, it implies recognition: that the land is a living, changing, entity; the source of food, water, and other primary resources essential to existence; but also a habitat in which none of these resources can be won without the operation of natural forces and organisms, of which we still have an imperfect understanding. In the past, though far more ignorant than he is today, man gained a living from the land more or less by rule of thumb, and suited society to his economic needs, and vice versa. He combined his business and his way of life, without having to distinguish too closely between them, if at all. He was not always successful in maintaining this vital balance. There were disasters; but so long as he respected what he did not know, he got by. When respect failed, he failed; and this accounts, for example, for the soil erosion of the Mediterranean seaboard, as a result of monocropping, the wholesale felling of trees, and the destruction of vegetation by goats. No sensible person suggests that we should put the clock back in the countryside in any slavish manner, or that we should stop invention or scientific research. That would be impossible as well as silly. But the principle remains of respecting what we do not know, and of tailoring our techniques to the limitations of our knowledge. By transgressing that principle, notably by over-specialisation in agriculture for economic ends (be it monoculture, the exclusive use of inorganic fertilisers, or livestock concentration), we have jumped into a maelstrom of dietary and environmental troubles. Sir George Stapledon, of whom more anon, wrote:

> Allow for what we do not know. The more powerful our weapons, and the more we use them to single purposes (the modern fashion: Nature abhors single purposes) so we plunge ever more deeply into inter-play of forces which we are not watching or are beyond our power to watch.[1]*

Secondly, integration means peaceful penetration to mutual advantage. Take two examples. Village society has declined ever since the town took away its industries. Agriculture was rarely, if ever, the sole employment in the countryside; and so the loss of alternative work disturbed and weakened the social balance. With good communications there is no reason why selected small industry should not flow back into

* See Notes, pp. 225–235.

the countryside, and establish modern units in villages and country towns. This would both relieve pressure on built-up areas and help reinvigorate country life, humanly and financially. True, this has happened already in parts of industrial England, where however the lack of planning and gross misuse of soil and landscape has resulted in a chaotic countryside. This is not the aim, and need not happen again. In deep or relatively unspoiled country, the process properly controlled would bring great benefits.

Conversely most townsmen need Nature on their doorstep. They demonstrate their preference by getting out of town at weekends and for summer holidays, and by enduring the tedium of commuting in order to have a home in the country or neo-country. Garden Cities and New Towns for permanent living; access to National and Country Parks; the creation of Nature Reserves and conservation areas; these are some of the solutions offered. They may go far towards success— towards alleviating the spiritual frustration of the age which derives, in large part at any rate, from sheer physical imprisonment.

Robert Waller, the biographer and interpreter of Stapledon, and a creative philosopher in his own right, develops the theme:

> Stapledon points out that the frustration of the need for wild and open countryside in modern man is as great as that of his sexual frustration and will in time probably become considerably greater. It is this frustration which accounts for as much neurosis as anything else in our neurosis-ridden age. To bring town and country closer together again without losing the character of either, to give the industrial worker the access to countryside that he had in medieval times, will be to restore a healthy psyche to contemporary man, renew his will to work and break down the massive and menacing consolidation of a proletariat that pursues affluence for its own sake, because it has no means of satisfying the basic emotions on which man—without realising it—has depended since time immemorial for his happiness.[2]

It is fruitless nowadays to argue that the civilisation of the countryside must remain inviolate and be perpetuated in past forms. The countryside lost its virginity long ago, the forms have largely vanished, and Giles is no longer with us. George Ewart Evans has recorded his customs and his character with accuracy and insight in his documentaries about East Anglia,[3] and in the same region the author of *Akenfield*[4] has described the metamorphosis of an agricultural community. The literature of the old life of the countryside is legion, and we have an abundant record of the skills, institutions, and attitudes of countrymen and women in all parts of the British Isles. We cannot recapture country life as it was, though we rightly revere and enjoy the relics.

Many farmers today are further away in thought and deed from their predecessors, than are townsmen. This does not prevent or excuse us however from respecting Nature, or through conscious knowledge from exercising wisdom in our treatment of the environment—wisdom which the old people possessed by intuition and experience.

The fact is that practically everyone today, townsman or countryman, is in varying degree a sophisticated person and lives simultaneously at two levels. At one level we depend upon and enjoy many of the material and other advantages of our age—electricity, cars, television, the printed word, piped water, packed foods, any amount of ready-made goods and useful services. The list is endless, and our ability to profit from these things is largely determined by choice and purchasing power. That is the level common to all, whether we live in a block of flats and sell insurance, or in a tied cottage and milk cows. The real differences occur at the personal level, where we are indeed beings apart, each with his or her intimate interests and relationships; and we need these differences in order both to alleviate collective pressures and make best use of common advantages. Of course today, as in the past, what we individually think and do is strongly influenced by inheritance, education and environment; but so far as the countryside is concerned, even those who live relatively remote lives are distinguished far less than formerly by the idiosyncrasies of their calling, or by ignorance of affairs. A visit to the nearest large town is no longer a seven-day wonder, nor is a trip to London or Birmingham the unique experience of a lifetime. To live in isolation is already an anachronism. The everyday world is becoming a wide and open place. This is to the good, for we shall need all our reserves of sophisticated knowledge and understanding in order to control our destinies—in order, in other words, to survive. The man of tomorrow must recognise that he does live on two levels. He will *consciously* have to combine his collective life with his individual life, and accept the fact that he is a hybrid: which means, in this tight little island of ours, being part-townsman, part-countryman, the balance swinging up or down according to circumstances. Many of us are in this position already. I for one.

*   *   *

When I was a young man, there was an inverted snobbery about being a countryman. A sense of superiority in defeat. It was, I think, a form of defence assumed by farmers and others dependent on the land, who were rightly resentful of the way agriculture had been abandoned after the First World War. The feeling is not totally absent today, and is present too in the minds of townsmen who feel cut off from the countryside and who hate the artificiality of their lives. In the 1930s it was but one fact of wider social discontent: expressed variously in politics, pacifism, and vividly to young people in the poetry of Auden, Spender and Day Lewis, especially of Auden. We felt we were living in a top-heavy country, run to fat, owned and controlled by a handful of rich men, who were literally consuming the capital accumulated in the past. How little times change! In those days however we were tamer, more submissive, more inhibited. We did not wear beards, go drugging, live openly with our girl friends, or march in many demonstrations. Some of us did join the march from Jarrow, attend unemployed camps, go social servicing in the East End or the mining valleys of South Wales, join the International Brigade in the Spanish Civil War, and generally were a nuisance to—rather than the despair of—our parents.

I was twelve years old at the time of the Great Strike in 1926, and grew up to awareness in the midst of massive unemployment and stark poverty in the meaner streets. With my expensive education at Winchester and Cambridge, and a comfortable home, I felt a parasite. I read Left Book Club books avidly and became, in theory only, a Socialist. I was not brave enough to go to Spain, not ready in my mind to break away and flout my parents, though I did cause them plenty of pain. Specifi-.cally I wanted somehow to get on to the land, live simply, and find the fundamental values. It was all very starry-eyed. My father, a regular soldier and a liberal-minded man, was very patient; and he made no objection to my switching to an agricultural course in my last year at Cambridge. I saw no future in continuing with the Modern Languages Tripos. What was the use of Norman French and Middle High German, compared to the realities of A. G. Street's *Farmer's Glory*?

But my father was cautious. Farming was not his world. He knew no farmers, and one of his brothers, my Uncle Edgar—a distinguished colonial administrator—had said straight, 'No gentleman goes into farming.' Having no capital to spare—anyway it was a mad thing to do at that time and without practical knowledge and experience—my father simply wanted to see me in a safe and congenial job, preferably a profession with recognised qualifications. He therefore suggested I should go in for land agency, and arranged for me to be attached to the agent of the Marquis of Bath at Maiden Bradley—a plum start in a very pleasant office. At the last moment I cried off, and cost my father a fat fee by way of compensation. It was the summit of ingratitude. I became a by-word among the Bonham-Carters for bloody-mindedness, and was written off as a bad hat. In fact no one felt more disgusted with myself than I; but in the midst of misery I felt that to settle down at Maiden Bradley was merely to tag along with the Establishment. I had no wish to face another four years of exams, deal with tenants, go hunting, make up weekend shooting parties, or play any part in the socially superior side of country life. All that seemed to me effete. Of course I should have made this clear long before, but my mind was far from clear. I simply felt I wanted to get close to the soil and live a simple life. Put into words even now it sounds silly; it sounded even sillier then. The ordinary run of back-to-the-landers were a pretty loopy lot; and the alternative would have been to find a farmer who would have given me work for my keep. No doubt I should have done that, without asking anyone's help or permission. But I could hear the amazed cries: 'What— become a farmhand after an education and upbringing that has cost thousands?'

But I did something else, entirely alone. I answered an advertisement for a learner on *The Countryman*, and Robertson Scott, owner and editor of the magazine, took me on. One day I shall record that experience, but not here. This is not my autobiography, and I have referred to Robertson Scott in a related context later in this book. Suffice it to say that, although our association was short, Scott gave me my start in the world I wanted, and I am grateful to him for that.

I was in London in quite different employment when the war started, but six years in the army did not diminish my love for the land; and I whiled away the tedium of many hours reading up the subject. George Henderson's *Farming Ladder* fired me, also Lady Eve Balfour's book on soil and organic husbandry,[5] Stapledon's work in Wales,[6] above all C. S. Orwin on the economics of farming and country life generally.[7] But reading after all is like stoking a boiler. It raises a head of steam— then what? In my case I already had a safety valve. In 1938 I had married Audrey Stogdon, and in that same year—while still earning my living in London—we managed to rent a farm cottage under Inkpen Beacon in the far corner of Berkshire. Soon afterwards we built a house close by, and during the war my wife cultivated a smallholding and milked cows. When peace came I managed to dig myself into village life, playing cricket, chairing the Parish Council, and even got myself elected to the County Council after an exciting re-count. Most important of all, I did the donkey work in securing, draining, sowing and fencing a seven-acre playing field for the parish. All this gave me plenty of insight into the inner workings of village life. Inkpen was still a fairly well-balanced community, though physically scattered. There was farm work, a sawmills, and some domestic and estate employment; while Newbury and Hungerford were not too far off for men to travel to work daily and retain their roots in the village. But the old life was visibly weakening. Church and chapel loyalties were on the wane; one of the inns had closed down, and the local baker had given up. The established families were being replaced by newcomers who did up their cottages, but seemed to take little interest in the parish as a community. I felt that the playing field—with football and cricket pitches, and a corner for the children—was the most hopeful sign for the future; and it certainly was popular.

In 1947 however we decided to go full out as farmers. Unable to expand our holding or pay the prices of the few local farms that came on to the market, we sold up and sought our fortune in the West Country. Eventually, after looking at nearly thirty farms, we ended up at Brushford near Dulverton in west Somerset. There we settled into a roughish 130-acre farm, hitherto ranched for beef and sheep, part of it heavy clay in the valley fields, all full of rushes and 'arse-smart' (*persicaria*), part of it shaley soil under old pasture on the side of the hill, with a few flat fields on top. This again is another story, to be recounted elsewhere. Briefly we converted the entire holding to dairy and pigs; drained, ploughed and re-seeded some fifty acres of scrub, adapted the tough old shippons, built silos, laid on water and electricity; and for twelve years worked ourselves to the bone with precious little return. But it was an experience that neither my wife nor I would have missed: physically strenuous, mentally exacting, and at times financially desperate. We felt ourselves to be pioneers, and at least had the satisfaction of leaving the farm to our successors in far better shape than we had found it.

During those years we both played an active part in the village. Brushford was far less scattered than Inkpen. For that reason, and because it was at least twenty miles from the nearest town (and 175 miles from London), indeed surprisingly unaffected by contemporary change, it was a far tighter, more integrated community. I soon found myself a school manager and parish councillor again, and my wife an active member of the Women's Institute. Indeed, in time, we both performed a remarkable number of roles. Thanks to a succession of good parsons of the old sort, the church was well filled and well run, and the focus of the village. The place hummed, and in the ordinary way I should still be farming there today.

For economic reasons however—for example, paying for the education of our two sons—I soon found I had to earn a second income. That led to broadcasting at Bristol, ordinary journalism, and writing books—my first, *The English Village*, a Pelican published in 1952, fortunately did well and helped square a lot of bills. Moreover writing deepened knowledge and broadened understanding. Having to write about farming, local history, and what made people tick in the countryside, gave me the opportunity to travel about the region and study contemporary problems in a way I would never have been able to do, if I had stayed on the farm day in day out. But the biggest stroke of luck followed a broadcast about the Dartington Hall Estate at Totnes, where the Trustees commissioned me to write a history of the enterprise, since its inception in 1925. I have given some account of this in Part Two. It meant visiting Dartington—some fifty miles away—about once a fortnight, to collect material and see people; and then coming home to fight off sleep before and after farm work in the intervening days, to write it all down and try and make sense of a very complicated subject. Dartington was and is an education in itself: that is, the entire enterprise of farms, woodlands, industries, school, arts college, and all the multifarious activities that make up the Estate. It took me six years to work out the basic story, another year to write the book, and a further eight to establish a records office and bring my history up to date. As related in Part Two, I have no hesitation in saying that Dartington is at the same time the most practical and the most visionary experiment in re-creating country life in an urban age.

The intention of these paragraphs is not to tell my own life story, but to illustrate a theme from personal experience. I am a hybrid townsman-countryman; and I believe that is what many of us are becoming and want to become. I still have my home in the West Country, but combine it with working in London to earn my bread and butter. I no longer farm, but I am deeply engaged in the affairs of Exmoor and, having been a farmer, believe that—working with friends and colleagues in the Exmoor Society and the National Park administration— I can contribute useful 'hybrid' knowledge: especially at moments of tension, when farmers on Exmoor resent the intrusion of visitors (and the damage that they do, often unwittingly), and when visitors do not see why they should be shut out from the wide moorland, in an area that is meant to be available for public enjoyment.

*   *   *

Foreigners are coming to Exmoor in larger numbers every year. I often wonder what they think, not only of Exmoor, but of the English countryside at large. England, as opposed to Scotland and Wales, is not highly rated as a holiday country in foreign terms. We have a long way to go yet in the standard of food and accommodation, and in making our countryside presentable and accessible. So I suggest it is salutary to try and look at our land and ourselves through foreign eyes. Fantasy often finds out truth.

I believe that to see England for the first time is an excitement. You peer down through the windows of the aircraft at the map-board below you, or stare over the side of the ship at the approaching cliffs; and you are curious. It depends of course on whom you are—North or South American, Australasian, European, African, Easterner—on how you have been indoctrinated, on what you actually know. At the barest you may have seen posters of the Changing of the Guard, bought a record of the Beatles, followed football, read Dickens or Ian Fleming. You are aware that the British once owned an empire but have now lost it; that none the less they still have stately homes with lords living in them, popular royalty, a social calendar, the academic aura of Oxford and Cambridge. There is a confusing conflict of tradition and iconoclasm: the City Englishman with his brief-case and bowler hat; the militant student with his vari-skirted girl friend. Hyde Park, Buckingham Palace, King's Road—where is the real England? For a foreigner it is difficult to resist the feeling that everything happens in London: or possibly in the lesser Londons of Liverpool, Manchester, Birmingham or Leeds. The English countryside—what there is of it—you may not be aware that any exists at all, unless you happened to see some of the serene Dorset downland so gorgeously revealed in *Far from the Madding Crowd*; but that was a film, and about the past, suspect therefore on both counts.

Let us suppose that you, as a foreigner, have come to look more closely and see for yourself. You will be surprised. There are many towns, it is true, some of them contiguous or continuous, London a vast sprawl; but there is country too, far more than you had realised and gloriously green. Farming is obviously an active enterprise, mechanised, lightly manned, and in great variety: cherry orchards and hop gardens in populous Kent, sheep runs in East Riding, stretches of sugar beet in flat East Anglian fens, corn prairies in rolling Wiltshire, mixed husbandry in many counties. Hedges and hardwoods may seem extremely English to you; but you will find familiarity in the softwood forests of Kielder in Northumberland, and you may be reminded of Alpine foothills in the Lakes. One thing is clear. England has an immensely variegated landscape and, for such a small and heavily populated country, it is still remarkably intact.

The historian will tell you that there is a paradox in all this. Although God made the land, man moulded the landscape. Even the intact areas, even the relatively wild stretches of hill and moorland where human impact is slight, but above all the pleasing complex of field and hedge-row punctuated by farmsteads—all these are the result of deliberate development, and derive in the main from a distant age. At least the agrarian alterations of the eighteenth century seem remote, and what happened before then even more so: separated not only by time but by the barrier of industrialism, which began the age we live in now. To judge by what you see, those distant developments were done by a sure hand with a sense of enhancement: the placing and proportion of the buildings, the harmony of materials, the ability to work with the contours of Nature.

It is the charm of these survivals that is most disturbing; the impression is one, not merely of nostalgia, rather of a countryside where man is losing his touch. Disharmony is made plain in a hundred ways. It may be an old quarry choked with tins, a cluster of plastic bags blowing about a field, or what was once a living hedge of beech and thorn—now a raw line of concrete posts and mesh netting. Contrasts tell the tale. They are more obvious in the country than in the town, for although many urban Saharas still exist, we are becoming aware at last that we have to suit our towns to human needs. The same lesson—once an axiom so manifest that no one questioned it—has yet to be re-learned on the land. Whereas a town draws strength from the very fact it is a town—a place of business and manufacture, and a centre of population which serves the needs of settled existence—the country is in quite a different situation. With far fewer people in it and a long record of decline, it has come to be regarded as the poor relation—fair game for anyone who wants to patronise or exploit it.

History shows—in England at any rate—that once man progressed beyond the bare struggle to survive, a dichotomy crept into his attitude to the land. At first no bigger than a baby's hand, yet it was there; and, like a cancer, it lay dormant until some new force liberated its growth. In farm politics it has become familiar in the catch query, 'Business or Way of Life?' Yet the same question troubled people in the fifteenth as in the twentieth century. Sheep runs destroyed feudalism, as later agricultural improvement and enclosure destroyed the English peasantry, when the lowland landscape was transformed from weedy open fields and commons into hedge-bound holdings, more or less as we know them today. Rural society suffered severely in the process, but as profit-making began to dominate agriculture after about the 1770s, it brought benefits too, culminating in the short period of prosperity following the Repeal of the Corn Laws in the mid-nineteenth century. It was only when commercial agriculture finally lost out to industry after the 1870s, that the real rub came.

By then great damage had been done—and much more was to come—not merely to the economy and hierarchy of the countryside, which anyway had glaring faults and were never immutable, but in a far more serious way: thoughtless destruction of natural resources, disfigurement of the landscape, and a loss of contact between man and the land. This is not a lament for pre-Industrial England, no nostalgia here, but a statement of historical fact, which we are seeing in perspective today. We are now beginning to assess the legacy of the past, while knowing full well that nothing could have stopped the Industrial Revolution, and that without it we should not now be enjoying the benefits and the affluence which we have come to regard as our right in this country.

The use of land for living and making a living is not only justifiable but essential. Land is literally the foundation of our existence. The problem is how to use it so as to satisfy both requirements without mutual detriment and, above all, without killing Mother Goose herself. In the past ignorance of science and belief in a divine morality kept the balance. Man stood in awe of the unknown, and that fact alone usually determined his behaviour, or at least set limits to the worst he could do. But when the barriers began to fall, first of science, then of the dogmas of religion (and of morality based upon religion), there was little left but habit of mind and the strength of tradition to stop man running wild. And he did run wild—and is still running wild—outraging the environment without regard to his neighbour or posterity, and multiplying in the process: so that as demand feeds on all that nurtures it, the pace of 'progress' escalates.

Later historians may regard the Second World War as a turning-point in the record of land use. I adopt that view—with caution. Nothing is ever finite in time, but when you take into account the ledger of earlier events and actions, the date will serve. Since 1945 we have, as a nation, begun to realise—first in one way, then in another, but not yet by far in every way—that we have to apply rules to our behaviour, especially in our treatment of the countryside. This is a matter of self-interest, let alone of morality. Yet we are still glaringly inconsistent. With one hand we restore agriculture as a national industry, with the other we saw through the branch it sits on, expecting it to yield more and more food from a diminishing area of land. This leads to the industrialisation of farming at all costs, with consequences deleterious it seems to both Nature and man. The need for control has been recognised in post-war legislation; but the business of making control work in relation to the right use of our resources is continually hindered, often nullified, by the sheer scale and diversity of the problems of existence: above all by the inexorable pressure of a rising population in an overcrowded island.

Is survival therefore first and foremost a matter of numbers? This is not rhetoric but a question which, some experts say, unless it is answered all else fails. The countryside will be extinguished in a hopeless race to contain and sustain our bodies. Yet this first and foremost problem is the last to be taken seriously by the Government.

Writing in the first issue of *The Ecologist*, Dr Aubrey Manning wants:

> A country with great variety: cities, towns, villages, farmland and empty wilderness with clear-cut divisions between them, a country with many relics of the past, clear and easy to study and with rich wild life—it would be difficult enough to get this if our population stayed constant, there is no hope if it grows much more. How can the planners be so myopic as not to realise that, to plan an environment for man, we must begin by planning the numbers of man himself.

Time is running out.

PART ONE

Business or Way of Life?

The history of the land is a good guide, not merely to rural society, but to all society. Most people in England take for granted there will always be food for their plate and drink for their glass. They have very little idea of how the means of life are produced; and they jog along in a pullulating population that is swallowing up land for other purposes. They even criticise farming in the terms expressed at the head of the page: as if the alternatives were valid and the answer was easy. It is not; moreover it does not affect farmers only. Ultimately land concerns everyone; and it is because we have lost sight of that fact, that the conundrum comes up at all.

In a peasant country, the question is unnecessary, because it is a matter not of alternatives but of identity. For the peasant his business *is* his way of life, and he would not grasp the point if you put it to him. This was true of England at least until the end of the Middle Ages, when land was acknowledged both as the physical basis of living and as the foundation of society. As a collective asset it was collectively controlled by land tenure and farm practice.

Social Farming: to 1500
The system derived in effect from the Anglo-Saxons who settled in England in the six hundred years between A.D. 449, when Hengist and Horsa arrived in Kent by invitation, and A.D. 1066 when William I landed in Sussex without being asked at all. Unlike the Romans, the Anglo-Saxons were a wholly rural people. They distrusted towns, camped outside the abandoned streets and colonnades, and set up a co-operative system of settlement and farming. As time passed their rude democracy developed into a loose hierarchy of landlord and tenant, with the king as the ultimate dispenser of law and power, closely watched by the Church. The man on the land was nominally free; and the Danish-descended peasant who had forced his way into the east of England during Anglo-Saxon times was better off still. Yet freedom for all tillers of soil and tenders of stock, whatever their grade and origin, was always relative. Theirs was a life of grinding toil, governed by the sheer necessity of tearing a living from the earth, and by the obligations of defence and social order. In return they received protection and the rule of law, however rudimentary. In the higher ranks duties were of different kinds, often of military service; while, throughout the state, there emerged the elements of a money economy and a fiscal system which gradually grew in complexity. Even so, after six hundred years,

the Anglo-Saxon-Scandinavian Englishman still lived and worked in a fairly free society of his own making. Other than a few landless labourers, he was not without rights. With starvation never far away, what mattered was survival. All men were aware that by sustaining each other, they sustained themselves; and that meant maintaining a manorial system founded upon care for the land.

The Normans did not abolish the old order, but hardened it and gave it a character of their own. While all land vested in the sovereign as before, William I introduced a far tighter system of allegiance and obligation, and re-distributed the estates between the Crown, the Church, and the ruling families who supported him. He further strengthened his hold by means of the Domesday Survey of 1085–6, a body of statistics about the occupation, resources and value of land over the whole country. Thus, although the anatomy of the state altered little, the tissue changed a great deal; and the effect was to diminish personal freedom. Freemen survived, especially in the Danish areas of England, in the border counties, and in other pastoral hilly regions where the peasants had hacked their own holdings out of the waste. Elsewhere, particularly in the midlands and the south, many farmers were degraded into a new unfree class of tenants, represented principally by the villein, who was closely bound to the manor and the soil.

The life of the villein was fettered by a forest of obligations: by week work and boon work on the lord's demesne, by enforced payments in corn and honey, and by an array of fines and galling duties. Beneath these burdens he and his family tilled their strips in the open arable fields and tended their stock upon the common grazings, in community with their neighbours: yet always lacking the liberty to move away from the village or dispose of the properties they served. So regarded the villein's life was one of near-slavery. None the less service was rendered him in the manor court, where most villagers played their part as jurors and officers, and justice in the shire court by the king's representative. All men, from the freeman to the serf, were countrymen in an overriding sense: the blacksmith who beat iron into ox and horse shoes, the tanner, the ropemaker, and all the craftsmen who fashioned goods and exercised skill; likewise the fishermen, the miners, the priests who farmed their own glebe, and even the lord's own servants and retainers. They all added up to a multitude of self-contained, very nearly self-sufficient, communities all over England. Land was every man's business and every man's way of life; while the ownership of it was the hallmark of prestige and aristocratic wealth.

Socially rigid as the manorial system was, various influences were soon at work which ultimately broke it down altogether. The movement was like a slow swell at sea, gathering force with the rise in population, the growth of towns, and the spread of trade by means of markets and fairs. There emerged an insistent demand for the surplus produce of the countryside, over and above what was required for local life. On many manors it encouraged the commutation of feudal services. In the twelfth century men began to pay their rents in money, while the lord used the cash to hire labour for the land. Besides this, the production of wool began to be highly profitable, not only for villagers and the lord of the manor, but—more to the point—for large-scale farmers who created immense sheep runs in the Cotswolds and the West Country, the border hills, northern dales, southern downs and eastern fens. The pioneer entrepreneur was the Church, especially the great monastic estates belonging to the Benedictines and the Cistercians, and certain orders of nuns. It used to be said that 'if the Abbot of Glastonbury could marry the Abbess of Shaftesbury, their first-born would inherit more land than the King of England'. Having trained administrators and the necessary capital, the Church was better organised even than the King to manage land and promote trade: applying its resources to corn-growing, stock-rearing, land drainage and reclamation, building, and wool production. In short it actively encouraged the conception of farming as a business, rather than a mere means of subsistence, though deprecating commercial enterprise at the expense of the community. And if at times the two ideas seemed to conflict, the Church could always point to its achievements as the founder of schools and alms-houses, and its general concern for men's souls.

English wool was of good quality, much prized by the weavers of France and Italy. Its export rapidly accounted for a large part of the nation's wealth, although at least by the middle of the fourteenth century the pattern of trade had begun to alter. As home manufacture displaced the export of raw material—and the work was chiefly done in humble cottages, prior to marketing in the towns—so a new element of industry entered into village life. Moreover, the success of sheep pro-voked a social as well as an economic revolution. Shepherding required few hands and a low investment, and led to sheep runs being so extended, especially in the midlands, that whole villages were oblit-erated. Elsewhere also lords of the manor began taking in large areas of the common waste for the same purpose, and so deprived the village farmers of an important part of their living—the right to turn out stock to forage, gather fuel, house timber and thatching materials. They also found it profitable to let off their demesne lands as separate farms, enclosing them with fences.

All this, however, was still at an early stage, when the security of a socially minded agricultural society was suddenly and brutally under-mined by the ravages of the Black Death. Between 1348 and 1350 the population was reduced by a third, possibly by a half. All over the countryside land lay untilled, cottages and hamlets deserted, and the price of labour rose quickly by fifty per cent. This had immediate consequences. It made the lord of the manor chary of commuting further services, and in some cases the process was reversed, as labour—even for hire—was hard to come by. In other instances land had to be sold freehold, since no man could be found to work it, nor any tenant to rent it. It also made life difficult for the sitting occupier in that, while the rent remained constant, his household and family—his earning power—had been diminished by disease. Finally it put the labourer in a position to bargain for better wages and conditions. Of this he took full advantage. Many broke the rules of the manor, left home and found work with any employer willing to pay more, no questions asked.

Parliament stepped in, and from 1349 onwards passed a series of Statutes of Labourers, designed to freeze wages and restore economic order: a policy dictated mainly by the yeomen, or substantial village farmers, who had made money in wool and in cultivating demesne lands rented from the lord of the manor. Desperate attempts were made to restore the *status quo*. Justices of the Peace were appointed by the Crown to assess wages locally and enforce the law: an action, ironically, that weakened still further the manorial system, for wage-fixing had hitherto been one of the main functions of the manor court. Yet the drift continued and tensions grew, culminating in the Peasants' Revolt of 1381.

Not all the rebels were peasants (in the sense of depressed country-men), but included all those who wanted the abolition of villeinage and of manorial dues and restraints, land to be let at a perpetual rent of fourpence per acre, with free buying and selling. There was a strong element of Christian Socialism mixed in with the movement, inspired by parish priests and friars who hated servitude and the privileges of wealth no less than the lowly layman. In the end the revolt was put down. Its aims none the less were achieved with time.

*　　*　　*

The Rise of Commercial Farming: 1500–1750
The Peasants' Revolt achieved no millennium. By breaking the bonds of feudalism, the peasant laid himself open to the fluctuations of com-mercial enterprise and gained a form of freedom that proved as arduous as the discipline of the manor. However the commercial age did not arrive overnight, for no new epoch is born and no declining system dies in a day. Although in character the Middle Ages overran the year 1500, time was already running out for those who thought that the divisions in society should remain fixed as of right, with the lower orders tied to the land; and that commerce required constant correction and control. Likewise it makes rough sense to look upon the sixteenth century as the beginning of modern times, since out of it emerged attitudes that have enjoyed acceptance ever since.

The whole Tudor period was one of revolutionary change, and of astounding vigour and pace. The philosophy of Humanism opened windows from which men could scan the horizon of their surroundings. It helped them rediscover antiquity and appreciate the pagan glories of Greece and Rome without any sense of sin. It set the fuse for the Reformation which, in England, meant something far more than a squabble over doctrine or breaking with the Pope or even seizing monastic lands. It provoked an aggressive sense of national identity; made religion intelligible, intensely interesting and personal; and sowed the seeds of the Civil War of the next century. It released the full force of the Renaissance, expressed in the flowering of literature and the arts, and in the genius of Shakespeare.

For all this there was a price to pay—the ascending power of a new section of English society, the middle class, which put a premium on economic effort and shrugged its shoulders at the inequalities of social change.

There was not a great deal of difference between middle-class Elizabethan Englishmen, whether they lived in town or country. Few places outside London exceeded 10,000 inhabitants, and all were countryfied in appearance and atmosphere. Merchants were essentially countrymen come to town, engaged in cloth or any one of a hundred other trades, living in solid half-timbered or stone houses, each with its large garden. The families dressed and ate well, were lettered, and the daughters learned elegant as well as domestic accomplishments. The bolder spirits ventured abroad. The more conscientious founded schools and charities, or conferred some practical improvement—such as a conduit or a causeway—on their town. They were well able to ride the rise in prices, caused partly by the influx of gold from the Americas by way of Spain, partly by Henry VIII's debasement of the coinage, and partly by the slow recovery in population after the Black Death. Indeed by good business they made good profits in an expanding market. In general they governed their own communities as burgesses, aldermen, and Justices of the Peace. They had little to fear from the old feudal aristocracy, most of whom had disappeared in the Wars of the Roses. Of the latter, though some survived in outmoded castles, others had sense enough to apprentice their younger sons to trade and the professions, and so re-enter the stream of English life.

The merchant's counterpart in the country was the yeoman, a term difficult to define with any precision. He might be a freeholder farming his own property, or a tenant occupying land on lease or at the will of the landlord, or a copyholder paying a fixed rent by title of a copy of the manor court-roll. Or again he might be a big capitalist farmer, who had got his hands on to a large slice of Church property after the dissolution of the monasteries in 1539. Already there were examples of yeomen farming several hundred acres and living like gentry, though the average holding was probably between fifty and a hundred acres, worked by the farmer, aided by his family and hired labour.

A yeoman's property might consist of unfenced plots parcelled out among the open fields; or it might be consolidated and enclosed; or a mixture of both. Farmers on the make preferred to fence for reasons of practical management and good husbandry. Some of them succeeded in enclosing by agreement with their neighbours: a process that continued slowly over the years and later provided the opportunity for scientific improvements. Others, as mentioned earlier, went sheep ranching, threw farms together, took in common waste, and swallowed up whole villages. The State frowned on actions of this kind, and endeavoured by statute to restrict enclosure for pasture. When the law proved ineffectual, men took it into their own hands. Led by their manor officers, villagers sallied out to tear down fences and scatter the encroaching flocks. Even so, it is estimated that by 1550 half a million acres of arable land had been lost to pasture, and some fifty thousand people put out of business by sheep enclosures.

Since for reasons of defence it was concerned to encourage *all* countrymen, Parliament was in two minds about the matter. A depopulated countryside weakened the nation's fibre, and 'shepherds be but ill archers'. Yet the yeoman—encloser or otherwise—was much admired for his vigour, his independence, and his success. It was men of his sort, and the thriving driving merchants,[1] who contributed most to the prosperity of the age: a glory still reflected in the noble churches and monuments, the strong serene houses, and the ample market places and halls, in places as far apart as Chipping Camden in the Cotswolds and Lavenham in Suffolk.

For all his admirable qualities, the yeoman was not sole master nor even main occupier in the countryside. Below him in the rural hierarchy ranged a variable class of smallholder: each with a cottage and five, ten, or twenty acres of land, rented or owned, with the usual common rights; and who supplemented his living by working for his neighbours. The craftsman might also cultivate a few acres and keep a cow, in addition to plying his trade. At the bottom of the scale stood the landless labourer, who had to rely entirely on his wages. If housed by his employer, he was probably better off than if he lived out. Sure of food and lodging, he was accepted by the household and earned two to three pounds a year, or about half the amount paid to other workers. Skilled men, such as stockmen, earned more still and were given privileges, while piece and casual workers might secure even better terms in the busy season, up to a shilling a day. Low as these rates seem, they enabled a countryman and his family to get by in an average year. In bad times however they were insufficient. The landless labourer was the first to suffer, and now that he was no longer tied to the manor, nor the manor to him, it was he who formed the bulk of the beggars who roamed the countryside. Yet farm servants were by no means settled in their station. Some saved enough to start up on their own, if necessary by squatting: that is, by reclaiming a piece of wasteland, and by running up a hovel with a chimney in a night, popularly accepted as evidence of title.

The village was changing in appearance: notably the yeomen's dwellings, small substantial farmhouses built of stone, or timber with cob or chalk in-filling and solid chimneys—a great improvement on earlier constructions, though mere cottages in modern eyes. But farming as a whole was little advanced. Open fields and commons still predominated in the lowland counties, cultivation was hide-bound and primitive, few cattle survived the winter, and there was still an immense stretch of scrub and waste. As to food, the quantity and variety of meat, corn and greenstuff depended largely on the success of the season. Storage and preservation were perpetual problems, while a bad harvest brought hunger and want. Fresh meat was exceptional, eaten only on feast days or at the slaughter of stock when the summer grazing was over. Game could often be had, legally or otherwise, in the winter months; and pigeons were reared in large numbers on the great estates. All else was salted down and stored. Often the poor man could not afford to eat his own pig meat, poultry, or eggs, but sold them for ready cash; likewise butter, cheese, and milk. In the ordinary way he fed his family on messes of porridge and skimmed milk, with a coarse bread made of barley and rye, mixed in with beans and peas. Wheaten bread was a luxury. Vegetables and salads were available and some herbs (for seasoning and cures), but potatoes were a later introduction and did not become popular for many years. Fish, fresh or salted, was another standby, the staple food in Lent when the stock of winter meat was running low, religious observance confirming practical convenience. Fruit also was grown in cottage gardens: the source of many home-made wines, besides cider, perry, a light beer brewed from barley, and honey drinks.

Although much that was medieval remained, by the year 1600 the English countryside had outgrown the chrysalis of feudalism, and attracted fresh troubles in consequence, mainly of poverty. For many years past the poor had been left to their own fate, and for various reasons: the gradual disintegration of the manor, the disappearance of the monasteries (great charitable harbours of the needy), and the dislocation of labour when numbers of ex-soldiers were thrown upon the market after the end of the Hundred Years' War with France. Bands of unemployed roved the land. The beggars became a by-word, the enemies of the village and the terror of the town. Few recognised that poverty was the product of the system; thus relief was only intermittently afforded and that by private effort—free food, child welfare, loans to business, a few hospitals for the sick, the orphans, the lunatics, and

THE GRANDEUR OF HUSBANDRY

Traditional all-purpose barn, with additions

FARM BUILDINGS

Modern egg factory

almshouses for the poor. At first Parliament resorted to repressive action. Penalties were imposed for unlicensed begging, and 'houses of correction' set up where 'sturdy' vagabonds were put to work. Later more humane methods were adopted, expressed finally in the Poor Law of 1601 which established principles that held good until the early nineteenth century. Its main provision was to make the parish (the church unit of government represented by the vestry) the executive body for all poor law administration, placing detailed responsibility upon the shoulders of the churchwardens and new officials called 'the overseers of the poor', all acting under the general supervision of the Justices of the Peace. It became the duty of these men to care for all poor persons, whatever the cause of their poverty, and to afford relief, employment and correction as the case demanded. Although a heavy burden upon village government and finance, the new system worked at first with some success. The army of beggars was reduced, and the worst cases of distress relieved. Rural poverty however remained a constant problem; and with the growth of commercial farming it was to return in acute form in later years.

It is generally accepted that peasant or subsistence farming offers few incentives for technical improvement, but that so long as it satisfies demand it is unlikely to be disturbed. Once however demand outruns supply, or otherwise alters in character, then change is bound to follow. In England the demand for wool was the direct cause of enclosure for pasture and large-scale enterprise in sheep. Production reached its peak in the mid-sixteenth century, stayed static for about a hundred years, and then in the latter part of the seventeenth century began to recede. Although the State stepped in, this time to boost wool not restrain it, and passed supporting legislation,[2] such measures were no more successful than the earlier restrictions on enclosure.

Meanwhile a counter-development was taking place in corn. As the population slowly recovered from the disaster of the Black Death and other recurrent plagues, reaching (it is thought) about four million in the later 1500s and five to six million by about 1700, so the demand for grain increased. Wheat prices rose from less than five shillings a quarter in 1500 to nearly forty shillings in 1600, pasture began to be broken up, and arable yields—after a hundred years or so of grass, cropped and dunged by sheep—responded remarkably. During the seventeenth century England became as well known in the Western world as a producer of corn, as it had been of wool; and in 1652 it was estimated that, despite the disturbance of the Civil War, tillage was already twice as profitable as grazing. Relatively little of the additional grain was grown in open field strips; most came from the enclosed farms of the yeomen or the ring-fenced properties of the larger landlords, themselves of yeoman or aristocratic stock, who were investing their wealth in urban as well as in landed enterprises.

B

The seventeenth century was the heyday of the rural middle class, ranging from the rising smallholder to substantial farmers, and to a few great families emerging as entrepreneurs on a scale similar to the abbots of old. Such were the Russells, Earls and Dukes of Bedford, who brought over Dutch engineers to advise them on the drainage of the Fens; who astutely developed their properties in East Anglia, the West Country, and London; and who married at the right moment into the controlling family of the East India Company. Along with other agricultural improvers of high standing, they were preparing to form the ruling squirearchy of the eighteenth and early nineteenth centuries, when success depended on the possession of large quantities of capital and land, shrewdly managed. Indeed the rise of the great landlords coincided with the decline of the yeomen freeholders (not the tenants), due to the need for large economic resources and to the burden of land tax imposed in 1692. Moreover landlords benefited most from the protection afforded to farmers by Parliament, through import duties on cattle and corn, and bounties on the export of grain.

Despite the rise in corn farming, methods were still primitive in the 1600s. There was a limit to what was or could be done, even on enclosed farms, for sheer lack of knowledge. English farmers distrusted theory, not entirely without reason, for medieval treatises on agriculture had been few and generally fallacious. In the Elizabethan age three writers made some stir. John Fitzherbert, an experienced countryman, advocated mixed corn and stock farming in his *Boke of Husbondrye* printed in 1523. Thomas Tusser published a best-seller in his *A Hundreth Good Pointes of Husbandrie* in 1557, enlarged into *Five Hundreth Good Pointes of Husbandry, united to as many of good Huswifery* in 1573. Tusser, a failed farmer turned preceptor like others before and after him, preferred to record custom rather than preach innovation; and he owed much of his success to the fact that he wrote in doggerel verse. Barnaby Googe, in his *Foure Bookes of Husbandrie* issued in 1577, was however a genuine pioneer. In this work—a translation from the German with personal additions—he explained some of the advanced techniques already adopted abroad: notably winter feeding of cattle by means of fodder crops and the cultivation of grasses. But Googe was long before his time; and since foreign practice was automatically suspect nothing further was heard of these outlandish matters for nearly seventy years, and then only by chance.[3]

Despite its depredations, the Civil War made a practical contribution to English farming: for it was due to the exile in the Low Countries of a royalist landowner, Sir Richard Weston, that Continental methods were first taken seriously. Weston was interested in rotations, particularly the practice of growing turnips for winter keep and clover for hay. After his return to England, he experimented with both these crops on his farm in Surrey, and published his observations around the year 1650. For various reasons his immediate influence was small. There was always of course the obstacle of conservatism. Besides this, winter cropping was almost impossible for open-field farmers since, according to the custom of the manor, all livestock were permitted to graze the stubbles and fallows from August round to February. Even tenant farmers with enclosed holdings were reluctant to improve their land, for without an agreement on tenant right, they were merely benefiting the landlord and raising their own rent. Thus—although some open-field communities did succeed in breaking their immemorial crop customs— it was usually only on freehold enclosed farms that tests could be made, and crops other than traditional attempted at all. The advantages how- ever were enormous. Root crops, such as turnips, were late sown in the fallow field, after a thorough cleaning and working down of the soil. They were then fed off, during the winter, to sheep and cattle which improved the ground by dunging and treading. Clovers and new legu- minous crops, such as sainfoin, yielded better and more plentiful hay and grazing; and enriched the soil by fixing nitrogen from the air. The effect of these innovations, once their value had been appreciated, was to revolutionise English farming. By carrying cattle and sheep the year round, instead of slaughtering all but breeding stock at the onset of winter, it made possible the support of a human population that doubled itself within two centuries.

Progress in cropping was only one part of the story. Soon a similar advance was being made in the design and use of implements, notably the drill and the horse hoe. These two tools, although not entirely original, were substantially the invention of Jethro Tull, a Berkshire farmer. In his book, *The New Horse-Houghing Husbandry*, published in 1731, Tull explained how he came to design the drill. He had been experimenting with sainfoin, wishing to sow it by a new method, but his labourers objected. So he constructed a machine, following the principle of 'the groove, tongue, and spring in the soundboard of an organ', which suited his purpose admirably. Later, after observing intercultivation in the French vineyards, he evolved the horse hoe. By using first the drill and then the hoe, he was able to sow both corn and root crops at a controlled depth with a quarter of the customary seeding, and after- wards keep the ground free of weeds.

Both Weston and Tull did their work in relative isolation. They were ignored, if not derided. Their popularisation was due initially to Charles, Viscount Townshend, prototype of the new aristocratic squires, who were to decide the fortunes of the countryside for at least a hundred years. Because he lost political office, Townshend retired from London in 1730 to devote himself to the welfare of his estates at Raynham in Norfolk. He was an enthusiast of Tull, revived the use of marl as a dressing, and adopted Weston's suggestions regarding turnips and clover, evolving a notable sequence of his own which became known as the 'Norfolk four-course' rotation. This consisted of roots—barley—seeds—wheat. Roots meant turnips and swedes, fed to stock on the ground or in yards, whence manure was returned to the fields. Seeds meant red clover, with or without rye grass or other grasses: the mixture being undersown in spring barley, or late sown after winter corn had been harvested. Once established, the sward was good for mowing and grazing for a year or two, before finally being ploughed in as a preparation for wheat.

Forty years after Townshend's death in 1738, another landowner in the same county took the lead. When Thomas Coke came into the family estate at Holkham in 1776, the rent roll yielded £2,200 a year. By 1816 it had risen to £20,000. Coke followed Townshend's example in reclaiming many of his farms himself. In other cases he tactfully and enthusiastically educated his tenants, guaranteeing them the benefit of their improvements by long leases. He introduced bone manure and cattle cake, and paid close attention to breeding and the selection of grass seed. He also held annual sheep shearings, originally meetings between himself and his friends to discuss farming problems, which ultimately developed into great gatherings of six hundred people or so, including distinguished guests from abroad. They were in fact agricultural shows.

Improvement in farm practice was not achieved of course equally over the country, nor simultaneously in every branch of the industry. Despite the economic importance of wool and the high population of sheep—about twelve million in 1700 is the estimate—evidence of selective breeding before that date, whether of sheep or of any other kind of animal, is scant. Again it was the rising demand for food and the new spirit of scientific inquiry that supplied the motive. Hitherto the cow had been considered an all-purpose animal, pulling a plough or cart, yielding milk, bearing a calf a year, and at death providing meat. By modern standards, an impossible feat. Again there was little hope of progress in open-field farming, in which all females were mated to the common scrub bull. The best chance lay with those farmers who could grow winter feed, and keep their herds apart on enclosed properties. Yet such were the advances made in the eighteenth century that by 1800 British breeders were already renowned the world over.

The foundation stock was not promising. There were the black cattle raised in Scotland, Wales and the English hills, long-horned or polled; and there were the reddish-brown cattle with shorter horns found in the midlands and the south, together with an improved piebald type brought in from the Low Countries. Otherwise there were no distinct breeds and much mongrelisation. Similarly among the sheep there were a few basic regional types. Nearly all were horned, small, hardy animals (where possible pastured out all the year round to the amazement of foreigners) with fine fleeces. The introduction however of winter fodder and of intensive folding over roots had complex results. While adding immensely to the fertility of the ground, and so benefiting corn yields, it coarsened the fleece and thereby accelerated the decline of the wool trade. On the other hand better feeding added flesh to the carcass, and this gave the line to the new generation of breeders who, by sacrificing wool for mutton, restored the market for sheep.

Although he owed much to the efforts of earlier pioneers, Robert Bakewell of Dishley in Leicestershire is generally regarded as the founding father of British stock-breeding. By in-breeding he established the New Leicester breed of sheep, an early maturing animal with a favourable ratio of bone to meat; also the Longhorn for beef, and a black carthorse breed imported from Holland. He hired out rams, bulls and stallions, and gained a great reputation for his ideas. Not all he did however proved successful. Owing to inherent limitations the Longhorns faded out, and like other pioneers Bakewell himself died in poverty. But his example was the important thing, for it enabled others to follow—and vary—his methods, and so attain better and more lasting results. In this way, for instance, the Colling brothers (pupils of Bakewell) developed the Beef Shorthorn, Thomas Bates the Dairy Shorthorn, Thomas Turnell the Lincoln Red (out of Colling stock), Francis Quartly the Devon, John Ellman Southdown sheep . . . and so the story continued far into the nineteenth century, indeed right up to the present day when the best British breeding-stock is still strongly sought by overseas buyers. In due course most regional types of cattle, sheep, horses, pigs and poultry were taken up, inferior characteristics bred out, and new or improved breeds fixed.

Stock-breeding began late in the cycle of agricultural progress which, taken in total, came only just in time to meet the market created by the Industrial Revolution. But this was not merely a matter of markets and rising population, nor even of agricultural techniques. Industry in the eighteenth century was still an infant force, destined within a century to transform the whole balance and character of English life. It would push farming off its pedestal as the main business of the nation, undercut rural trades and undermine rural society; and in so doing alter the very attitudes which dependence upon the land had created in earlier time.

❊ ❊ ❊

Farm Fortunes and Social Neglect: 1750–1850
In 1801 the first official census returned the population of England and Wales as just under nine millions. By 1851 it had reached nearly eighteen millions, about half the people living in the country, half in the towns—a breakneck rise and a significant shift in distribution. During those fifty years 'Merrie Englande' virtually disappeared: in the sense that by 1851 it was no longer a country led by landowners and

dominated by countrymen. The peasantry had been brutally extinguished and folk culture was dying. How did it happen?

The immediate impulse was, as always, the demand for food: aggravated and accelerated by the expanding factory towns of the west midlands and the north. It was there that eighteenth-century industrialism began—expressed in coal and iron mining, steam power, and the development of machinery, particularly in the textile trades. This demand would, of its own volition, have altered the economy of the countryside in time; but any gradual adjustment was rendered impossible by the wars with France. Once Napoleon had mastered Europe, home acres were compelled to yield all the food, timber, and many other raw materials that were required. Drastic changes were therefore imposed by necessity, and the improvement of land came to be regarded as patriotic as well as progressive behaviour. Above all it proved profitable, hence the willingness of landowners all over the country to invest their money in this kind of enterprise. Such men were often involved in industry as well, so that the two Revolutions—Industrial and Agrarian—were in that sense complementary, both being fertilised by similar sources of finance, the one providing a market for the other.

Progressive farmers knew that land had to be enclosed before it could be improved. Enclosure was of course no new thing; much had been done by mutual agreement since Tudor days. But now the time had gone for amicable and leisurely arrangements; instead a new 'instant' system, designed by landowners for landowners, was given the blessing of Parliament. In a typical lowland village, where enclosure was intended, a warning notice would be posted in the church porch, and objections invited to the Bill to be introduced—not a great risk, since those most affected (small open-field farmers and graziers) were rarely capable of formulating their own case. Three-quarters of those interested had to give their consent before the Bill was passed; but since this proportion was calculated by property value, not by counting heads, there was rarely any difficulty. The Act then nominated three Commissioners (often neighbouring gentry or their factors) to investigate the claims and allocate the land: also to decide such matters as liability for fencing and access to the new farms.

In theory every occupier of land received his due share, provided he could establish the validity of his title or claim in law. This was the nub of the problem. Many occupiers were unable to produce the requisite legal document, because in all probability they had never had one. Copyholders, for example, suffered severely since their title resided in the existence of manor rolls or records in which the conditions of their holding had once been written down. Most of these rolls had disappeared in the natural course of time; and so, it was argued, the title had vanished too. Even though the unwritten 'custom of the manor' had been respected for centuries, the lawyers' arguments and landlords' power proved too strong for the mass of peasant farmers enjoying customary and common rights. Sometimes a concession was made to the past by allotting a piece of unwanted land for the benefit of the poor; in other instances the new properties were too distant or inconvenient to be of value to a villager, who in any event could pay neither the fencing nor the legal costs incurred—a matter, perhaps, of twelve pounds an acre. So placed, a poor man had no alternative but to sell out to his more prosperous neighbour.

Looked at simply as an historic event, the Great Enclosures appear inevitable. They enabled millions[4] of acres of poor grazing, indifferent arable, and wasteland to become productive. Without this addition to tillage, under the pressure of population and war, the country would have neared starvation long before Waterloo. Moreover enclosure benefited agriculture as a whole. It not only ensured better crops and stock, but spurred invention and the use of improved implements, encouraged the application of fertilisers and the selection of seed, raised fertility, and exerted influence on industry and trade at large as well as upon the ancillary employments of agriculture. Most important, it led to the accumulation of wealth, and stimulated a spirit of scientific inquiry among farmers and landowners. Finally, out of all the turmoil of change, emerged an ordered and prosperous pattern of fields and farmsteads much as we know it now—that distinctive type of English countryside of which we are so proud.

But of course there was another side to enclosure, and not a pretty one: in sum, a selfish scramble for other men's land, a legalised grab sanctified by Parliamentary procedure. Only the Haves benefited. For many smallholders, and for most cottagers and squatters it meant actual loss of living and independence; and there quickly arose a large class of landless labourers who had to rely entirely upon their wages for existence. Since wage rates rarely exceeded 1s. 6d. a day, it was not possible to make ends meet on anything but a starvation scale. In the past, earnings had always been supplemented by milk and butter from a cow grazing the stubbles and the commons, by pigs and chickens foraging the waste, and by the produce of a strip in the open fields. All that now had gone. The rich became richer, the poor poorer, and much of the countryside came to be peopled by two main classes, the employers and the employed.

This was the England so violently deplored by William Cobbett, political journalist, the son of a Surrey smallholder. At heart a Tory radical, he ridiculed the plough-up and fence-in mania, and never ceased to fight 'progress' in its assault upon the old order of rural society. It even horrified realistic and reasonable people such as Arthur Young, first Secretary of the Board of Agriculture (founded in 1793), who approved the new methods of farming, but who wished none the less to alleviate the social misery they caused. If the labourers had shared appreciably in the new wealth, the problems of poverty would indeed have been mitigated, despite rising prices and the loss of common rights. But enclosure threw a lot of men on the market at once, as did the industrialisation of certain handicrafts and cottage skills; while after 1815 matters were further aggravated by the demobilisation of servicemen from the wars. By taking advantage of the labour surplus to keep wages down, the employers not only made misery worse and promoted a legacy of violence and hate, but—by pauperising the labourer— ran up a financial debt they themselves had to settle in the end.

Although the Poor Law of 1601 had diminished the army of beggars that roamed the countryside in Tudor times, it never extinguished poverty. With the rise in population, the problem returned in an acute form; and new devices had to be introduced to assist parish overseers in their unending task of caring for the aged and sick, finding work for the able-bodied, and maintaining pauper and bastard children. Each device became more hateful and inhuman in its turn—the test of Settlement which confined every man to his birthplace unless he could prove substantial means of support; the establishment of workhouses; the hiring out of pauper labour at bargain rates; the apprenticeship of children, by which the formalities were demeaned to a mere entry in the parish books. Ultimately, beneath the sheer weight of unemployment and hardship, a new system was adopted—well-intentioned but disastrous. On the initiative of the magistrates of Speenhamland in Berkshire, meeting in May 1795, out-relief became available in the form of supplements to wages, paid from the rates. A sliding scale was drawn up, related to the price of bread and the size of man's family: so that, as the subsidy rose automatically with the price of food, a large family became a wise investment, and it paid just as well to be kept by the parish as to earn an honest living.

The repercussions were catastrophic—except in the north where wages stayed steady or actually rose by reason of competition with industry; and in certain 'horticultural' regions, such as the fertile Lincolnshire fens, where land was freehold and in the hands of small owners who made a good living out of small acreages. Elsewhere Speenhamland caused havoc. It pauperised the labourer and destroyed his morale. It actually encouraged employers to pay low wages, knowing that the deficiency would be met from public funds. And it crushed the ratepayers, who had to pay out of their own pockets what the farmers should have paid out of theirs. As for the farmer-ratepayers, it was the middle and smaller sort who suffered from their own folly, not the larger men who weathered everything.

Meanwhile parish rates rose with the cost of food, wherein the controlling factor was the price of corn. Ever since the seventeenth century the Government had been at pains to ensure an adequate supply of grain at a just price, both for the consumer and the producer. The method was in times of scarcity to let foreign grain in, in times of plenty to encourage the export of home grain by means of a bounty. As a result Britain managed to feed herself without difficulty at least until the end of the eighteenth century. By then—for reasons of war and the rapidly rising population—the food situation was becoming precarious, in anticipation if not in fact. Since imports had virtually ceased, and home harvests happened to be meagre for fourteen out of the twenty-two years between 1793 and 1814, corn prices began to rocket. The average annual price of wheat rose irregularly from 49s. 3d. per quarter in 1793 to a record level of 126s. 6d. in 1812 and 109s. 9d. in 1813. At one moment in 1812, the price touched 155s. The Corn Laws had ceased to offer any protection, and the price was crudely determined by supply and demand within the country.

It was not a pretty position. Despite a genuine increase in the cost of production, the system still yielded large profits to the corn grower, but disseminated misery among the poor, and contributed directly to the sharp rise in the cost of living. When the price of wheat plummeted after Waterloo to 74s. 4d., and the grain market was freed again, a small but powerful minority of landowners in Parliament forced through a new and effective Corn Law, which made the import of foreign wheat uneconomic until the home price reached a minimum of eighty shillings per quarter (less for colonial wheat). It is hard to regard this as anything but naked self-interest, although there was some justification in the argument that if corn prices fell too far, then all agriculture would suffer, employer and employed alike. One thing was clear however. The 1815 Corn Law made no attempt to establish a just price for the consumer, but merely protected the interests of the producer. Even in this it did not entirely succeed, for the smaller corn growers—along with other smaller farmers—faced ruin when all prices collapsed in the first few years of peace.

This was the beginning of the end of the reign of the large landlord, although it took at least another generation to do away with agricultural protection. By then—the late 1840s—power was already passing into the hands of the industrialists, and by the last half of the nineteenth century England had become a predominantly manufacturing and trading country. What happened was inevitable because it was an economic process working itself out. You cannot resist the majority indefinitely, but the pace of change was hastened by the persistent egoism of the landlords and large farmers—seen in the story of the Great Enclosures, the Corn Laws, the Poor Laws, and the code of criminal legislation which hanged a hungry man for stealing a sheep or transported him to Australia for trespass.

By 1832 the poor rates were costing the country eight million pounds a year, and Speenhamland was reaping a whirlwind. A multitude of small farmers, bankrupted in the depression following Waterloo, had swelled the ranks of the pauper labourers, and thousands of acres were temporarily abandoned for lack of tenants. Having forced through the Reform Act of 1832, a landmark of Liberal legislation, the Whig Government of Lord Grey was determined to deal equally drastically with the problem of poverty. The dilemma here was to replace a demoralising system with one that combined humanity with common sense: in other words to get rid of 'parish money', and so induce employers to pay a living wage for an honest day's work. The solution offered was the Poor Law Amendment Act of 1834, which grouped parishes into 'unions' for the maintenance of a common workhouse and enforced the test of in-relief. This meant that henceforward only the aged and infirm might receive charity at home, while able-bodied persons had to enter the workhouse and endure its rigours to obtain support. The new Act worked only too well in an inhuman way. It halved the poor rates within seven years, and forced wages up to the lowest statutory level. But the level was so low that it made barely any difference to the labourer's lot; while the workhouse, always an indignity, became part of the new folklore of the countryside—as an object of abhorrence.

William Cobbett made no bones about it.

> Let us set regularly to work. I will do my duty, if the friends of the working people will do their duty; and their duty consists in the following things:
>
> 1. Wherever the Poor Law Commissioners are at work, send me word of it by letter, and give me the name of the Commissioner very particularly, and the thing or things he is about to do.
>
> 2. Give me the name or names of any lords, baronets, or such people that are co-operating with the Poor Law Commissioners; and tell me the place of their residence in the country.
>
> 3. Where there is any UNION, as they call it, give me an account of the number of parishes, and the probable extent and population of them.
>
> 4. Tell me who is the chairman of any committee or body of persons who are pushing on the thing.
>
> 5. If there be any regulation about separating man from wife, or children from parents, let me have them, and particularly if they be put in print.
>
> 6. Give me their dieting scale; and give me any other particulars that you think will be useful.
>
> Unless I be thus assisted, it will be impossible to do justice in the discharge of my duty. I desire that all statements made to me be perfectly true; and it is desirable that the writers should permit me to put their *names*, unless they can refer me to somebody that I know.[5]

Cobbett was a man of paradox—a reformer in reverse. In his humanity he did not look forward to some socialist solution, but backward to the old order before enclosure, when the countryman had a measure of independence. This battle of course was already over, but it had not been lost without action other than the sound of Cobbett's loud voice. Men and women whose memory of former rights was still green rose in riot in the summer of 1830, first in Kent, then in Sussex, Hampshire, Berkshire and Wiltshire: the next year Dorset, Gloucestershire and East Anglia were involved. In the south the outbreaks seem to have been organised; elsewhere action was disunited and sporadic. Men smashed machines in protest against loss of work, and fired ricks as an act of vengeance against employers. Instead of ten shillings a week or less, they wanted half a crown a day; and in some districts they got a good deal of sympathy, frightened though the farmers were. The Government however took a different view; and the Home Secretary, Lord Melbourne, sent troops to quell the disorders and Special Commissioners to try the offenders. Although only one man lost his life in the riots, and he a rioter, 450 men and boys were transported, nine executed, and scores of others imprisoned. Repression did not cease when the rick fires finally flickered out. In 1834 six labourers of Tolpuddle in Dorset were sentenced to transportation for trying to form a Trade Union, as a more effective means of securing a living wage. It was this notorious case that roused public opinion at last, and obtained a free pardon for the men. By that time however the peasant had lost his rights and his land, and the medieval heritage of the countryside had passed away.[6]

✻   ✻   ✻

Although farmers might grumble and compare notes on the bad times, some saw a break in the clouds overhead. Progress was again a watchword as it had been in the heyday of improvement in the eighteenth century, when societies for the advancement of knowledge in agriculture and other sciences had sprung up in several counties, allied to cattle shows, ploughing matches, and the like. Although many had declined or disappeared in the bad years after Waterloo, some important institutions remained, notably the Bath and West Society founded in 1777, and the Smithfield Club in 1798. The renewal of faith in farming was marked in 1838 by the foundation of The Royal Agricultural Society of England (R.A.S.E.), which held its first Show at Oxford in the following year, and was incorporated by Royal Charter in 1840 with Queen Victoria as patron. It attracted into membership the best brains and the most enterprising landowners and farmers, and quickly established its authority. It fostered invention and research, and stimulated practical progress in almost every branch of the industry— crops, stock, manuring, farm building and farm practice as a whole, especially machinery. Farm mechanisation in Victorian times is a story by itself. Steam was applied to cable ploughing and threshing; while new or improved implements, such as cultivators, rollers, drills, reapers, mowing machines, horse-rakes, elevators, turnip and chaff cutters, and a multitude more were regularly advertised and acquired. Another innovation—porous clay pipes for land drainage, invented by John Reade in 1843—was widely adopted after the middle of the century, and put heart into many acres of wet and acid land.

Other important institutions were founded at this time. For example, the Experimental Station at Rothamsted in 1843, and the Agricultural College at Cirencester in 1845. With the former are associated the names of Sir John Lawes and Sir Henry Gilbert. These two men were primarily concerned with agricultural chemistry, basing their work upon the discoveries of Justus Liebig in the field of plant nutrition; and it was Lawes who started the fertiliser industry, combining 'practice with science' in the best Victorian manner.

In the nature of things a progressive Victorian farmer was able to do far more than his Georgian predecessors, having greater knowledge and more effective means at his command. Besides this, the rapid spread of the railways was opening up town markets all over the country: so that the continuing increase in population was reflected in the higher demand for home-produced food. The root reason for recovery, therefore, was a readjustment of supply and demand, sharpened by quicker communications; and it was this form of economic pressure that by the early 1840s was restoring confidence in farming and attracting capital back to the land.

It was mainly men with large resources that made early Victorian farming prosperous: some of them long established and well founded; others new men who had made money in industry and bought their way into the land for the purposes of investment and prestige. Their attitude was often one of characteristic ambiguity. It comprised a passion for physical improvement—model farmsteads and service cottages on restricted rents, equipped with gardens or allotments, a new school, a reading room, and sooner or later the restoration of the parish church: permeated throughout by a moral paternalism, expressed in village charities,[7] clubs and annual feasts. It also comprised as strict an application of business to the management of the land, as to the trade by which the city owner had made his money. This made him an active landlord, for it involved a respect for science, a worship of efficiency, and a readiness to experiment.

*   *   *

One of the most invigorating and illuminating examples of early Victorian enterprise concerns the reclamation of the Royal Forest of Exmoor by John and Frederic Knight, father and son.[8] 'Forest' here is a misleading term, for it was not woodland but in the main a great tract of open land, where originally deer and other wild game had been reserved for royal sport. Until the sixteenth century it had been looked after by a Warden on the king's behalf; but from 1508 onwards it had been leased at an annual rent of £46 13s. 4d., and the Warden empowered to make what he could out of letting grazing and other rights. All this came to an end between 1815 and 1819, when the 20,000 acres of the Forest were enclosed, the land allotted and most of the customary rights extinguished. By 1820 virtually the entire area—including Simonsbath, the only steading on the moor—had been purchased by John Knight, an ironmaster from Worcestershire, a man of great energy and substance, but totally unacquainted with Exmoor.

For twenty years he poured effort and capital into the land. A devotee of East Anglian arable farming, particularly the Norfolk four-course rotation, he dreamed of converting the heights of Exmoor into prairies of waving corn: despite high winds off the Atlantic, sixty or more inches of rainfall a year, and a common elevation of 1000 feet. Yet he achieved much—roads, gates, a Forest wall twenty-nine miles long, a lake at Pinkworthy (for irrigation?), deep channels for drainage, subsoil ploughing by teams of oxen to rid the land of waterlogging, and by liming and burning to prepare the land for over 2000 acres of crops. His attempt to establish the Norfolk system failed, however, nor were his importations of 'foreign' stock any more successful—West Highland bullocks and Herefords that wintered poorly (and on one occasion at least ran amok), sheep ranching with Cheviots, and the crossing of native Exmoor ponies with Dongola Arab stallions to improve size and quality. In themselves John Knight's ideas were often excellent, and some were re-adopted later with success. What went wrong was his attempt to farm on a grand scale all at once, without adequate staff, and without compensating for the rigours of the climate.

In 1841 he was succeeded by his son, Frederic, who was determined to profit by his father's mistakes. Employing a succession of two good agents, he gave up ranching the estate as a whole, and carved out separate farmsteads at Honeymead, Cornham, Emmett's Grange, and eight other places. He attracted tenants by offering twenty-year leases with low initial rents, and made other allowances to encourage improvements on the holdings. He abandoned corn for a simple rotation of roots and grass, grazed by Devon bullocks and folded off to Exmoor Horn sheep, the native breeds; and he kept reclamation going at a slower pace by successive crops of rape, followed by subsoiling to break the iron pan below the peat. All this proved itself in the end, although it took another twenty years to stabilise the economy of the farms and find the right tenants. He also engaged in three other interesting projects. One was to plant mile upon mile of beech hedging on top of the high boundary banks to serve as windbreaks. Another was to import

5000 Blackface and Cheviot ewes from Scotland—his father's idea again, but with one important difference, for the sheep came with their own shepherds. Both these ventures went well. The third did not—the leasing of mining rights to the Dowlais Iron Company and the surveying of a light railway from Porlock Weir to Simonsbath. Iron ore was found in several sites but none proved profitable, and after a few years the whole enterprise had to be abandoned.

In 1879 Frederic Knight lost his only son at the early age of twenty-eight, and after his own death in 1897 the estate passed to the neighbouring Fortescues at Castle Hill. But it had been a great piece of pioneering: the creation of hill farms out of a wilderness, and the ultimate partnership between holdings, climate, and thousands of acres of unreclaimed moorland. Besides this, a new parish was established at Simonsbath, with church, school, and inn: and by 1880 the Forest was supporting as many as 300 people. The Knights were venturers, hardheaded, yet with a strong streak of the gambler in both their characters, like many others thrown up by the Industrial Revolution. In this they were true representatives of the age.

*   *   *

Although the land was showing signs of revival, the 1840s were years of want and anxiety and, as we can now see, they proved to be the watershed of British farming due to the repeal of the Corn Laws in 1846. It was not of course an unexpected development. By maintaining duties on foreign imports, the Corn Law of 1815 had succeeded in protecting home-grown grain at artificial prices, but at a time when demand was outstripping production. Repeal was but one angle, though an acute one, in the gathering conflict between Protection and Free Trade, and in the general clash between town and country skirmishing with each other ever since the end of the wars with France. The prophet of Free Trade, Richard Cobden, recruited a large middle-class following in the towns; and the foundation of the Anti-Corn Law League meant that the issue could not be delayed indefinitely. In agitating for repeal, the townsmen argued that the free import of foreign corn would provide cheap food for the working classes, encourage the sale of British manufactures abroad, and discourage the setting-up of foreign industry. The farmers denied that Free Trade would do any such thing; rather, they said, it would enable employers to reduce wages and ruin agriculture at the same time.

In the end the issue was settled by the Irish potato famine of 1845. Foreign corn then had to be admitted as a measure of emergency; and it was this that forced the hand of Sir Robert Peel, Tory Prime Minister who—though personally converted to Free Trade—led a strongly Protectionist party in parliament. With the help of the Opposition, Peel had his way; and thereafter import duties on corn and other farm products were reduced by stages until they vanished altogether. What happened next was history at its most ironical, for it confused the experts on both sides. At first, as anticipated, corn began to slide and a mild panic ensued 1848–52. Then prices recovered, levelled out, and the prospect of disaster disappeared. The prophets of doom, it seemed, had been utterly confounded: even Benjamin Disraeli who, denouncing his own party leader, had in forthright terms foretold the ruin of the land. In the end he was not proved wrong however; for although disaster did come in the 1870s, it was delayed so long that almost everyone— Disraeli included—had forgotten the warnings uttered some thirty years before.

✶   ✶   ✶

Free Trade and the Fall of Farming: 1850–1900
Between 1853 and 1862 agriculture enjoyed a decade of expansion and prosperity, extended though ebbing until 1874. The causes were part-economic, part-political. At home as always the population continued to rise—by six million 1850–75—with townsmen outnumbering country-men by a widening margin year by year. More food was needed and there was more money to buy it with. International trade was being fertilised by the discoveries of gold in Australia and California. Britain, still the workshop of the world, was able to forge ahead because other important countries were industrially undeveloped and politically disturbed. Throughout Europe the Revolutions of 1848 had, for a time, weakened confidence in Continental commerce. Russia, not yet a serious com-petitor and temporarily deprived of her corn cargoes by the Crimean campaign 1854–6, was engaged in internal reforms and imperial expan-sion towards the south and east. Though rising afresh as a colonial power, France was trying unsuccessfully under Napoleon III to regain her place as the dominant country in Europe. Germany, still disunited, but a new force on the make, was involved in a series of amalgamations and aggressions before consolidating into a single state in 1871. Across the Atlantic, America was torn by the Civil War of 1861–5. All these events had a multiple effect. They stimulated British exports (already finding new outlets in colonial expansion), absorbed surpluses of foreign food, and benefited industry and agriculture alike.

It was the age of High Farming. Seasons were generally good, crops and stock flourished, inventions and improvements came into their own, and prices remained high in almost all branches of husbandry. So did rents. Rural landlords were enjoying an Indian summer of prosperity and power. In 1851 it was calculated that most of the farmland in Great Britain was owned by less than 35,000 persons who—despite the reforming legislation of the 1830s and the repeal of Protection in the 1840s—still exerted almost absolute influence in the countryside. The traditions of squirearchy, both good and bad, were still very much alive

and practised at all levels in a mixture of public duty and private privi-
lege. Large landowners did service in Parliament without thought of
pecuniary reward, in the same way as lesser men acted as Justices of the
Peace, Guardians of the Poor, and in other positions connected with
local government. At the same time they hunted regularly and passionately without fear of trespass, preserved large quantities of game
under the protection of the law, and evicted tenants without difficulty
if they voted the wrong way.

As to care for the land, much was being done in practice and much
being thought out. I have already described the ventures of the Knights
on Exmoor; but the *Journal* of the R.A.S.E. reveals many other examples
of agricultural enterprise, indicative of the confidence felt in farming.
Philip Pusey, Eton and Christchurch, enlightened landlord of 5000
acres in Berkshire, was a man of mark: liberal in outlook, many-sided,
with a probing scientific mind. He had supported Peel in Parliament
and was convinced that agriculture could survive without the Corn
Laws, provided it put its house in order. 'Chemistry and mechanism,'
he said in 1852, 'have beaten politics and protection.' A very different
personality was John Joseph Mechi, born in London of Italian origin,
who purchased some heavy waterlogged land at Tiptree in Essex in
1844. He drained it, reorganised the layout of the fields, applied
manures, invested in machinery and new buildings, and published his
accounts. Mechi was as foreign to the English countryside as Pusey was
a part of it, but both set out to demonstrate that science could overcome
tradition.

Sheer business ability however could not operate without an adequate
supply of capital; and this was where a number of entrenched families
were at a disadvantage owing to the system of entail, by which in
effect each successive owner became a tenant-for-life. Unable to raise
money by the sale of property, a pushing young heir might find the
estate saddled with family settlements or similar charges, in addition to
the service of mortgages and loans. In such cases the land languished,
and although the situation was eased by legislation after 1855, it
continued in such cases to impede active management.

None the less the prosperity of farming in the 'golden age' permeated
country life in a hundred ways. Village trades were reinvigorated; the
blacksmith, by the demand for shoeing, as horses replaced oxen for
farmwork even in the remotest parts; while numerous workshops—
family concerns, usually—manufactured implements and serviced
machinery, including steam engines, in villages and small towns,
especially in the arable counties. Building also flourished all over the
countryside in a bewildering variety of styles, for ease of transport was
by-passing dependence upon local materials and local architecture.
Sometimes whole villages were reconstructed, as at Bourton in the Vale
of the White Horse, recorded in all its rosiness by Alfred Williams.

The following extract should not be written off on that account, for Williams was no stranger to poverty. Born and bred in a neighbouring village, he walked daily into Swindon to operate a steam hammer in the G.W.R. works, and in his spare time educated himself in literature and the classical languages.

> Here every house and building is of stone, well made, with large gardens, and plenty of room and light; it is altogether a model village. This was brought about by a beneficent landlord, who came a stranger, and sympathised with the poor; he had all the ruinous cottages removed and filled their places with substantial modern dwellings. Nearly every cottage has gardens and parterre in front; these the occupants tend with great pride and care, vying with each other in the production of beautiful blooms.[9]

The mention of gardens is important, for they were certainly a great boon to working men, and a number of landowners offered allotments as well. The idea was not new. As the word 'allotment' implies, it derived from the process of enclosure and was regarded as a substitute for the loss of common rights and holdings. Ironically many of the new allotments were carved out of the residue of common land; indeed commons continued to be enclosed by Parliamentary sanction until well into the 1870s—614,000 acres being absorbed in this way between 1845 and 1869. It was thanks only to an urban organisation, the Commons Preservation Society (founded in 1865), and to the growing realisation of the value of open spaces near towns, that wholesale enclosure was finally brought to an end. As this was one of the earliest expressions of amenity, it is worth a word in parenthesis.

For the first few years of its existence the Commons Preservation Society concentrated on saving commons round London: notably Hampstead Heath, Epping Forest, and at Blackheath, Barnes, Hackney, Wandsworth, Wimbledon, and other places—now unthinkable as anything but public open spaces. There was also the epic adventure of Berkhamsted, where Lord Brownlow's agent attempted to expropriate 434 acres by *force majeure*, erecting two miles of iron fencing five feet high and extinguishing all public access and enjoyment. As local people feared to take action, the Society hired a contractor with a force of 120 navvies armed with hammers, chisels, and crowbars to remove the obstruction. A special train arrived at Tring at one thirty a.m. with the men and their equipment on board—unfortunately without the contractor himself, for he had already subsided in alcohol in a public house near Euston Station. However the Society had dispatched a confidential clerk to watch the proceedings; and sensing the situation this splendid man took immediate charge, formed up the navvies and marched them into action. By six a.m. the job was done and all the fencing levelled to the ground; but it was only after four more years that the case was won in the courts. In 1876 rural commons in general were brought under protection, and soon something was being done to save rights-of-way as well.

Admirable as all these actions were, they constitute a different aspect of the subject of common land, being in effect an epilogue to the story of peasant occupation and a prologue to that of amenity, to be described in Part Two, and which—it can never be said too often—though urban in origin, was to do so much to rescue the rural heritage.

Behind the rosiness of Bourton, the revival of employment through machinery and estate development, and other undoubted manifestations of prosperity, lay the raw reality that, in southern England at any rate, the agricultural labourer was little better off than in the past. He did not share adequately in the harvest of wealth. In 1860 the average basic wage was around 11s. 6d. a week, in 1870 12s. 2d.: in the north and north-west, owing to industrial competition, rates were higher than this; in the west midlands and south-west, they were lower. In all barely better than in the depression days of the 1820s–1830s. The periodicity of work was a severe handicap. In winter and other slack times, a man often had to depend on the assistance of his wife and children to make ends meet. His family, if a large one, might earn more than he did. In the eastern counties there developed a system known as 'gang labour'—troops of men, women and children, without homes, wandering about doing field work under the direction of gang masters. It was due to their labouring, and to general over-employment and under-payment on the land, that the arable fields were kept so clean, well hoed and free of weeds (acres picked over between finger and thumb): a phenomenon observed by perceptive foreigners who visited England at this time. Ultimately public opinion was aroused and excessive exploitation reduced, first by the Gangs Act 1868, and then by various Education Acts after 1870, by which all children up to the age of fourteen were sent to school, none to be employed on the land except by permission at busy periods of the year. Even then the rule was frequently broken, as school attendance registers showed.

For a first-hand portrait of labouring life in mid-Victorian England, it is still best to turn to the first of three letters written to *The Times* in November 1872 by Richard Jefferies, then an unknown Swindon reporter. As the son of a small (unsuccessful) tenant farmer at Coate, Jefferies knew his subject—the Wiltshire labourer—down to the bottom button; and although his letter was drenched with condescension, it remains a fine example of social reporting. Too long to reprint in full, a few sentences supply the sense and quality.

> The labourer's muscle is that of a cart-horse, his motions lumbering and slow. His style of walk is caused by following the plough in

early childhood, when the weak limbs find it a hard labour to pull the heavy-nailed boots from the thick clay soil. . . . His food may, perhaps, have something to do with the deadened slowness which seems to pervade everything he does. . . . It consists chiefly of bread and cheese, with bacon twice or thrice a week, varied with onions, and if he be a milker (on some farms) with a good 'tuck-out' at his employer's expense on Sundays. . . . Vegetables are his luxuries and a large garden, therefore, is the greatest blessing he can have. . . . There is scarcely any limit to the power of absorbing beer. I have known reapers and mowers make it their boast that they could lie on their backs and never take the wooden bottle (in the shape of a small barrel) from their lips till they had drunk a gallon. . . . Corduroy trousers and slops are the usual style. Smock-frocks are going out of use, except for milkers and faggers. Almost every labourer has his Sunday suit, very often really good clothes, sometimes glossy black, with the regulation 'chimney pot'. . . . The women must dress in fashion. . . . The poorest girl . . . must have the same style of dress as the squire's daughter—Dolly Vardens, chignons, and parasols for ladies who can work all day reaping in the boiling sun of August! Gloves, kid, for hands that milk the cows! . . . The fairs are the chief cause of immorality. Many an honest, hard-working servant-girl owes her ruin to these fatal mops and fairs, when liquor to which she is unaccustomed overcomes her. Yet it seems cruel to take from them the one day or two of the year on which they can enjoy themselves fairly in their own fashion. The spread of friendly societies, patronised by the gentry and clergy, with their annual festivities, is a remedy which is gradually supplying them with safer, yet congenial, amusement. . . . The children help both in haymaking and reaping. In spring and autumn they hoe and do other piecework. On pasture farms they beat clots or pick up stones. . . . Dairymaids are scarce and valuable. A dairymaid who can be trusted to take charge of a dairy will sometimes get £20 besides her board (liberal) and sundry perquisites. These often save money, marry bailiffs, and help their husbands to start a farm.[10]

For the labourer patronage, however generous and disinterested it might seem, could not continue indefinitely as a substitute for justice. Amid all the prosperity of High Farming and the few pleasures that came his way, life was hard for a man earning eleven to twelve shillings a week and fettered to a depressed station in society. Whatever Jefferies might say, there were few chances of getting out of the rut. Before the Education Acts of the 1870s, there were no State primary schools and only sufficient voluntary elementary schools, run by religious denominations, to cater for about half the child population. Secondary and adult education were not yet for the countryman, and that was why the labourer, turned in on himself, so often found solace and strength in the Dissenting chapel. It was at the same time a religious refuge and a social stronghold. Jefferies wrote:

> A grimly real religion, as concrete and as much a fact as a stone wall; a sort of horse's faith going along the furrow unquestioning. . . . This great building, plain beyond plainness, stood beside a fir copse. . . . If all the angles of the architects could have been put together, nothing could have been designed more utterly opposite to the graceful curve of the fir tree than this red-bricked crass building.[11]

Another writer, Reg Groves, has related that by its agency

> . . . innumerable small groups came into existence, governing their own affairs, having their own unpaid teachers and preachers and paying their own way. In the chapels the labourers learned self-respect, self-government, self-reliance and organisation; here men learned to speak, to read, to write, to lead their fellows.[12]

Here lay the springs of revival tapped by Joseph Arch, Methodist preacher and, by reason of his skill as a workman and agricultural contractor, independent in his business. Following the legalisation of Trades Unions after 1871, Arch founded a local union at Wellesbourne in Warwickshire. It was the first overt association in the countryside since the Tolpuddle disaster of 1834, and a thousand people attended Arch's initial meeting in February 1872. The bonfire lit that day roared into conflagration, and out of it soared the National Agricultural Labourers' Union, the first national organisation for farm workers. Other unions leapt to life, and within two years membership overall reached 150,000, Arch retaining his pre-eminent position as leader and spokesman of the whole movement. The objects were simple: 'to raise wages, shorten hours, and make a man out of a land-tied slave.' The vote was demanded. The labourer, it seemed, was coming into his own at last.

However, trouble was at hand. In 1873 a number of farmers in the eastern counties threatened union men with dismissal. Lock-outs followed and the unions began to weaken. Many men emigrated overseas and were helped to do so. Within a few years membership declined disastrously. By the end of the century all was over, and Arch retired, an old and disappointed man. What really killed the unions was the catastrophic slump that hit agriculture at the very moment when the labourers began to combine. It was the start, furthermore, of something far more serious than any of the periodic recessions that had affected the countryside in the past.

*   *   *

It had been explained how national subsistence farming went out with the Corn Laws, and how for adventitious reasons agriculture then entered a period of prosperity. It was still doing well when, in 1874, a general trade depression struck Britain and other countries as well. In the United States it accelerated the drive to settle new lands in the middle and far west, a movement of profound significance to British agriculture. In Britain itself farming first felt the wind through a series of bad harvests. The summer of 1879 was a disaster, the wettest season on record; but any rise in the price of grain was forestalled by a flood of cheap imported corn, grown in a favourable climate on the virgin soils of the newly broken prairies of America. Arable farming, hampered by lack of landspace, uncertain weather, and the disabilities of tradition, never recovered and the bottom fell out of corn production. The home market, wide open to foreign food, carried to the ports on railways built often by British capital and then transported on British owned ships, was no longer the private outlet of British farms. Moreover, with the advent of refrigeration, horn followed corn. From 1890 onwards dead meat from Argentina, America and Australasia poured into the country; likewise cheese, butter and wool. Savings accumulated in the era of prosperity on the land were now running out, and the only hope was to reimpose tariffs and return to protection. But this was no longer possible. Free Trade had been elevated into a dogma as sacrosanct as the Mosaic Law. It was the oracle of industry, which had so developed as to depend for its very existence upon the export of a vast volume of manufactured goods. And, in simple economics, these had to be paid for by the import of raw materials and cheap food emanating from the customer countries. In this way foreign food helped keep the export trade alive, and British industry retained an interest in the depression of home agriculture.

Here then was the moment of truth. The rift between town and country broadened into a gulf because their *business* interests conflicted. Sophisticated society rests upon an economic base: particularly so in Victorian England where the rule of self-help and commercial viability, within a framework of free trading, free of Government interference, reigned supreme. In other words, if farming could not pay its way—for whatever reason—then the countryside had to take the consequences; and take them it did. Between 1871 and 1901 corn declined by nearly three million acres, and the stubbles fell back to coarse weeds and grass. Buildings decayed, hedges grew out, and many farmsteads were abandoned. More significant, the people themselves began rapidly to leave the land. Agricultural labourers alone decreased by over 300,000 in thirty years; and there were many casualties among the tenant and freehold farmers. It was the kind of rough-and-ready adjustment approved by *laissez-faire* economists, who insisted it was better to staunch the wounds with charity than ward off the assault altogether with such mechanisms as subsidies and protective duties—an attitude that persisted almost up to 1939. That land might have values other than those dictated by the vagaries of the market, was not allowed to upset the theory. When things went wrong, humanity had only a small place in the thinking of Free Traders; but their influence was so strong as to prohibit all political alternatives for several generations.

Although brutally wasteful of men and resources, the effect of the depression was not totally detrimental. At severe cost it forced agriculture into different channels which, by reason of climate, the suitability of soils and communication, and new enterprise, flowed in the course of time into a new economic mould. In the normal run however it was done by sacrificing the standard of living in the countryside. Many family farms, for example, survived simply because sons and daughters worked for nothing more than their board and lodging and a pittance of pocket money; and they married late if they married at all. None the less as arable acreages diminished and the production of fatstock declined, so increasing attention was paid in appropriate areas to the raising of crops for seed; the breeding of pedigree stock for export abroad; intensive market gardening, orcharding and hop growing; the management of pigs and poultry (hitherto regarded as sidelines); above all grass growing, particularly for the production of milk and its distribution to town dairies by fast rail.[13]

Reorganising the structure of agriculture raised many formidable difficulties. For example, to convert an arable into a grass farm for dairying, neither the landlord nor the tenant in a traditionally arable area was likely to have the necessary capital, nor was the bank keen to supply it during a slump. Yet it was essential to pay for seeds and machinery for grassing down, lay on water, construct buildings, and buy foundation stock. Labour too was often unwilling to learn new skills, for—in the farming fraternity—cow-keeping had always been a despised form of employment. Leases likewise contained restrictive clauses concerning rotations and farm practice, derived from decades of corn and root production. Necessity of course called the tune in the end; and sheer adversity attracted many newcomers not bound by tradition but prepared to experiment. A few men, such as George Baylis of Newbury, defied the trend of the times and made a fortune out of growing thousands of acres of corn and grass, without livestock, in order to sell grain and hay for cash.

One of the most interesting examples of large-scale enterprise, evolved out of the depression, took place on the Lockinge estate in northern Berkshire.

*   *   *

The story concerns Lt.-Col. Robert James Lindsay, V.C., hero of the Crimean War, a member of the Scottish family headed by the Earl of Crawford and Balcarres. On his marriage to Harriet Loyd[14] in 1858 he adopted the surname Loyd-Lindsay, and was later created Lord Wantage in recognition of public and political services. His wife was the grand-daughter of Lewis Loyd, a self-made millionaire banker of Welsh origin, who had accumulated large holdings in Northamptonshire. His son, Samuel Jones Loyd, was no less successful, a strong Liberal and Free Trader, and a lifelong friend of George Warde Norman,[15] a director of the Bank of England. The Loyds had first purchased land in Berkshire in 1825, but it was not until 1854 that they began acquiring property at Ardington and Lockinge—relatively a late start in the history of Vic-torian landed empires. However after Lindsay's marriage to Harriet they moved fast, at least until 1870. After that date—except for one large purchase in 1890—they continued their acquisitions at a slower pace, in-filling and consolidating until the 1900s. In the end they got together over 20,000 acres in a compact block, the largest individual estate in the county; and it is fortunate that a thorough study of this enterprise, the principal personalities, and the impact of their ideas, has been recorded in two books,[16] from which this account is drawn.

When the Loyd-Lindsays moved into Lockinge House in 1859, the Berkshire Downs country was in many ways a relic of the medieval past, and Harriet described it in the following terms:

> Farming in those days was primitive, roads off the turnpike high-ways were mere cart-tracks impassable in winter . . . the cottages were fast decaying hovels through whose 'wattle and dab' walls a walking-stick could easily be thrust. The better dwellings, sur-rounded by muck-yards and rough homesteads, were occupied by the now almost extinct class of small owners and yeoman farmers, true sons of the soil, on which their limited interests were con-centrated. The speech of village folk and hill shepherds, an Anglo-Saxon patois, terse and pregnant, was difficult to understand, and many of their habits and customs were as primitive as their talk. The village school was oft-times held in a cottage parlour by the parish clerk, who added to his other duties that of imparting elementary instruction to a group of children who clustered round the old table on which he perched with his birch-rod beside him. Village boys followed the plough with their fathers from the age of seven . . . and many an old labourer can boast of having worked over seventy years on the land. It was a hard life, but the lads did not dislike it, and had no aspirations for town life.

With agriculture doing well and with plenty of family capital behind them, the Loyd-Lindsays launched early into a vigorous programme of improvement and reform—two primary schools (nine years before State education began), most of Lockinge village resited and rebuilt (with model 'Gothic' cottages), the setting-up of an estate yard for construction and repair with a staff of a hundred men, and the installation of two active clergymen in livings formerly served by absentees. As to farming, although most of the estate was let out to tenants up to the 1880s, there was a home farm where Robert Lindsay dumbfounded the neighbourhood with innovations, including a Fowler steam plough and cart horses imported from Normandy. But Lindsay was no playboy. In the good times his wheat and his beef steers sold at top prices; and in the bad—beginning in the late 1870s—he showed both courage and a masterly grasp of affairs. Harriet wrote:

> A series of bad seasons, co-operating with other causes, resulted in a prolonged period of depression which culminated in 1879, the worst year as regards low prices and low produce, and which proved disastrous alike to Landlords and to farmers. It was a despairingly wet and cold season; in Berkshire the harvest did not begin till September 1, and was, as might be expected, a very indifferent one. The worst cases of distress were in farms on the low-lying lands, where sheep rot set in with alarming severity; the hill farms at first fared somewhat better, but later on they also suffered greatly, as depression increased, and trouble pressed heavily on all. An entire change in the system of management on the Berkshire estate became necessary in order to avoid the evil of allowing much of the land to go out of cultivation, with the inevitable result that nine-tenths of the populations would find themselves forced to leave the district and endeavour to find employment elsewhere. Farms the leases of which had been eagerly competed for, a few years previously, could be let no longer. Offers of fresh leases there were none; rents began to tumble down; those tenants who desired to remain could only do so at a reduction of about fifty per cent. Many landlords would have let the tenants go, but Lord Wantage kept them on and helped them liberally through bad times.

None the less a growing number of tenants did give up, and Lindsay had no alternative but to take their land in hand. By December 1893 he was farming 4427 acres himself, and by November 1895 nearly 13,000 acres—or about two-thirds of the entire estate. It was the way he dealt with this situation that marked him out as a man apart. Commenting on the advantages of large-scale farming, he said:

> In the first place you get a superior sort of agriculturalist to manage the land, a better man in knowledge, both theoretical and practical, in training and in capacity, than the neighbouring farmers, so that he can set an example to the whole country round; farmers see the work better done, and the labourers are not slow to find it out. I employ

one head bailiff only for all the land I have in hand. He buys everything and sells everything, and under him are only ordinary working
foremen. In farming on a large scale there is a great economy; you can
use machinery more advantageously; and you can diminish the
number both of labourers and horses.

Lindsay also appointed a personal friend as resident agent. By these
means he secured overall control both of the farming operations and of
the other activities of the estate. To keep the former afloat, he grassed
down much of the arable, watered and fenced great stretches of the
downland, and concentrated on livestock—cattle, sheep and horses. This
paid off, once the initial cost had been met; and even with 2000 acres
under the plough he still managed to show a small profit. He described
the financial results as 'not altogether disastrous', the land bearing a
rent equivalent of about £1 per acre, and the whole estate yielding
around five per cent on the capital invested. But Lindsay was far more
than a shrewd businessman. Tory by tradition, Radical in outlook, with
an intelligent interested wife of Liberal stock backing him up, he became a social pioneer: launching profit-sharing, cooperative marketing,
savings bank, health insurance, and other communal self-help schemes.
He even put suggestion boxes in the fields, and made himself the friend
of his men, encouraging public discussion of affairs. Not all his ideas
worked out well in practice, but the cooperative stores at Ardington did.
Based on the Rochdale[17] system, and well equipped with a slaughter-
house and bakery, it induced its customers to give up cheap imported
food for some of the fresh produce they themselves had helped to raise.
   It was said that Lindsay was well able to afford all he did, because he
had plenty of money from sources outside the Lockinge estate. Quite
true. The same was said of Leonard and Dorothy Elmhirst at Dartington
in Devon, a generation later.[18] There was a strong similarity between the
two estates, in that both were launched shortly before an economic
depression, both drew on urban investments to finance and revive a
rural enterprise, both were permeated with social intentions, and both
made mistakes. This does not diminish their achievement by one iota.
How many rural owners, well found in the City, used their resources in
the way Lindsay did? What happened mostly was that an estate or farm
belonging to a rich man was simply subsidised by urban profits or
dividends: the annual loss being borne as part of the price of having a
place in the country, and of enjoying the prestige, the sport and all the
other delights that went with it. That was a very different thing from
trying to make a part of the countryside pay, or to revitalise its village
life, as Lindsay did. Free Trade, it is true, had long made it difficult for
individuals, even wealthy ones—who were not exceptional men as
Lindsay was—to do anything effective. But the point had been reached
at which most people had become conditioned to rural insolvency.

Confidence had lapsed, and so the basic attitude towards agriculture had deteriorated into one of defeatism.

Alternatives to Agriculture

One type of insolvency bred another. Forestry, the principal alternative to farming among the primary occupations of the land, had run a parallel historical course. The early settlers of Britain had come into a country blanketed with scrub and woodland, treeless probably only on the higher hills and downs. Before the use of iron for axes, they cannot have made much impression upon it. Persistent progress however was accomplished by the Anglo-Saxons and Scandinavians, who hacked out their holdings and cleared the ground for tillage and pasture: so that, at least by the end of the first millennium A.D., it had become necessary to reserve areas of uncleared territory (more or less covered with trees) as 'Royal Forests' or hunting grounds for the sovereign and his supporters —a system perpetuated by the Normans who preserved the game, mainly deer, by draconian laws.

At the same time local farmers were granted common rights—grazing, turf-cutting, wood gathering for fuel, etc.—similar to those in operation outside the Forests, as described earlier in this book. By the end of the Middle Ages a number of these Crown preserves had been 'disafforested': that is, the game laws had been suspended and the land passed to a private magnate, who thereafter exploited it for his own purposes—for sport, and for the timber requirements of his estate and neighbourhood. Enclosure followed in the course of time, just as it did in other parts of the country: conflicting often with the interests of villagers, who struggled to retain their rights in waste and woodland so long as the manorial system lasted.

Wood was of course the commonest raw material to hand for farm and household needs—fencing, firewood, furniture, utensils of all sorts, the building and repair of houses and barns, the fashioning of cart wheels and bodies, and use in a hundred other craft employments. In certain districts also it was heavily exploited for industrial purposes. Iron smelting demanded quantities of charcoal, tanning needed bark, and shipbuilding absorbed thousands of tons of oak and elm. In this way, over the centuries, great stretches of ancient woodland had been cleared; and deep inroads made into remaining reserves in such areas as the Weald of Surrey, Sussex and Kent, Sherwood in Nottinghamshire, the Forest of Dean in Gloucestershire, and the New Forest in Hampshire.

By the Restoration of Charles II there were still some sixty-eight Royal Forests in existence, largely in a neglected state.[19] But national concern was at last being aroused, partly by John Evelyn's plea for afforestation in his *Silva*,[20] published in 1664, and partly by official realisation that the Navy was running short of timber for ships.

Although Government action was never more than spasmodic, private enterprise stepped into the breach; and from then on, aided by favourable economic conditions for planting, landowners entered with enthusiasm into making good the devastations of the past. All during the eighteenth and early nineteenth centuries, an 'improving' landlord would plant trees in the same spirit and endeavour as he would clover and roots in his field rotations, or in-breed his cattle—but with this difference. Safe in his heritage, with the prospect of indefinite security ahead, he was prepared both to plant slow-growing hardwoods for the benefit of posterity, and enhance the existing landscape—by massive physical alteration if necessary—for the sake of amenity. 'Trees for use' became synonymous with 'trees for beauty'. Thus the whole of this period is justly renowned as one of aesthetic as well as silvicultural achievement, brought about by the genius of such landscape designers as Kent, 'Capability' Brown and Repton, and other humbler estate officers and gardeners working for enlightened patrons, who also built superb country houses in a setting in which they succeeded miraculously in moulding Nature into Art.

All this activity increased the wealth of owners, added substantially to employment in the countryside, and re-established a reserve of maturing timber. Most of the new trees were hardwoods: found either as replacements in depleted forests, or freshly planted in woodlands, parks, shelter belts and clumps, or in the thousands of miles of hedges raised for the purposes of enclosure towards the end of the eighteenth century and after. Nor were conifers entirely absent. Certain species were introduced both as nurse crops for the slower-growing deciduous trees, and for practical use as well—Scots pine (already native and important, especially in Scotland), Norway spruce, and European larch, the latter intended as a substitute for oak in shipbuilding. So Evelyn's call was answered.

> Naval timber was produced in quantity and helped to maintain England's sea power in the wars against the French. . . . Wood-working crafts and industries of every description were generally well supplied from home sources and, as the woodlands matured, so the furniture maker's art became more refined and elegant in the hands of masters such as Chippendale and Hepplewhite.[21]

As the nineteenth century advanced, however, tree planting and landscaping began to decline. The causes were complex, but at the root of everything lay the revolution in industry. Iron displaced timber in shipbuilding, and by 1870 it was estimated that 'the tonnage of iron ships launched, excluding warships, was more than five times that of wooden craft'.[22] At the same time coke was replacing charcoal for smelting, and chemical and other substitutes tan bark in the leather trade—two changes that struck a double blow at the traditional practice of oak coppicing. Most serious of all, the home market contracted yet further with the collapse of agriculture in the late 1870s and the growth of the trade in imported timber (mostly softwoods for cheap building)— all part of the pattern of *laissez-faire*, whereby it paid better to exchange industrial exports for foreign food and raw materials than nurture primary production at home. Nor was this the end of the lament. Many private woodlands stagnated because, under the terms of family settlements (which treated trees as part of the capital assets of an estate), felling was prohibited. This meant inevitably that forestry proper stood still, and woods came principally to serve as pleasure parks and preserves for pheasants, with the forester turned gamekeeper. They also provided an incidental reserve against the payment of 'death duties' and other taxation.

By 1900 nine-tenths of our timber requirements were being imported. However a handful of owners were already aware of the dangers of such dependence and, as in agriculture, the revival of interest in forestry had its origins before and during the depression—thanks largely to private pioneers.

> They felt that the woods should be replanted with commercially attractive species and foresaw that, if home supplies of softwood were to meet only a proportion of the new demands, the afforestation of large areas of new land with conifers was a further requirement in this country. . . . Much of the information gained during the second half of the nineteenth century about the performance of conifers under varied English conditions of soil and climate, may be attributed to the practical work of such men. They tried out new ideas in the management of woods, employing already well-known softwoods, such as the Scots and Corsican pines, Norway spruce and European larch, on a much more extensive scale than in the past. Many experimental plantings of freshly discovered conifers were also made. Trees were constantly being introduced from abroad by plant hunters such as David Douglas and John Veitch. Those species destined to become foremost in importance to forestry in this country included Douglas fir, introduced in 1827, Sitka spruce, which arrived in 1831 and Japanese larch, the seeds of which were first imported in 1861.[23]

Other species, such as the Giant *Sequoia* or *Wellingtonia*, dating from 1853, were adopted for ornamental purposes, and as Roger Miles points out 'it became fashionable to plant collections of many species of conifers together to form a pinetum or, if hardwoods were represented as well, an arboretum'[24]—as at Westonbirt in Gloucestershire, first established in 1829. Miles concludes:

> In these several ways sample groups and specimens of a large variety of softwood trees were established throughout the country.

When the twentieth-century forester was faced with the task of restoring England's timber resources as rapidly as possible with fast-growing conifers, valuable examples of the performance of different species under numerous geographical conditions were already available. Many of the conifers had become acclimatised to English conditions, but the failures were as instructive as the successes.[25]

Eventually the Government was roused. In the early 1900s land was acquired for State forestry in Gloucestershire and Monmouth, and a school set up for foresters in the Forest of Dean—nearly twenty years after Sir William Schlich[26] had opened a private school for forestry at Cooper's Hill in Gloucestershire.

'In 1905 this was transferred to Oxford University where it has since become the most important centre of forestry knowledge in England and the Commonwealth countries.'[27]

Finally in 1909 the newly formed Development Commission[28] was made responsible, among several other duties, for promoting forestry. By 1914 however the basic situation in England had hardly changed. Only five per cent of the land was under woodland, mostly hardwoods, mature and ageing. Virtually all softwood timber was still imported; and the stage was set for a frantic wartime demand that cleared about one-sixth of the acreage under trees, and consumed about one-third of the volume of timber standing at the outset of hostilities with Germany.

*   *   *

The decline of forestry and farming was not the whole story. Certain other primary or extractive industries, now ordinarily regarded as urban, began and remained for many years rural in character. That is, they were operated in small units and served by small communities which, apart from the peculiarities of their trade and other local distinctions, differed little from other settlements in the countryside. They ranged, for example, from the local chalk or clay pit, to the myriad stone quarries in the limestone belt (wrapped round England from East Yorkshire, through the Cotswolds, and down to Dorset), the early iron and coal fields in the midlands and the north, the Staffordshire pot-banks, and the tin mines of Cornwall. In a similar category were the coastal villages which depended on fishing. In many instances the men, aided by their families, were smallholders on the side. Whatever its nature, the particular industry supported a number of ancillary trades and skills, without which the village would have lost its meaning. Farming found work, for example, for the miller, hedger, and smith; forestry for the carpenter and wood turner; quarrying for the mason, brickmaker, and builder; metals maintained a multitude of employments, large and small. The impact might be purely local or broadly regional. At one time, for instance, the spinners and weavers of East

Anglia populated a whole textile region, with a wide intake of English wool and an extensive export of finished goods abroad; yet the work was all done domestically in the cottages of Norfolk, Suffolk, and neighbouring counties. It was the diversity of skills and the interplay of primary and secondary employment that underpinned rural society, and which in turn only declined when the economic balance was permanently disturbed.

Decline was irregular and protracted. Already by the mid-eighteenth century new industrial techniques were developing, soon to transform the entire economy and turn Britain (England in particular) from an agricultural and handicraft nation into an industrial one: multiplying many times the towns and their inhabitants. Just as enclosure destroyed the peasantry in the open-field districts, so machinery and steam power eliminated one cottage craft after another. It is true that in time fresh jobs were created on the land by mechanisation and new methods in agriculture: so that in the prosperous days of High Farming there was still plenty of work for craftsmen serving farms and the large estates; but in most other rural trades there was little respite. In some—wool, for example—collapse was complete within a generation. Everywhere craftsmen found it daily harder to hold up against the tide of mass production. The very essence of craftsmanship—its individuality, its emphasis on quality and on the performance of the *whole* process of manufacture—placed it at a disadvantage commercially, and rendered it ever less competitive.[29] And as the nineteenth century advanced, the village community became more accessible and more vulnerable to change. The old monopolies had not been difficult to maintain in the absence of good communications; indeed their very isolation had been a source of strength. But all this began to evaporate before the turnpikes, the canals, the great trunk roads built by Thomas Telford and John Macadam, and finally the railways. It seemed only a question of time before the impetus of urban industry forced all the remaining mills, kilns and village workshops to close.

By 1900 the business side of country life had become fatally unbalanced, not merely because farming and forestry were in the doldrums, but because the alternative employments were facing extinction. Moreover the economic equilibrium has never been regained; for however successful the recovery of farming and forestry (and in 1900 this was still a long way off), the march of mechanisation on the land meant that primary employment must decline—let alone find jobs for displaced craftsmen or their sons. A chain reaction occurred, one loss or failure in rural business detonating another, with far-reaching effect.

*   *   *

The End of the Old Order, 1914
A live society is powered by work. Once the jobs have gone, then the

community they created is bound to disappear. An early symptom in England was the disintegration of folk life. With the passing of the peasant, it was inevitable that the native culture of the countryside should drift towards its demise. Folk dances, folk songs, local customs, dialect, the very values and attitudes characteristic of countrymen—in all their vigour and variety, deriving ultimately from man's intimacy with Nature–weakened and waned. Here are a few examples. The last 'Scouring' of the Uffington White Horse took place in 1857. The Mumming Play, once a piece of pagan ritual, hi-jacked by Christianity and livened with local allusions, deteriorated into meaninglessness. Again, as labour left the land or moved more easily about, it became customary to advertise for work—at any rate to seek it in ways other than by attending Hiring Fairs which, shorn of their *raison d'être*, deteriorated into oblivion: as did the festivities that had turned them into traditional holidays, traditionally enjoyed.

Although survivals lingered, lustily in places, they remained survivals. There are today whole libraries of folklore, and important societies devoted to the study of folk art. These are sophisticated institutions, founded by collectors who moved in just in time to write down words and tunes from diffident minstrels, record dance movements, save by-gones for museums, and publish dictionaries of dialect and place-names.

Indeed we owe our scholars and field workers a great debt, for other-wise a valuable part of our national heritage would have vanished into oblivion. Theirs was a work of salvage, not resurrection.

The story is full of fascination. It was on Boxing Day 1899 that Cecil Sharp happened to see the Headington Morris Men, accom-panied on the concertina by William Kimber, himself an excellent dancer and then still a young man. The team was performing out of season, Whitsun being the proper time, but work was slack and money was short. For Sharp the performance was a revelation, and he was inspired from that moment on to devote the rest of his life to recovering and recording the heritage of English folk dance. A year or two later, in September 1903, while staying with his friend, Charles Marson, per-petual curate of Hambridge in Somerset, he took down the words and music of *The Seeds of Love* from the gardener, John England; and that was the beginning of his part in saving folk song.[30]

It is a sad thing, but whenever a collector starts work, that very fact is a sign that whatever he is collecting is approaching the end of its natural span. Sharp aimed, and largely succeeded, in giving his dis-coveries new life by introducing them into the curriculum of schools; and that is where they, remain today in association with the admirable work of the English Folk Dance and Song Society (which Sharp helped to found).[31] Yet no one would deny that this is revival, not survival, conscious, sophisticated and enjoyable, but artificial because obviously it is no longer the product of a self-sufficient rural society. More pertinent perhaps is the influence of folk art upon contemporary art, expressed in radio ballads, pop music and pop painting; but that is outside the scope of this chapter.

In sum, as man lost his awe for the mystery of Nature, so he lost interest in the art of honouring it in ritual and entertainment. Science and sophistication killed tradition, just as they weakened faith in the dogmas of religion. And—as with the economy of the countryside— once the heart had missed its beat and the blood ceased to flow freely, then the whole body of rural society suffered in every part. The remedy moreover hastened the decline. In this case quicker communications made the town as easy to reach for entertainment as for work; and what was discovered there—by reason of its novelty, of being ready-made, of its aura of superiority—came to be preferred to the customary attractions of the village, which depended wholly upon the inventiveness and the participation of those that attended them. Thus further damage was done to that sense of self-sufficiency, which had hitherto permeated all of rural life.

As to social services, ironically even the benefits conferred by Liberal legislation—by the Old Age Pensions Act 1909, the National Health Insurance Act 1911, and the growth of other schemes for mitigating the evils of poverty and unemployment—had parallel repercussions. As Whitehall and County Hall took the place of the manor and the parsonage as the main sources of social aid in the countryside, substituting —as democracy demanded—public right for private discretion, they did so at the expense of what had been worthwhile in the old pattern of patronage and self-help. Personal benefactions, curious charities attached to church and chapel, especially village friendly societies—with their distinctive emblems, bands, banners, feasts and rituals—all declined or died out altogether. In other official ways too the town intruded into the fabric of country life. In administration the village had been governed by the vestry since the Act of 1601 until, under the pressure of change, it lost in the nineteenth century one local responsibility after another— Poor Law business in 1834, followed by highways, police, and other matters. In 1888 County Councils were established, in 1894 Rural District and Parish Councils, which deprived the vestry of its remaining civil powers and returned it to its original place as a unit of Church government.

As to education, before 1870 about half the children in the entire country were never taught at all, despite vigorous efforts by private pioneers and philanthropic societies to provide schools. The Education Act of 1870 was the bottom rung of a new State ladder, at first supplementing the voluntary and fee-paying institutions, and then gradually supplanting them, a process still working itself out today. Soon after 1870 therefore every village had its elementary school, State or denominational; and this was followed thirty years later by the adoption of the

Traditional stock farm

FARM BUILDINGS

Modern barn for 1200 sheep

Grazing land by the Roman Wall

FARMSCAPES

Fenland arable

County Council as the local education authority, with powers to set up secondary schools, to which a limited number of elementary pupils might gain admission by means of scholarships. There is no need to continue the tale. The point is that it installed the town in a commanding position in yet another vital sector of rural society. Education became town controlled and town conceived. The curriculum of the village school was soon divorced from its environment, dialect gave place to grammar, and bucolic customs denigrated in a hundred ways. A child with aptitude and ambition might receive efficient secondary schooling only in the nearest town: so that, from an early age, opportunity became synonymous with exodus from the land.

The message of urban superiority was conveyed most strikingly perhaps in sheer physical improvements. Main water from the tap was more convenient than hauling up a bucket at the village well; gas and electricity gave better light than lamps and candles; a water closet was more hygienic, more refined, than an earth closet; a straight tarred road, kerb lined and wire fenced, was preferable in every way to a dusty track winding between high banks and overgrown hedges that had to be hand laid and hand trimmed. Such things came to be accepted automatically for their obvious visible advantages.

*   *   *

Decline did not, and cannot ever, continue in a vacuum. The very weakness induced by economic change encouraged the town to exploit the country for its own purposes in a positive and far-reaching manner. For the old order the consequences were disastrous. The lack of opportunity at home had long been sucking the young and enterprising out of the countryside, so that villages lost their manpower as well as other means of revival. At the same time urban expansion accelerated, partly to accommodate growing population and industry, partly to seek ways of escape. The two stages were successive, then simultaneous. Each year building absorbed thousands of acres around the towns, engulfing the peripheral villages in suburbia. As communications improved, the pace quickened and the impact of town life was felt farther and farther afield. In an attempt to capture the charm of the country, without being involved in its realities, businessmen began to settle their families in places up to thirty miles or more from their offices, and commuted. It meant that, in the course of time, what were once recognisable rural communities, with their own sources of employment and social institutions, became dependent dormitories, pale imitations of town or village, without the vitality and identity of either.

Before the motor car, this kind of dispersal was relatively restricted. When Soames Forsyte built Robin Hill, at Mapledurham in the Thames Valley, his method of travel was train and cab; and that was how Young Jolyon, who bought the house off him, went up and down to London before the First World War. In other words, so long as the horse or the bicycle dominated the road, commuter building in the countryside was confined to existing communities, or their immediate neighbourhood, which were served by rail. It was not until the 1920s that the new motor age began to open up the rural areas at large and at speed, introducing an era of ribbon building and other forms of sporadic development, which are the ultimate negation of social existence.

A similar situation was induced by 'retirement', a matter of much importance in a wealthy urbanised society. Seaside and cathedral towns, spas and watering-places, had been the first to attract large residential colonies of *rentiers* and others living on pensions and savings. Brighton, Scarborough, Winchester, Harrogate, Bath, Cheltenham, Chichester, Bournemouth—the list was already long by 1900, and lengthened steadily as people then discovered the advantages of settling in country towns and villages. A pleasant accessible location was of course essential, preferably well away from areas of industry and urban squalor, which ironically often yielded the very dividends that made retirement possible. By their nature retired people tended to congregate together, being of an age, without children, and belonging to a similar social background. Their aim was seclusion, absence of noise and traffic, and a surrounding that combined town comforts and facilities with rural intimacy and quiet. At least that was the idea. A garden was a necessity and a view over fields; but so was the tradesman who called twice a week, a lending library, and a fast train service for occasional expeditions to 'town' or abroad. Roots rarely dug deep because the link between residence and retirement was so tenuous. In general a retired person had no compelling need to live in any particular place, other than personal preference or a desire to be near relations and friends. It did not compare with the sense of identity felt by the man who lived over his business or farmed his own land; and this too constituted the common factor between commuting and retirement, which might be described—if not as rootlessness, at least as mobility. In neither case did the person concerned feel bound by overriding economic ties to the place where he lived.

Wherever colonies of this kind existed in strength, then they tended to weaken the host community. If they predominated, they often altered it out of all recognition. Ordinarily a village or small town would draw its vitality from two main sources: first, from the work it offered and the stake held by its inhabitants in the various businesses that provided the work; secondly, from the variety of ages, classes, and interests that composed its society—evident in its administration, schools, clubs, inns, places of worship, and all their associated activities. In a village the connection between work and society was especially close. It had to be if the community was to function at all, for sheer lack of numbers. Everyone had a job to do and a place to fill—squire, parson, schoolmaster, the farmers, craftsmen, traders and labourers—within the hierarchy evolved out of their occupations. Whatever the defects, the system worked in its fashion for centuries; and when it finally began to falter because the economy had contracted, the imposition of a colony of urban residents provided no ready-made solution. The village remained a ghost.

By 1914 the old order of country life—weak within and under siege without—was fast collapsing.

The Way back to Protection: 1900–1947

For the countryside the four years, August 1914 to November 1918, were both an end and a beginning. Much of what remained of traditional life and ways was obliterated, at the same time as bold new undertakings were being born, or others recently started forced on in the hothouse of war.

Farming for example was already on the mend at the turn of the century; 1895 had been the pit of the depression. Thereafter prices rose slowly, due partly to an all-round improvement in trade, and partly to radical changes in farm practice. Between 1871 and 1901 more than three million acres of arable land in England and Wales had been turned into pasture,[32] mainly for milk; and for this trade, in which the railways played a vital part, the sky was the limit. Likewise market gardening (glass culture and certain field vegetables, flowers and fruit)—despite keen competition from abroad—was becoming a specialised and successful enterprise in such areas as the Vale of Evesham, and parts of the Thames Valley, Kent, Bedfordshire, Cornwall, Lancashire and the Fens. Here then were two important shifts in production away from immemorial arable and mixed husbandry, that took full advantage of the climate and of the proximity of markets in the ever-expanding towns. Even so the new pattern depended heavily on imported feeding-stuffs and fertilisers, while the nation continued to buy most of its meat, butter, cheese, and bread grain from overseas.

Slowly and painfully agriculture was adapting itself to new demands, though—however you looked at it—it no longer rode high in the economy of the State. In 1867–9 it had contributed about one-sixth of the national output, in 1911–13 less than one-fifteenth.[33] The number of male farmers and farmworkers in England and Wales fell from about one and a half millions in 1861 to around one million in 1911.[34] Men left the land as a matter of course, not only to find better-paid jobs in the towns and overseas, but because—owing to rising productivity—home agriculture had to do without them. A smaller labour force made possible a slight rise in wages, from one to two shillings per week according to the district between 1882 and 1910, the best weekly rates ranging from fourteen shillings (or less) in the south to eighteen shillings (or more) in the north, plus perks.[35] Mechanisation in the modern sense was making some impression too: not merely improved horse-drawn implements such as haymakers and corn harvesters (notably the self-binder), but several thousand stationary oil engines for pumping water and for driving barn machinery, more steam sets, the occasional early tractor, and a pre-historic milking machine or two. None the less in 1914 farming was still a horse and muscle industry, and it was the war —and the aftermath of the war—that revolutionised the mechanics of it.

Better prices and fewer hands encouraged improvement in other ways, converting new-fangle into necessity: the use of basic slag (a by-product of the steel industry developed in 1879) to regenerate old pastures; silage (grass and other crops harvested green) a laborious business and hard to mechanise but better than bad hay; experiments with seeds mixtures; concentrates for balanced feeding; milk recording, etc. Moreover it was in this, the technique of farming, that the Government —uninhibited by the politics of Free Trade—was able to give substantial help: by measures concerning the quality of feeding-stuffs, fertilisers, and dairy produce, the purity of seeds, the control of disease, tenant right, finance for capital improvements, the easing of local taxation, and the provision of smallholdings and allotments.[36]

Most important was the fact that after 1890 public money became available for agricultural education and research. Before then progress had depended on private initiative and finance.[37] Even the renowned Experimental Station at Rothamsted, founded by Sir John Lawes in 1843, had had to be endowed out of the sale of his fertiliser business. There were other benefactors too, but the new impetus came through the County Councils and the Board of Agriculture, which set up groups of colleges and departments of agriculture at universities, offering one- to three-year courses for diplomas and degrees. At first suspect among ordinary farmers, it was not long before graduates from these places made themselves felt, and in time an academic training came to be accepted as a necessary complement to practical experience. This was well illustrated by the career of A. D. Hall (Sir Daniel Hall), one of the great names in British agriculture. Starting as a school science teacher, he became in 1891 one of the first external lecturers under the new agricultural education scheme. In 1894 he was appointed the first Principal of Wye Agricultural College, founded by the County Councils of Kent and Surrey, where he was singularly successful in all his contacts with local, highly critical farmers. Eight years later he succeeded Sir John Gilbert, the first Director of Rothamsted.

Hall was keenly aware that original research, as well as education, was essential to progress in agriculture. At many of the colleges the teachers themselves were carrying out their own investigations and finding money from their own resources. By keeping in touch with each other's work and by publication,[38] they were gradually building up a body of expert information. Even so this kind of work was too important, too fundamental, to have to depend on private effort. Ultimately in 1910, thanks to the Development Fund Act promoted by Lloyd George, Chancellor of the Exchequer, funds were forthcoming for the organisation of agricultural research on a national scale. Hall became a Development Commissioner, and so did—among other notables—R. E. Prothero (Lord Ernle), author of the classic history of English farming.[39] The plan adopted was to allot one or more Research Institutes to a particular branch of the subject. For example Rothamsted became the centre for soil study and plant nutrition; Cambridge had two centres—one for animal nutrition and the other for plant breeding; dairy research was concentrated at Reading; agricultural economics at Oxford; fruit growing at Long Ashton, near Bristol. All these and other Institutes were independent within the general framework of State support, and the number was increased as time passed. The only centre directly under the State was the Veterinary Research Station at Weybridge, which was necessarily involved in day-to-day problems concerning the control of animal diseases.

It is significant that at a time when agriculture was still in the doldrums, the Government began to treat it in a new and responsible manner. If the dichotomy of land use was to be resolved in favour of business rather than a way of life, then the business of farming must have a fair chance, and the subject be treated as a science of infinite complexity requiring the best brains in its service. This was action of a fundamental kind, for it heralded a complete change in public attitude. Science was not solely responsible for the transformation. Amenity was another influence of critical importance, to be described later. But the changes that overtook farming, forestry, and land use generally in the next few difficult decades, could not have happened without science. Technical support preceded economic support. In other words all the steps taken by the State before 1914 paved the way for the purely protective legislation that started to put agriculture back on its feet in the 1930s.[40]

Research and education did not of course stand still after the First World War. Although farming slumped in the 1920s, due to the fall in world food prices and the withdrawal of Government guarantees, science was not abandoned. On the contrary the work expanded, and to good effect. At Aberystwyth for example, at the Welsh Plant Breeding Station, the grass and clover strains developed by Professor Stapledon (Sir George Stapledon) so revolutionised hill husbandry that they altered farm practice in general, and contributed directly to the success of food production in the Second World War. Indeed research was moving on so fast that in 1930 the Agricultural Research Council came into being to co-ordinate all the activities that were proliferating—an astounding escalation of effort in barely twenty years, and far ahead of practical farming. Progress in education was less dramatic. None the less it developed into a comprehensive, possibly over-elaborate, system covering the whole country, and at all levels. At the top a provincial advisory service attached to the colleges and university departments provided farmers with the expert services of agricultural specialists. At the bottom the county farm institutes offered them lectures and practical demonstrations, and also trained young people in farming. This was a good investment and a piece of social wisdom, for it was aimed at the next generation of farmers and farm workers, and equipped them with knowledge their parents never had the chance of acquiring. It took away too some of the stigma laid on the land, mostly by towns-people who dismissed agriculture as the kind of work only done by those who had not the wit to do anything else.

A pertinent criticism was that so few college graduates went into farming proper. This was largely a matter of money. Although capital had been available for some years to buy farms, or carry out improvements, by means of mortgages—and after 1928 it became possible to raise cash on the security of farm stock as well—yet no one without some money of his own could make a start. In any event, to have to carry a huge load of loan repayments and interest at the outset was a severe handicap to a young farmer, as well as being a depressing thing. The only alternative was to go into management, but the number of farms capable of carrying a manager was limited, and in early days at least there was a common prejudice against college trainees, who were thus compelled to crowd into the administrative side of agriculture or into the occupations that supplied and serviced farmers. Restraint on entry for these reasons did farming no good. It discouraged initiative and put the profession at a needless disadvantage with industry and other kinds of urban employment.

*   *   *

In other ways however agriculture was conforming to industrial practice, e.g. in collective representation and bargaining, and this took into account three interested parties—farm workers, farmers and landowners.

Although the union movement launched by Joseph Arch in the 1870s had petered out, it was eventually replaced by two new workers' organisations in the early years of the new century. One—the precursor of the National Union of Agricultural Workers (N.U.A.W.)—was pioneered by its Secretary, George Edwards, a remarkable man, already in his fifties. At first fostered by the Liberal interest, it broke away in 1911 and became affiliated to the Trades Union Congress (T.U.C.). Edwards was a dogged organiser. He quickly accumulated members, and with the help of the railwaymen won an important dispute in South Lancashire over Saturday half-holiday and overtime pay. In other instances he was able to negotiate a settlement without strike action.

The second organisation to recruit farm workers was the precursor of the Transport and General Workers' Union (T.G.W.U.), with George Dallas as the responsible official. Dallas started work a few years after Edwards, and concentrated on building up branches in different parts of the country in order to regulate wages and conditions—particularly because wide variations occurred between one county, even one parish, and the next. This was the principal task of the two unions—to secure minima and reasonable uniformity in wage rates, to contest all forms of victimisation, and to win recognition for themselves.

The strongest of the three parties were the farmers, who also combined. The National Farmers' Union (N.F.U.) grew out of the Lincolnshire Farmers' Union, founded by a Scotsman, Colin Campbell, in 1908. Representative both of tenants and owner-occupiers, the farmers had already secured wide freedom of action under the law. Thanks to successive Agricultural Holdings Acts, they were no longer fettered by restrictive leases which dictated the way they should farm (except here and there to preserve high-grade pasture). On the other hand they were entitled to outgoings when they left the farm, and later to compensation for disturbance if given notice to quit. By 1914 they had become a powerful political force, with whom the Government was glad to treat in the emergency of wartime, and after.

In some respects the landowners found themselves in the weakest position of all. Although a number benefited from their dual role as owner-occupiers, those in possession of large estates let off into tenant farms were no longer free agents. They had lost the commanding status of the past, and they had suffered severely under the depression. Investment in agricultural land was barely profitable; and when rents returned less than three per cent it was difficult to do more than a minimum of maintenance to land and buildings. For necessary expansion and redevelopment, capital had to come from outside. While these conditions lasted, country landowning attracted for its prestige and its pleasures rather than for any economic reason—not a good image in a country that was growing steadily more conscious of the inequalities of society. Because of this, and because land still rested in relatively few hands, largely by inheritance, owners faced a series of political assaults, starting with the imposition of estate duty on agricultural property in 1894. Not onerous at first, the rate rose steeply after the Liberal Budget of 1909, which also planned taxation on the increase in value of undeveloped land. Lloyd George, Chancellor of the Exchequer, was particularly threatening in his attitude. Nationalisation of land was in the air, and the crisis developed into a national issue affecting the powers and privileges of the House of Lords.

By this time the owners too had decided to combine—in 1907, one year before the farmers—forming the Central, later the Country Landowners' Association (C.L.A.). The first honorary secretary was

Charles Bathurst, later Lord Bledisloe, a great agriculturalist, and a man of vision and wide sympathies who was justly honoured during his life for all his services to the countryside. Paradoxically it was the break-up of many of the great estates after the war that brought strength to the C.L.A. This shifted the emphasis of membership to owner-occupiers with 500 acres or less, and greatly increased their numbers. The C.L.A. also played an important part in post-war legislation and ultimately, in 1947, was awarded statutory recognition as a partner in agriculture.

*   *   *

It is clear that in the generation before 1914 much was happening that was to determine the character of the countryside after 1918. Farming was trailing in the wake of industry, though very much in its own way and at its own pace. That was inevitable. Its very variety resisted rationalisation. And however compulsive the new drives and incentives, it was no small thing to break away from centuries of tradition—in this instance a compound of empirical but tried farm practice, mixed up with paternalism in human relations and an intuitive respect for the forces of Nature. Even progressive agriculture in the nineteenth century had not removed or replaced the basic inheritance of 'land sense'. Nothing dies harder than country custom, and even in the 1960s it was possible for George Ewart Evans to record from living witnesses the ways people had farmed and served the land in the pre-industrial age in East Anglia.[41] They were ways that had far more in common with the origins of settled farming a thousand years or more earlier, than what is happening in that region today.

On the other hand the gradual rationalisation of farming was inevitable, and it led to a change of heart inside the country community itself. Thus the 1890s were the real Rubicon between one era and the next. The division was not merely one between countrymen and townsmen, for that had already appeared under Free Trade, but between the new generation of farmers and the old. The gap widened year by year, since science and economics reacted upon each other and combined to secure a rising return per acre and per man from a diminishing area of land. However so long as peace lasted and exports flourished, the pace of rural change was restrained. Heavier imports satisfied the higher demand for food, and the country was able to let agriculture go on fending for itself, and so continue to afford social survivals from an earlier age of rural life.

The First World War was 'the great divide', not only because it accelerated changes already evident in the countryside, but because it introduced Government controls on a scale never known before. This did not happen at once. For the first two years the official attitude towards agriculture was one of extraordinary complacency. Unlike the other carefully laid plans of the Committee of Imperial Defence, no preparations had been made before the war for the increased production of food at home. Farming had not been besieged for ninety-nine years, but back in 1815 England had been able to feed herself entirely out of her own resources. In 1914, with four times the population, she could only supply about one-third of all her food requirements. The Government simply assumed that imports would continue to arrive without fuss under the sure guard of the British Navy, and that Allied shipping as a whole would always suffice to offset losses by enemy action. But this was not the only area of complacency. The idea that all would be over by Christmas, each successive Christmas—though Lord Kitchener thought and said otherwise—took a lot of shifting. As things turned out, the war lasted very nearly five Christmases, jolted the structure of industry as violently as it did agriculture, punctured the Imperial idea, and shook the nation out of its easy assumptions in almost every department of existence. But it took two years, i.e. until the end of 1916, to reach a sense of reality, a near-naval defeat at Jutland, a horrifying offensive on the Somme in which Britain's first real citizen army suffered 400,000 casualties in four and a half months, the loss of half a million tons of shipping in the last quarter of the year—and worse which was to come.

Suddenly food was in the forefront; but unlike industry which under pressure can be mobilised in a matter of months, farming cannot; and by the time Lloyd George had replaced Asquith as Prime Minister and injected a dynamic change into the conduct of the war, agriculture had fallen frighteningly behind. One-sixth of all the farm workers in England and Wales had already enlisted or disappeared into other jobs. Farms were short of labour, horses, fertilisers, machinery and other equipment, while facilities for servicing and repair had also run down. Besides this, farming had to compete with massive manpower calls by other services: nearly one million demanded by the Army alone, and 300,000 for munitions. To add to the gloom, the harvest of 1916 had been poor, and the succeeding winter was proving long and cold. France had already lost many thousands of acres of fertile farmland by invasion, and even in Britain the acreage of winter-sown wheat had heavily declined. The need was desperate but all too clear—to plough up millions of acres of grassland and get back to the intensive arable husbandry of the 1860s. How to do it?

The Government was not entirely unprepared. In June 1915 a Committee had been set up under Lord Milner to make recommendations, should the war last beyond the harvest of 1916. The Committee worked fast, and within a month proposed many of the things that had to be done eighteen months later—mainly a guaranteed minimum price for certain crops, and the control of farm operations by local committees. In the event some of the committees were formed, otherwise nothing effective was done and the report pigeon-holed. At the end of 1916 however the situation was such that it called for total planning and control of all national resources, human and material. *Laissez-faire* was thrown overboard, and although already too late to affect the harvest of 1917 to any serious degree, State control of agriculture was imposed almost overnight. A Food Production Department came into being, alongside the Board of Agriculture, on 1st January, 1917, and was made responsible for a crash campaign, which in the end achieved remarkable success. County Agricultural Executive Committees (C.A.E.Cs.) were set up to assess potential production in sixty-one areas, and ensure (by compulsion if necessary) increased output from existing tillage and the ploughing-up of pasture. By the end of the war, the Department had recruited (training many of them) 120,000 male workers (soldiers, prisoners-of-war, volunteers and schoolboys) and 300,000 women, including a full-time Land Army, 16,000 strong. It supplied 4,200 tractors, 10,000 horses, and many thousands of implements; and secured large quantities of fertilisers, feeding-stuffs and seed. The results were impressive—an extra three million acres ploughed, most of it for wheat, oats and potatoes; while the number of vegetable allotments was trebled. By the autumn of 1918, despite the reduction of grassland and a shortage of feeding-stuffs, milk and meat had been fairly maintained, while the production of grain and potatoes (the energy foods) had gone up by about fifty per cent. One authority estimated that in terms of calories the nett output of home-grown food in 1918 had risen by approximately twenty-four per cent in comparison with that of 1909–13.[42]

Behind these facts and figures lay the necessary legislation, mainly the Corn Production Act of 1917. This guaranteed minimum prices for wheat and oats for the following six years and for potatoes for the 1917 harvest; set up an Agricultural Wages Board, which fixed minimum rates at not less than twenty-five shillings per week—in fact both prices and wages well exceeded these levels; held down rents; and provided the powers to control cultivation. In 1919, in the euphoria of victory, the old Board of Agriculture was modernised into a Ministry; consultative machinery was established, representative of all interests in agriculture; and in 1920 came the Agriculture Act which, by and large, placed the provisions of 1917 on a permanent footing. These measures, and all that was achieved on the land, were positive and inspiring. People really felt that the long depression was over at last, and that Government interference was a small price to pay for a renewed and reasonably prosperous farm industry. After seventy years, Protection had come back.

But had it? In the event the whole structure, so painfully erected, collapsed within twelve months. The war had affected every part of the world, and stimulated the global production of food, especially of wheat. In consequence grain prices fell steeply in 1921, so that all the agricultural price guarantees had to be repealed. Even the Agricultural Wages Board was abolished. Wages sank from around fifty shillings to thirty shillings per week, all the wartime ploughland was lost, and farming dropped back to where it had started. Worse still, all the confidence and enthusiasm instilled by the war evaporated, leaving a legacy of deep distrust among country people of every sort.

✳   ✳   ✳

One of the most vivid descriptions of the 1920s was recorded by a Wiltshire farmer, A. G. Street, in his book, *Farmer's Glory*.[43] It is a story told from the inside. Following the death of his father, young Street took on the tenancy of the farm at Michaelmas 1918 at double the normal rent.[44] It was a large mixed holding—400 acres of arable, ninety of downland, forty of water meadows, 100 of pasture, carrying two milking herds and a breeding flock of Hampshire Down sheep. All the cultivations were performed by horse and hand, and normally there was a staff of over twenty men. That was how things had gone before the war. Street was not accepted for the Army, but helped his father run the farm in traditional style, albeit with one or two significant changes. The breeding flock, around which all the operations seemed to revolve, was sold and replaced by stores[45]. Grain growing absorbed more and more of the land, swallowing up the fertility banked over the years by the folding of the flock.[46] As the staff diminished, so many things that used to be done as a matter of course, went by the board. In particular the hedges and ditches were left to look after themselves. Instead of singling, and hand-hoeing, the roots had to be thinned out by repeated harrowing, and looked thoroughly dirty as a result. The farm became daily more like a food factory, and an untidy one at that—a fact deeply resented by master and man alike. 'But there it was. There was only barely enough labour for essentials and the frills had to be cut out. From 1916 the farms in the countryside were allowed to deteriorate or to "go back".'[47]

Then suddenly it was all over.

As all the world knows, the war ended in November, and it was as if a heavy weight had been lifted from the whole country. The reaction to this was that the whole population went pleasure mad. All classes indulged in a feverish orgy for all those sports and pastimes which had been impossible for four long weary years.

Rural communities were no exception. Hunting, shooting, fishing, and the like, suddenly reappeared in our midst. In the summer tennis parties became the order of the day. Farmer's Glory was going to be as splendid as of old, only more so. More so because we all had money to burn. I find this hard to write. It is not a pleasant thing to set down on paper what a tawdry life one lived in those few years immediately after the war. But the majority of farmers took no thought for the morrow, their only idea was to have a good time. Instead of living for one's farm, the only desire was to get away from it and pursue pleasure elsewhere . . . It seems incredible now, but we began—God forgive me—to have late dinner in the evenings . . . In short, farmers swanked. . . . For this, I blame the motor car. Its advent marked an epoch in rural affairs rather more definitely, I think, than in urban ones. . . . Farmers now went away from home for frequent holidays, to seaside resorts and to London. They discarded the breeches and gaiters of their ancestors for plus-fours of immaculate cut, incredible design, and magnificent bagginess . . . Personally I started golf in 1919, and in 1921 I was the proud possessor of a handicap of eight, which statement tells only too plainly the amount of time I must have spent on the game.[48]

It was on the crest of this wave, with a high horizon still in sight, that many tenants purchased their farms at inflated prices. They were joined by newcomers of two kinds—Servicemen prepared to invest their gratuities and borrow the balance, and town traders who had done well in the war, ready and able to pay substantially more than the ordinary farmer, whether to buy or rent.

It was in 1921 that the first suspicion of anything wrong in the farming world was noted. In spite of the bonus paid under the Corn Production Act that year, money was a little tight. The harvest of 1922 left no doubt in my mind that things were going—no, had gone—wrong. It was a wet summer, and the price of both corn and milk had slumped badly. I found that I had a great difficulty to pay my interest and meet my other liabilities.[49]

It was the beginning of the new slump and Street summed up the change that came over prices and profits:

Take the case of any farm that changed hands at Michaelmas 1920, and again say in 1927. At the first change the incoming tenant would have been forced to stock the farm on the basis of the prices realised at the outgoing tenant's sale, cows at £60 each, horses at £100 each and sometimes more, and the other stock and implements at similarly inflated prices. His rent would also have been based on the prosperous condition of farming at that date. . . . At the second change of tenancy in 1927, the incoming man would have purchased his cows at about £24 per head, and his other stock at a similar depreciation. In addition, the landlord would have had to reduce the rent of the farm considerably, in order to get a tenant, and, in the case of a large arable farm, would have probably grassed and fenced a large portion of it as an added attraction.[50]

What Street did was to turn to grass farming and outdoor milking, but that is a later part of the story.

Comments of a different kind, no less pithy, about country life at this time, were made by J. W. Robertson Scott in his book, *The Dying Peasant*.[51] Though never in practice as a farmer, Robertson Scott had a rural background, the son of Lowland Scots parents settled in Cumberland. An energetic trenchant journalist, friend of George Edwards (founder of the N.U.A.W.), and a strong Labour man, he propaganded all his life for rural reforms. At the age of sixty he started *The Countryman*, publishing it single-handed with his wife from their Cotswold manor house at Idbury in Oxfordshire. Although he made a place for himself as the editor of a successful quarterly, as Justice of the Peace and County Councillor, Scott remained an outsider in the countryside. He had strong prejudices. The fact that he hated blood sports, did not smoke, never drank, rarely ate meat, and always poked fun at the Church, made him an uncomfortable man, not much liked by his neighbours. The passage that follows was probably compounded of Idbury and surrounding hamlets.

Not one of the Nether Gloaze old men, within reach of their pensions, after a burdened, harassed life of making ends meet and continuous discouragement, is wanting land. Younger men in Nether Gloaze, short of physique or of gumption for the railway or the police or the Dominions, or in such a hobble of shiftless parentage and domestic squalor that some of the grit they had has been worn out of them, do not look beyond weekly wages, and sometimes, no doubt, doing no more for them than they have to. . . . Before the war, the village had no great faith in what its betters told it about the land or religion or anything else. Now it has hardly any. . . . These Nether Gloaze folk have not been masters of their own lives. Other people have been. . . . It is not despair, but hopelessness and ignorance which afflict these people. These people are not in despair, are not desperate. If they had been, they would have struck a blow for themselves. In a parish where they can still see the baulks of the open fields of their Saxon forefathers, they do not seem, within living memory, to have lifted a hand on their own behalf. Not one of them was in Joseph Arch's Union. Today it is doubtful if one of them is a member of the National Union of Agricultural Workers or of the Workers' Union.[52] These people are supine.

Their lives have been leading them nowhere in this world, and, more and more, they have been inclined to discount the parson's allegations about another world. . . . Some of the younger men have either given up church-going, except on wet nights, or in order to see the girls, or have never begun it. They are on firmer ground, some of them feel, with the *News of the World* than with parsonic news from any other world.[53]

I worked for Robertson Scott on *The Countryman* for a short time, a few years after he had published the foregoing; and happened, on the very first Sunday after arrival, to meet my future wife at tea at his house. Quite apart from differences of age and sex, the contrast between the two—country-wise—could hardly have been greater. She had lived for several years with a landowning family in the East Riding of Yorkshire, a territory of great estates, with sizeable tenant farms, solid stone houses and cottages, where people spoke plain whatever their station. No social soap, no Nether Gloaze there. You were seldom allowed out of a Yorkshire parlour without a glass of milk and a slice of plum cake; but equally the groom who taught Audrey to ride and jump put her through it bluntly without frills, shouting, 'Set back, miss, doan' jump before t'hoss.'

There was little surface evidence of poverty thereabouts, even in the 1920s and 1930s. Although the owner derived most of his income from coal, and had come from the same stock as his tenants, his wealth was not resented; nor the fact that he and his family did themselves well in the way of pleasures—hunting and shooting in the winter, fishing in Ireland in the summer, a party of guests most weekends. Grouse bred in the moors, partridges settled in the roots grown specially for the purpose, and pheasants populated the woods. To grow trees seriously was hardly the thing, for the keeper was a more important man than either the forester or the farm bailiff. A host of servants kept the large house and extensive gardens in good order. They were not well paid, but they lived comfortably and contentedly together. Indeed almost everyone in the neighbourhood depended on the estate, whether as employee or as local trader, and when the post-war depression was at its deepest and unemployment in the village at its worst, the owner started a small factory to take up the slack. This man therefore occupied a dual position of obligation and authority, and he responded generously to it; as did his wife. It was however the Indian summer of landed affluence, sustained not by farm rents and the profitability of agriculture but by industrial investments, a direct result of the fall of farming fifty years earlier, but bearing all the overtones of paternalism. It was not to last and the owner knew it. Meanwhile he held on tightly to what he had. Town tourists were trespassers in his eyes; and the idea that everyone had a natural right to enjoy the countryside, whoever owned the land and in whatever quantity, was socialistic anathema. No National Parks or waymarked walks for him. It was the calm before the storm.

In another county, Rutland, where we also had connections, the situation was changing fast. Though a rich hunting and grazing country, not dissimilar from the East Riding in that much of the land was in the hands of moneyed townsmen, our friends were business farmers from the Fens. In defiance of tradition they broke up the rich pastures for

potatoes and sugar beet, the son ploughing all night in the busy times.
The father did his selling to merchants by telephone, and the produce
was loaded direct on to trucks in the railway siding that ran right into the
farm. Wages were not high, but there was plenty of piecework, and the
land was of a kind that by intensive methods could be made to pay.
Further east, on the other hand, in the arable sheep and corn areas of
Norfolk and Suffolk, there was dire distress. Grain growing had collapsed in the 1920s. Farms had to be forgiven rent for years to keep
them tenanted, and there was a tithe war to add to the bitterness. In the
south-west, at the pit of the depression, a mid-Devon farmer recalled to
me recently the following prices: 5d. per gallon for milk, 30s. per ton
for cider apples, 3½d. per pound for wool, about £5 per ton for oats,
and slightly more for wheat. His best Devon Long Wool ewes realised
only 24s. each, and his best Devon cow £17 10s. Yet he farmed
through it somehow; and that has been the keynote to every era of
hardship on the land—somehow.

*   *   *

The slump was not of course confined to farming.[54] Industry at large
suffered too. The trouble was rigidity and a vain attempt to revive the
pre-war pattern of trade, relying on massive exports of coal and the high
earning capacity of staple industries such as textiles, steel and shipbuilding. Not enough had been done to diversify production, and there
was a dangerous dependence on returns from foreign investments to
rectify the adverse balance of trade. Meanwhile the world had moved on.
Some of Britain's best customers were building up their own industries
—India, for instance, was producing cotton goods and importing a
cheaper article from Japan—while basic changes in technology were
also having an effect. Coal, for example, was giving ground to oil and
hydro-electricity as a source of power. To make matters worse, the
return to the Gold Standard in 1925—in an attempt to restore credit
and the status of the pound sterling—added further to the difficulties of
exporters. Between 1913 and 1930 British exports fell by almost one-
third, while unemployment rose to sixteen per cent of the total labour
force; by 1933 it had reached twenty per cent. After the Wall Street
crash of 1929, and with tariff walls rising everywhere else in the world,
the position deteriorated so rapidly that it became impossible to maintain an open door for trade as of old. And so, with the imposition of the
Import Duties Act 1932, the great classic century of British Free Trade
came to an end. Like the fall of Constantinople in 1453, the hinterland
that supported the capital had long been lost.

For a variety of reasons home agriculture took a long time to recover.
The war had raised the output of food overseas as at home, and glut had
been the main cause of the fall in world grain prices in 1921, leading to
the repeal of price guarantees in 1921–2. Arable farming was then

largely abandoned as described, although some benefit was felt by meat and milk farmers, in that they relied on cheap imported feeding-stuffs and on a grass husbandry with a low labour and capital outlay. Britain therefore retained her traditional role as the chief purchaser of foreign food, and on paper this was still thought to make sense. It was of course the old story re-told in different words, but the plot remained the same: namely, agriculture was to be left to fend for itself while industry was expected to earn the currency needed to balance the national accounts. In the event the nation had the worst of both worlds. The balance of trade was not made good, while farming slipped back into depression. Towards the end of the period prices fell so fast—a drop of thirty-four per cent, 1929–32—that numbers of farmers failed to make any profit at all, let alone finance new methods to meet the situation. Much land was abandoned, and in many districts it had value only for uses other than agriculture. In this way 2·7 million acres were lost to farming between 1918 and 1939, and the earlier pattern of decay was repeated. Buildings and equipment deteriorated, fields went back, while low wages and lack of prospects accelerated the endemic exit from the countryside.[55]

Farming however was not utterly abandoned after 1921, and within a few years the State was being forced back step by step into a role similar to the one it had played during the war. For example, agricultural land and buildings were de-rated under two Acts of 1923 and 1928. The control of wages and working conditions was re-established in 1924 by means of County Wage Committees. The Land Drainage Act of 1930 set up Catchment Boards to regulate rivers and watercourses, with good effect upon low-lying farmland. Under the Agricultural Credits Act 1928 loans for capital improvements became more manageable and less expensive, and working capital was also made available against the security of farm stock. All these however were peripheral forms of aid. Paradoxically agriculture did not immediately benefit from the imposition of tariffs in 1932. Food from abroad continued to flow in, for owing to Empire Preference the proportion of imports was merely weighted in favour of countries within the Commonwealth at the expense of those without. Nor did attempts to limit the world production of food have much success.

Far more effective was the action taken to subsidise certain crops and to regulate the market by means of producer organisations. The first crop to benefit was sugar beet. The home growing of sugar had started experimentally in Norfolk in 1911, and was kept going after the war, first by the remission of excise duty and then by a subsidy guaranteed for ten years. In 1935, after difficult discussions, State assistance was made permanent and the British Sugar Corporation set up to operate the subsidy and exercise control. This gave positive help to the hard-pressed arable economy of the eastern counties; likewise the Wheat Act 1932, by which a small charge on imported wheat was added to the growers' price of home-grown wheat, then a depressed crop at only 1·25 million acres harvested in 1931.

Of wider application were the two Agricultural Marketing Acts 1931 and 1933, which empowered producers in any branch of farming to regulate their own production and distribution, and at the same time benefit from the control of imports. Marketing Boards on these lines were formed for hops, milk, potatoes, pigs and bacon; and were supplemented by similar bodies (on which the producers had representation but not control) for wheat, sugar and livestock. The fact that these organisations were not identical in function was due to the nature of the product, the variability of demand, and the complexity of marketing. In essence however the objects were the same—to rationalise supply and demand, expand the market wherever possible, fix fair prices for producer and consumer alike, and administer whatever inducements by way of subsidies and price insurance were offered by the Government. Despite the difficulties they encountered—not least among the farmers—these innovations proved themselves beyond doubt. Not only did they make it possible to earn a living at many types of farming, but the experience gained during the 1930s proved invaluable when it came to feeding the nation during the Second World War.

Indeed what had started as action to promote self-help and economic protection in peace became, as the situation in Europe deteriorated, strategic insurance against war. Thus the Government moved further and further into the farms and fields. Under the Agriculture Act 1937 it extended deficiency payments to oats and barley, and for the first time influenced farm practice itself by subsidising the application of lime and basic slag. This was the direct outcome of the Land Fertility Scheme, in which soil testing was carried out all over the country by Advisory Chemists attached to agricultural colleges and university departments. It was only one benefit—although a striking one—derived from the agricultural research and education programme, costing in all a mere three million pounds per annum. Farmers, not only the progressives, were thus induced to swallow their distrust of academic theory by sheer practical results. The farming press was also a powerful persuader.[56] In many households, apart from the Bible, a handful of textbooks and the Women's Institute literature for the wife, the only reading matter was the local paper and the weekly farm magazine, and this was read from cover to cover for business, information and pleasure. Moreover by accepting advice and co-operating with the experts, farmers ventured ahead of their own volition and through their own organisations. This was evident in the cumulative support given to better breeding techniques, to recording, rationing, and farm-management schemes, to mechanisation, and to the control of plant and animal diseases—the latter boosted by the establishment of a national veterinary service under the 1937 Act.

By 1939 the State was involved in agriculture to a degree unprece-
dented in peacetime, and this was a mere preliminary to what was to
come. Yet despite everything, farming as an industry was still depressed,
both by comparison with urban industry and in the basic element of
confidence. The events of 1921–2 were too close and too bitter to be
easily forgotten; while the return to Protection was too tardy and
empirical to instil any permanent feeling that the nation at large—
which meant, in effect, the urban vote—would not abandon the land
again, once the emergency was over. A casual observer would have noted
that, in the common view, anyone who tried to earn a living off the
land was rated at the bottom of the scale; that about 15,000 farm
workers left their jobs each year; that farm land diminished by about
100,000 acres annually; that almost every other field was riddled with
rabbits or abounded in thistles, docks, bracken, charlock, and ragwort;
and that in aggregate home agriculture produced only about one-third of
the country's food. A close observer however would have acknowledged
that, none the less, farming was undergoing a profound change; that,
despite losses of men and land, it had already altered course towards
meeting the higher demand for such health-protective foods as
milk, eggs and meat; that crop yields per acre were up in every case;
and that, other than sheep and poultry, the livestock population had
increased.

*   *   *

My own memory of 1939 is of a fine southern summer, of village
cricket on Saturday afternoons, and of a sense of foreboding whenever
military aircraft—though only trainers—flew overhead. It was a sense
sharpened by contrasts, of peace and pain side by side. The movement
of the sun as it seeped along the line of the downs beyond Inkpen
Beacon; the wealth and scent of hedges thick with thorn and honey-
suckle; rolling chalky fields yellowing under barley; the sound of
spinneys alive with game; and then the radio ranting with Hitler's
bullet-sharp speeches, all too clear without having to understand a
word of what he was saying. One longed to hold tight to it all, especially to the things that, war or no war, were bound to go. The basket-
maker, for instance, who still cut his own withies from a neglected
osier bed; the old man who mended bicycles in a back shed and sold
us, in excellent condition, a Dursley-Petersen racer of about 1900;
the baker who kept the inn as a sideline—or was his bread the
sideline?

Every village had its relics, not only rural ones. In parts of the north
and midlands particularly, there was plenty of small-scale industry in
the countryside. Some of it—such as shoe-making in the villages round
Wellingborough—was directly descended from the early years of the
Industrial Revolution. Some of it was flourishing, some not; but I was

not thinking of industry in that sense, rather of the crafts and trades serving, or closely associated with, the land. It was easy to multiply examples. I had only to think of half a dozen hamlets between Newbury and Hungerford, where I could find deserted limekilns and chalkpits, a shuttered wheelwright's shop, a woodland ride that had once been a ropewalk, a smithy with smashed windows tenanted one day a week by a peripatetic smith. Even the village shopkeepers were diminishing; and no wonder when I watched our local grocer (who saw no reason to spend good money on gadgets) sawing off slices of bacon, as undulating as corrugated iron, with a huge knife in his aged trembling hands. The wonder was that, since the First World War, any such businesses had survived at all.

I was aware of course of the work of the Rural Industries Bureau, a Government-sponsored organisation financed by Treasury grants from the Development Fund, which had done much to keep afloat all kinds of small businesses—saddlers, thatchers, farriers, brickmakers, and many more—by finding and training apprentices, by accountancy services, and by classes of instruction in oxy-acetylene welding and tractor repairs to enable blacksmiths serve the needs of mechanised farming. In addition, thanks to a Loan Equipment Fund, money had been provided for the purchase of modern tools and machines. I realised too that, largely due to urban penetration of the countryside, a luxury market was springing up for the products of artist-craftsmen—potters, weavers, cabinet-makers, and the like, who were settling in villages and trying to make a living there. It has since become the fashion to scoff at such people for aping the simple life. Although their activities can never by themselves restore the balance of rural society, yet they constitute a sign, a protest if you like, against the loss of pride in personal skill exhibited by the craftsmen of the past. I quote C. S. Orwin, one-time Director of the Oxford Agricultural Economics Research Institute, never a man to shut his eyes to the realities of rural life:

> In the ordinary work of the farm, there is not the fine finish by which once it was characterised. There are corners in the field which the ploughman cannot reach, and these at one time were forked by hand. The stack was not finished when it had been put up and thatched, for then a man would brush its sides with a scythe-blade, trim the eaves with shears, and he would adorn the ridge with some fancy device in straw. . . . And who today would expect to see the farm horses, where such still remain, with their tails and manes plaited with straw and ribbons, on the days on which they are to deliver produce in the market town? Neglect of some of these things does not indicate, necessarily, a falling off in production from the land, but they suggest a slackening in the artificer's pride in his work, which is to be regretted.[57]

Orwin was writing in 1945, a few years after my nostalgic reflections on the approach of war, but the situation was substantially the same, although the war itself had hastened the pace of change. He wrote too with realism of attempts to restore the small man in agriculture:

> Up to the present time, land settlement has been striving to supply two needs. In its oldest form—the small holdings created by the County Councils under the Small Holdings Act 1908 and subsequent Acts—it was intended to provide an economic ladder for the farm worker, and as such it has failed. There is no general history of progress to larger farms amongst the tenants, and this activity in the subdivision of land, extending over forty years, has not sufficed to maintain the total number of small farms in the country, in the face of the opposite tendency towards absorption and amalgamation dictated by economic pressure. More recently, attempts have been made to use land settlement as a remedy for industrial employment, under voluntary organisations aided both by public and by charitable funds. Fifteen years' experience has shown that it offers no solution.[58]

Orwin was too sweeping, as are most writers on small farming. It was true that the number of smallholdings (i.e. small farms of fifty acres or less) had declined—from about 450,000 in 1870 to 384,000 in 1934. Yet in 1934 the number of smallholders still represented about two-thirds of all occupiers of agricultural land in England and Wales. Although the amount of land was less than sixteen per cent of the whole, these figures show that smallholdings were meeting a need, if mainly social. It sprang of course out of the human desire for independence, descended partly from the peasant era and surviving—despite everything—into an age when the peasantry as a separate class had long been replaced by the pattern of employer and employed. This instinct was belatedly acknowledged, first privately by a handful of owners who offered land on easy terms, then publicly by the Government towards the end of the nineteenth century. By then it had become a matter of political conscience, which sought to restore some of the land filched by enclosure and give the agricultural labourer the chance of becoming a small independent farmer.[59]

The first effective legislation, the Small Holdings and Allotments Act 1908, empowered County Councils to acquire and equip parcels of land of not more than fifty acres in extent, and let them to suitable tenants. The Act was successful. By 1914 over 12,000 holdings had been taken up at relatively small cost to the Exchequer. A second Act in 1919, designed to settle ex-Servicemen on the land, also went well. Another 16,000 holdings were created, and although the percentage of failures rose, it had not exceeded fifteen per cent by the third Act in 1926, which was intended to maintain the supply of land and money.

From this point however the impulse slackened, mainly due to higher costs of building and establishment. While therefore a surprisingly large number of smallholders were able to make a modest living, at much personal effort and some public expense (i.e. the statutory small-holders), Orwin was correct in asserting that this form of farming did not normally enable the labourer to climb the ladder to full-scale husbandry and a higher standard of life. None the less smallholdings survived, and small farming as a whole is by no means dead today. In his other reference, Orwin was confounded by events.[60]

At the pit of the depression in the early 1930s, a separate scheme was formulated to settle industrial unemployed on the land. This was an outright attempt at social reclamation, organised by the Land Settle-ment Association, and financed partly from Government and partly from private sources, with a substantial contribution from the Carnegie Trust. Because the prime purpose was social, the L.S.A. took care at the start to insure against economic disaster by instituting compulsory co-operation. As the chairman, Sir Arthur Richmond, wrote in retrospect in 1960: 'The men could not just be given holdings, lent money to equip them and then left to themselves to do the best they could. That would inevitably have led to failure.' The plan proposed—and in essence it evolved in this form—was to establish holdings of five to ten acres each, located in groups, contiguous wherever possible, each group acting as an administrative unit with an estate manager in charge. All holdings were rented, and the relationship between the smallholder and the Association was secured through the tenancy agreement in specific detail: whereby all produce was brought to a central packing station for grading and dispatch; all supplies were bought in bulk; and all machinery was owned and maintained by the Association for use by hire. This ensured that the centralised services of the Association, managerial as well as technical, were employed to the full and actually paid their way, as an integral part of the plan to secure efficiency and profitability on each holding. This, it is claimed, would not have been possible if left to voluntary co-operation. The size of the holdings allowed them to be run by small family units—a man and his wife, if no more—but the normal handicaps of small size were offset by the collective advantages described. Some of the early tenants soon gave up, as expected, but by 1939 there was evidence that 'with careful selection and some training, many men with no previous experience of agriculture could adapt themselves to the life provided on the Association's estates and earn a satisfactory living'.

The subsequent history of the L.S.A. is instructive. Industrial unemployment disappeared with the war, and although a residue of 'industrial' tenants remained, almost all newcomers were required to have a country background and a little capital of their own. In 1948 all the land was vested in the Ministry of Agriculture, with the L.S.A.

acting as executive agent, and a number of additions and modifications introduced by way of internal finance, technical aid, and production planning. Otherwise the structure of the scheme has not been altered. Experience has shown that not less than fifty and not more than sixty holdings make up the most satisfactory group; and the Association now has fourteen such groups with over 500 holdings. Latterly almost all production has been switched to horticulture, and the average nett farm income made by the tenants rose from £636 in 1958 to £1,973 in 1968. Clearly, what started as a heavily subsidised social experiment, in which the aim was to achieve a personal income slightly above that of the farm worker, has become something quite different. The L.S.A. scheme is one answer, and a highly successful one, to the question of smallholdings. Since however it is limited in scale, specialised in nature, and depends on a high degree of compulsory association, it is unlikely to be the sole solution. None the less it is a beacon light in the general dusk of small farming, in which other types of smallholders, and even of farmers, who struggle along on 50–200 acres of poor land, can only make a living by means of massive subsidisation.[61]

*   *   *

When Hitler marched into Poland in September 1939, home agri-culture—like the rest of the country—was not even half ready. To be fair this was not due to lack of forethought on the part of the Govern-ment in relation to war, for farm and food planning against just such an emergency had started as early as 1935. It was due rather to a deeper cause: to the fact that it was impossible to reactivate at short notice a diffuse and diverse industry, abandoned for at least a decade after the First World War, that had lost confidence in the politicians and, to some extent, in itself. There were material losses too, and in that sense the position was far worse than in 1914. Since that date, more than two and a half million acres had been taken out of farming; and out of nearly fifty million acres of farmland in the U.K., no less than thirty-nine million were under grass of varying quality, leaving a bare nine million in cultivation. Thus many farmers and farm workers had lost, or never known, the arts of arable husbandry. The majority were stock-men, raising animals on cheap imported feeding-stuffs, and using grass-land as much for exercise as for grazing. They were not producing from the soil at all. Nor was the land generally in good heart. Although pasture acted to some extent as a fertility bank, through root growth and absorption of animal manures, much of it was weed infested and sour; and the deficiencies of lime and phosphate had only begun to be made good under the subsidies provided by the Agriculture Act 1937. Man and horsepower continued to fall, and there were as yet only some 50,000 tractors in use. To sustain a population of forty-six million, it needed all that home agriculture could do, plus an annual import of food, feeding-stuffs and fertilisers amounting to nearly twenty-three million tons. It was a daunting prospect for a country that had to face a second world war within twenty-one years, under-equipped, under financed, and well aware that shipping was no longer the safe solution to supply as in 1914.

The problem then was this: what should—or could—be imported to feed the nation on a properly balanced diet? What was the maximum effective output of 550,000 British farms and holdings of widely varying capability? How best to organise the campaign and achieve the target? Although the details of planning had to be altered as the situation in Europe worsened, the basic thinking—derived from the experience of the First World War—did not change. It was, first and foremost, to grow a maximum of crops for *direct* human consumption, e.g. wheat, potatoes and sugar beet, and to maintain animal products at a safe minimum, viz. milk, meat and eggs. This meant ploughing up an immense acreage of grass, improving the yield and quality of the grazing that remained, and sustaining the fertility of all arable ground so long as the war lasted. All this had to be matched with manpower, machinery, the supply of seeds, fertilisers, fuel, and all other essentials to production; in addition, it had to be knitted into the availability of overseas resources and the sheer physical possibilities of shipping space. To illustrate: milk was acknowledged as a vital element of diet, bacon—though less important nutritionally—was a popular and necessary food. Cows required more labour and equipment than pigs, but (like other cattle and sheep) they made good use of grass and were economical converters of feed. They also dunged the land as they grazed. Pigs (and poultry) on the other hand depended primarily on cereals, which either had to be imported or grown on precious home acres. The answer adopted was to obtain the maximum quantity of milk from the minimum quantity of grass and concentrates, and import the bulk of bacon and eggs.

Wartime farming began in earnest with the Agricultural Development Act 1939 which offered farmers two pounds per acre for ploughing up permanent grass. This had an immediate effect, yielding an extra two million acres of arable by April 1940, this form of subsidy continuing for many years as one of the principal incentives to improved husbandry. Once the war had started, other measures followed fast, many of them direct descendants of 1917–18. War Agricultural Executive Committees controlled the conduct of farm operations in each county, all important agricultural supplies were rationed, heavy orders for tractors and machinery were placed, implement and labour pools were formed, prices and wages were fixed by national agreement at rising levels as the war advanced. There is no need to recite details at length, but a few facts and figures are necessary to measure the achievements of agriculture during the Second World War. The peacetime import of nearly twenty-three million tons a year was drastically reduced. At one stage, in 1943, it was down to an annual rate of just over six million tons, and in all some forty million tons were saved. This was done partly by strict food rationing, and partly by ruthless agricultural effort. By 1945 nearly six million acres of grassland had been ploughed, and almost two-thirds of all accessible farmland (exclusive of rough grazings) had been turned into arable. This included a substantial area of ley or temporary grasses—the outcome of Professor Stapledon's teaching that, wherever possible, grass should be treated as a crop and not as permanent ground cover provided by Nature. Food grown for the table increased by twenty-two million tons over six harvests, exclusive of vegetables, etc., raised in the 'Dig for Victory' campaign. Livestock products declined, as expected, but thanks to improved techniques the sale of liquid milk to the public was up by almost fifty per cent over pre-war. One further yardstick. In terms of calories the nett increase of home-grown food in 1918 over pre-war had been twenty-four per cent. The corresponding figure for the Second World War was more than ninety per cent.

In a word agriculture 'made it' again, on less land and in more difficult circumstances, though the Government itself was better prepared. But the great difference between the two wars was this. Whereas in the First War all expedients to higher production proved temporary, in the Second War they contributed to radical changes in farm practice and to establishing permanent relations between agriculture and the State, as formalised in the Agriculture Act 1947 and contingent legislation. Since this was but the outcome of reforms begun shortly before or during the war, 1932–47 must be regarded as the most critical period in the whole history of rural life. Not only did the State reassume its role as the protector of agriculture, but the degree of protection was far greater than at any time in the past. It amounted in fact to participation, and this had far-reaching consequences after the war—as described in Part Three.

*   *   *

It is a depressing paradox that as farming—the central activity of the countryside—becomes more efficient, it declines in importance as a source of employment. The battle seems lost either way. When farming slumps, the drift to the town for work and wages is accelerated. When it prospers and incomes improve, then mechanisation and higher productivity all round reduce the number of jobs. For that reason the revival of forestry between the wars was of vital importance. As a primary employment on the land forestry remained the principal alternative to farming, since as explained earlier other primary industries—such as quarrying, mining, and even sea-fishing—though originally rural, could rarely for reasons of scale and changes in technique continue to be so defined. Mineral extraction of whatever kind requires heavy capital investment. Thus operations such as the mining of coal and iron-stone in the north and east midlands, or of china clay in Cornwall, duly grew into urban industries with characteristic communities of their own. Their connection with the countryside was fortuitous and their impact on the landscape so destructive that restoration remains a major problem today. Thus any possibility of integration with country life was prevented by the very nature and size of the operation concerned: in the same way as many a manufacturing industry, starting as a village work-shop and developing into a major enterprise, has converted its neighbour-hood from countryside into town. Quarrying on the other hand, e.g. of sand, gravel or stone for building and road-making, remained often localised and relatively small in scale. In such places work at the site or on haulage would be an important outlet for rural employment, and a useful alternative to other jobs on the land.

To return to forestry, with which I close this part of the book. In 1914 only five per cent of the land surface of this country was under woodland, mostly hardwood, and over ninety per cent of the national requirement of timber, mostly softwood, had to be imported. The 1914–18 war was nearly lost for several reasons other than defeat in battle. Shortage of timber was one, and in four and a half years half a million acres out of three million acres of trees were felled, or about one-third of the total volume of standing timber. By such measures, by reducing imports to a minimum, and by every kind of substitution and make-do, the country came through; but it was a close-run thing and the lesson was not overlooked. A Committee appointed in 1917 and chaired by F. D. Acland, M.P. (Sir Francis Acland), recommended a long-term plan of afforestation, whereby two million acres (mostly softwoods) would be planted over the following eighty years. The plan was accepted by the Government, and the Forestry Commission formed in 1919 to take the necessary action. In general private owners, whose woods had been devastated by the war, were expected to make good the fellings and render their existing plantations more productive. The State would do the rest.

Unlike farming, forestry was not jettisoned when prices fell in 1920–1. Despite cuts and restrictions, the Commission went ahead with massive conifer plantations, notably in Scotland, Wales, East Anglia and the Border Country: so that by 1939 it had secured eighty-eight per cent of the land and completed seventy-five of the planting pro-gramme scheduled for the first twenty years. In so doing it became the largest single landowner in the country, with more than one million acres; and this included nearly 121,000 acres of woods and other lands taken over from the Crown in 1923–4, within which lay the residue of the old Royal Forests, notably the New Forest, which were largely hardwood in character. This was a remarkable achievement. The

Commission had generated fresh rural employment, was building settlements in the countryside, and was well forward in creating a large reserve of growing timber that, given time, would save currency and act as a strategic reserve against a new emergency. In fact the Second World War came too quickly for the harvest that was hoped for. The bulk of felling, 1939–45, had again to be borne by private woodlands which—for financial reasons associated with landowning at large—had by no means made good the devastations of 1914–18. For a second time the total volume of standing timber was reduced by about one-third, and this included a substantial quantity of thinnings and immature conifers from both private and State forests.

> In effect, all and more of the new area afforested in the years between the wars was cancelled out by these clearances. . . . Most of the best hardwoods were felled and certain categories, such as prime ash and veneer beech, were virtually exhausted. . . . Finally any semblance of an orderly arrangement of age-classes in British woods, never a satisfactory feature of their structure, but necessary to proper management and supply, was completely disrupted by wartime inroads.[62]

So once again the forestry industry had to make a fresh start, and again the Government—through the agency of the Forestry Commission—began drafting plans for peace halfway through the war.[63] This time the target was much higher.

> The overall proposals aimed at securing an ultimate total of 5 million acres of fully stocked, well-managed and productive woodland in Britain during the half-century after the conclusion of the Second World War. It was expected that, of this total, 2 million acres would be obtained through the proper management of existing woods by landowners, adequately supported and encouraged by the State, and 3 million acres through new afforestation undertaken by the Commission. Impressive targets of land acquisition, from the rough grazing land of the country, and of planting and replanting were set. Corresponding expansions of other branches, including research, education, roads, housing and forest parks, were envisaged.[64]

These proposals involved not merely a great increase in the acreage of trees, but radical alterations to the landscape. 'For instance, for economic reasons, the Commissioners had in mind the development of forest regions containing both State forests and private woods and characterised by relatively few species, mostly coniferous in type.'[65]

This meant that, whereas any private plantations that lay inside a forest region would, by conforming to the general plan of management, enjoy financial assistance, any that lay outside would not. Described as 'small woods, amenity, shelter belts, beauty spots and so on', they would have to be 'written off as being individually of an uneconomic size and unsuitable for inclusion in the master plan—or for grant aid for replanting'. Since much parkland and hedgerow timber was also coming under the axe in favour of intensive agriculture, it seemed likely that within a few decades the traditional pattern of field and hardwood hedge and spinney would be replaced by bare lowland stretches of plough and grass, interspersed with blocks of conifers, or heavily afforested hills.[66]

Whatever the economic or other advantages of the Commission's proposals—and they were as bold, in their way, as the concepts that created the enclosure landscapes of the eighteenth century—they were in this initial form bitterly opposed. Private woodland owners felt that, for all the fine words, they were being steam-rollered out of their fair place in forestry; and it had to be admitted that the chairman of the Commission, R. L. (Lord) Robinson, never liked private forestry. Hill farmers too feared the continued invasion of trees, while those concerned with wild life and the beauty of the countryside had long criticised what they regarded as a hostile, over-uniform, intrusion into the native landscape. Accordingly the Government took further advice: so that, in the Forestry Acts 1945 and 1947 and subsequent legislation, sufficient modifications were introduced at least to include private forestry on terms reasonably acceptable to the owners.

This however was but the beginning of a slow process of adjustment, not merely between the public and private sectors of the industry, but as between forestry and other uses of the countryside, especially agriculture and amenity. It was understandable that those in charge of State forestry should seek to justify their plans on financial, strategic, and other grounds. However economics, as the main motive for tree-growing, was opposed not so much by social arguments—which was the dichotomy of farming (expressed in 'business or way of life?')—as by aesthetic and ecological ones. Thus forestry preceded farming as to the impact of its techniques upon the landscape and upon the environment at large; and in this matter opposition derived largely from townspeople for whom the countryside was not a business but a source of refreshment.

PART TWO

The Approach to Amenity

What is Amenity?

In a sense the town has always been invading the country, ever since man adopted a settled existence, though for many centuries the impact was small. Although there have been great cities in the past—Rome is an obvious example—where the inhabitants were able to live their lives more or less detached from the countryside, yet in general and in Britain in particular most towns before the end of the eighteenth century were countryfied places. Few of them were so large that you could not walk, or at any rate ride, into open country within an hour; and in every town there was a patchwork of gardens, meadows and open spaces recorded today—to take London as an example—in such names as Smithfield, Hatton Garden, or Lincoln's Inn Fields.

It followed that most townsmen were essentially countryfolk who happened to be engaged in urban pursuits. The wealthy were landed proprietors who kept town houses for the winter season or to attend Court or Parliament; but many of more modest means also owned or had access to property outside. Even working people moved in and out of town without difficulty, providing they were not paupers. In Portsmouth, in the seventeenth and eighteenth centuries, it was a common thing for dockyard craftsmen to be absent in the summer, 'having gone into the country to make hay'.[1]

Britain, then, before the Industrial Revolution, was broadly a rural island dotted with small towns and villages. London was an exception, by virtue of its size and status as a capital and trading centre; even so, as late as 1830, continuous development outside the City was bounded by Westminster, Knightsbridge and Paddington to the west, and by Regent's Park and Regent's Canal to the north and east. Although life anywhere in town or country had always been characterised by dirt, disease, and unattractive habits, it had not altered man's attitude to his environment. Now and again there arose a crisis in resources. A quarry was worked out, a mine exhausted, or as happened in the seventeenth century the shortage of hardwood suddenly became serious; but in every case an alternative was found, or fresh provision made, without undue difficulty. In agriculture centuries of experience had yielded an adequate store of skill and knowledge. Man could not go far wrong. Whatever he did not understand or could not cope with in Nature, he fatally accepted; and if he sought the ultimate answers to phenomena, he attributed them to the Almighty. As to the beauty of the world, that too was a divine thing, everywhere about him, a constant source of wonder and inspiration. It was an attitude reflected in man's own activities, so that almost all his works communicated a quality of harmony, as much in buildings, furniture and implements, as in the ways he moulded the landscape. Art and use were indivisible.

Then came a profound change. By the end of the eighteenth century, industry and the application of steam power to manufacture were already transforming English life. The population was rising fast. Men, women and children were toiling in abject conditions in factories and mines; and they were congregating in urban slums on a scale hitherto unknown, cut off from the countryside. The misery, squalor and sheer ugliness so created erupted at times into violence and repression, and after *c.* 1800 the nation was subject to forces it seemed often unable to control. In short it was the inhumanity of industrialism, unchecked by dependence on natural forces, that degraded man's morality and altered his attitude towards man and Nature alike.

When the reaction against industrialism began, it operated with most effect through reforms *within* the structure of society. Social reformers worried about schools, prisons, factory hours, sewers, and hospitals rather than about what man was doing to the world around him. The idea of conserving the countryside would have seemed ludicrous before the 1860s, when the survival of common land suddenly became a burning issue. Most people thought that Nature was infinite and private interests paramount. Apart from penalties for poaching (an offence against property), the only regulations affecting wild life were those connected with sport. The purpose of a close season was to enable breeding to take place undisturbed for the better enjoyment of hunting, shooting and fishing. Selective control by culling was conducted for the benefit of the pastime. Any species not classified as game was 'fair game', and it is known that by the late nineteenth century several native breeds of birds and mammals had been wiped out.

For similar reasons it was not thought immoral to assault the landscape. If the land was yours, you could do what you liked with it. The great farmers and gardeners had turned that philosophy to good account; but the reverse was equally possible, and destruction was not regarded as a moral issue. Pioneer methods of extraction—coal, iron ore, clay, tin, copper, salt, gravel, chalk, stone—were particularly crude and wasteful: often of the deposit itself, almost always of the overmantle of soil, leading to loss of fertility and biological disturbance. The industrial aftermath has been a deadly wilderness of destruction and disuse—towering tips, gaping pits, 'hill and dale' desolation of surface mining; the dereliction of abandoned sheds, tracks and yards; even large areas of undeveloped land damaged by industrial processes or by mere proximity to manufacturing enterprise. All this adds up today to at least 150,000 acres of despoiled land, just one raw physical reminder of industrial irresponsibility, and the bill is by no means complete.[2] Whereas now we have suddenly become aware of the problems of reclamation and the need to conserve land, in the past 150 years there was no such understanding. Any acreage absorbed by development was written off against economic gain. No thought was given to land as an asset of existence, regarded either as a source of food or in the wider associations of environment.

Damage of this kind was condoned by ignorance. In the eighteenth and early nineteenth centuries the environmental sciences were confined to their own compartments, and mainly concerned with describing and classifying species. Although Charles Darwin and Alfred Russel Wallace revolutionised the basis of botany and zoology, and demonstrated the interdependence of different disciplines, it was a long time before ecology was recognised as 'the science which seeks to elucidate the principles governing the interactions of the natural processes of land, water and all living things'.[3]

The resources of Nature cannot however be divorced from the activities of man. The two are totally interdependent, which means that concern for environment must take account of every element and influence —a comprehensive concept only now emerging. And because the relationship between man and Nature is complex and interlocking, the public attitude has been confused, and still is. Terminology is fluid. Until recently the keyword was 'preservation', whether it be a section of the coastline, a species of plant, or an old church. As however the idea came to be associated with negation—to preserve from change, and so to sterilise or mummify—'preservation' has been replaced by 'conservation', a wider, more flexible term which implies survival within the world as it is, an ecological concept applied to both human and natural resources, whether they be living organisms, inanimate deposits, or man's own constructions. Conservation can therefore be attached to geological remains; or to historic buildings which are furnished imaginatively and thrown open to visitors, or converted to contemporary use as offices, colleges, assembly halls. In similar sense museums themselves are becoming dynamic institutions, thoroughly in tune with modern methods of communication, presenting the past as part of today rather than a relic of yesterday.

Conservation so understood cannot be left to chance however. There has to be control, otherwise it would be impossible—amid all the forces at work within and between Nature and man—to sustain the impetus of conservation or maintain it intact. Beyond that again there is a further concept, summed up in one inadequate word, 'amenity': in its literal sense, a slight term denoting 'agreeableness arising from beauty of site, pleasantness of climate, suitability of design, etc'.[4] Although often used portmanteau-wise to mean almost anything in the context of human surroundings, from a beautiful view to a public lavatory, amenity is

Hook and crook

FARMWORK—
HARVESTING HISTORY

Sail-reaper

Self-binder

Tanker combines

acquiring a far deeper significance—not so much to describe the environment itself, or some aspect of it, as the purpose behind it. In other words amenity is coming to mean enhancement of life through the agency of environment, and by the creative use of that environment, whether by conservation or by constructive development.

How does this apply to the countryside?

Looked at historically the movement towards amenity embraces all kinds of disparate activities. Take first the conservation of wild life.

✻   ✻   ✻

Wild Life

The full story has yet to be written, but all accounts agree that people in Britain have always found it difficult to distinguish between their protective and their destructive instincts, and this has led them into impossibly illogical situations. The tale needs no prolonged re-telling here. Until about 200 years ago wild life in this country was so various and plentiful that no one thought about conservation at all, other than for purposes of sport. In this matter however there were rigid rules. William the Conqueror enlarged and firmly fixed the boundaries of the Royal Forests or hunting preserves, begun in a small way by his Saxon predecessors, and he established a strict administration over them. Penalties for poaching deer were fierce, but exceptions were made in the case of predators, such as wolves, whom anyone might kill and receive a reward for doing so. As, during the Middle Ages, the absolute power of the king declined and the demand for land and liberty increased, so many areas were 'disafforested' or released from hunting prohibitions. Most of them diminished in size under enclosure and encroachment; others were leased to large magnates who maintained almost as strict a monopoly as the king—Exmoor, for example, remained virtually intact until 1818; and in such instances landowners built peripheral park walls or banks to fence the deer in, and often preserved fish, rabbits, and other game as well. Otherwise the remaining Forest areas continued as 'waste' or uncultivated no-man's-land, where wild life took its chance.

In these conditions some species were extinguished, others virtually vanished. The wolf and the wild boar were early casualties, while the pine marten and the wild cat survived only—and still do—in the farthest corners of the island. The greatest depredations occurred where control was entirely absent. Game survived in the Royal Forests and private parks, because they were deliberately preserved for the larder and for sport. Elsewhere they were exterminated, unless there was sufficient wild land to afford them refuge; and by the end of the seventeenth century in England such refuge was already becoming scarce. One reason was the substitution of the gun for the crossbow; another the wholesale felling of trees; another the progressive reclamation of land, e.g. drainage works in the Somerset and East Anglian Fens which, aided by the assaults of the wildfowlers, greatly reduced the number of marsh birds and drove some species out of the country altogether.

Paradoxically the eighteenth century presented a more hopeful out-look. Landscaping and the planting of private parks increased the quantity of cover. Similarly, despite the loss of commons, open land and waste through enclosure, the new pattern of spinney and hedgerow gave great encouragement to rabbits, foxes, and many sorts of birds. On the other hand, as the nineteenth century advanced, killing became more general and efficient. Owners combined to allow hunting over their estates by private or subscription packs of hounds, and as guns got safer and easier to handle shooting parties became larger and more organised. Such pastimes however were limited by expense, only to be afforded by men of substance who took good care that sufficient game survived for the following season.

The observance of a close season for breeding, rearing, and the intro-duction of occasional new species (e.g. the red-legged partridge in *c.* 1770) were all means to this end. Most important was the rise of the gamekeeper, who became an indispensable member of the estate staff. His task was two-fold: to rear young game, and to destroy anything that attacked his charges at any stage of their lives. The effect upon wild life is hard to determine. It certainly involved the killing of large numbers of rabbits, rats, stoats, weasels, crows, and other 'vermin', but many proliferated none the less because their predators were killed too, hawks above all. Destruction was therefore selective, though hardly scientific, while no amount of casuistry can describe the record bags of birds slaughtered in the last century as 'conservation'. Shooting too un-doubtedly killed off some rare birds, such as the great bustard and the osprey, for no reason other than 'sport'; and in other instances it was done deliberately to protect young farm stock and crops. Even so, while some pastimes ensured a careful balance of survival among particular game or wild life in general, and while others were indiscriminate, yet by their very popularity field sports tended more to conserve than condemn, and in recent years they have improved markedly in this respect.[5] This is still a hot subject, and because it rouses emotions it is hard to keep logic clear of the mud. Moreover people are inclined to support two contesting views simultaneously without being aware of it. Yet it is important to realise that the essence of the objection to field sports lies, not in killing as a necessary method of control, but that it should be done for the purposes of pleasure. That raises another principle altogether; but it cannot be said that wild life in the past in this country suffered *solely* at the hands of blood-lusting sportsmen.

A much more serious danger at one time was the passion for collecting. As Brian Vesey-FitzGerald has pointed out,[6] it was not so much the

ordinary amateur who was dangerous, as the professional who robbed
the nests of rare birds and supplied precious plant specimens to museums
and private collectors. This was a skilled and profitable business, but the
fault lay as much with the system as the man, the one producing the
other. Before the popularity of photography, or the development of
Reserves where Nature might be studied in action, or even the growth of
bird watching as we know it today, many earnest naturalists felt compelled to rob or kill in the interests of study. Animal artists too usually
worked from dead models, because they had to. The only practicable
alternative was to re-create a natural habitat in the artificial and confined
space of a zoo or a botanic garden—but this was an expensive undertaking, only possible in exceptional cases. Nothing therefore was sacred
for a while among all the native fauna and flora of Britain, whether for
scientific ends or to satisfy the mania for ownership. To quote Fitz-
Gerald, for his remarks apply to everyone who acted in this way: 'It is all
too easy, from this distance of time, to blame them, to say they should
have known better . . . In fact they were men of their time: and their
time was not ours.'[7]

Recently a far deeper and more insidious threat to wild life has arisen
out of chemical and other intensive techniques in agriculture; but since
this is inseparable from the whole complex of cultivation and conservation which has thrust itself upon us since the last war, it must be left to
consideration elsewhere. Meanwhile let us look briefly at the history
of Nature conservation as distinct from the implications of sport, a
subject not easy to record since it has to be discerned within the
spectrum of scientific progress.

The story begins with the medieval herbalists, whose interest in
certain plants was primarily medical and dietary, and whose observations were laced with poetic, even metaphysical, comments. It leaps
forward in the seventeenth century with the work of John Ray, the first
great English naturalist who, in a life of amazing accomplishment, concentrated on systematising and classifying species. It continues with
Carl von Linné (Linnaeus), the Swedish naturalist, who devised the
scientific naming of plants and animals, and after whom the Linnaean
Society of London was founded in 1788. By laying the foundations of
fact and method in Nature study, these—and other lesser men—prepared the way for conservation. Even the publication of Darwin's *Origin
of Species* in 1859 was of less consequence in this context, for by then the
great upsurge of educated interest in Nature was already under way.
Victorians were avid 'bug-hunters'—to use the term generically.
Natural history societies multiplied in every part of the country, their
members busily observing and recording—field work was the particular
enthusiasm of amateurs—so that well before the end of the nineteenth
century the study of the natural environment had ceased to be a purely
academic preserve. Furthermore it was amateur, added to professional

interest, that gave birth to the various national associations concerned with Nature study. The Linnaean Society was an early example, the Selborne Society another—founded in 1885 to perpetuate the memory of the Rev. Gilbert White—while important specialist bodies started at this time include the Zoological Society of London (1826), the two national Botanical Societies founded in 1836, and the Marine Biological Association of the United Kingdom (1884).[8]

Part of the purpose of organisations such as these is to inform public opinion, mobilise it at times of crisis, and exert pressure on Parliament when legislation is needed: usually after one or two pioneers have laboured on their own. This pattern is briefly outlined in the case of birds.

One hundred years ago, in an age when egg-collecting and the shooting of birds for specimens were at their peaks, members of the Yorkshire Naturalists' Union were instrumental in the formulation of the first Act to protect birds for other than sporting purposes. The Act, the Seabirds Preservation Act, 1869, was passed to protect the seabirds at Flamborough and Bempton.

The tradition of bird protection in Britain stems from the efforts of Charles Waterton, of Walton Hall, near Wakefield. In 1817 to prevent illegal shooting and intrusion, he erected an eight-foot wall around the three-mile perimeter of his estate. Keepers and dogs were forbidden in the woodland and boats were not allowed on the lake in the autumn and winter. Unfortunately he never saw the Seabirds Protection Act as he died a few years before it was passed.

Further Acts giving legal authorities power to apply bird protection orders were passed in 1880 and 1887.[9]

Thereafter came more good work by the Yorkshire Naturalists' Union, the founding of the Society for the Protection of Birds (Royal in 1904) in 1889, the British Trust for Ornithology in 1932, and a succession of statutes until the Protection of Birds Act 1954 (extended in 1967) simplified and codified the law, treating the subject as a whole.

A similar story might be told about other kinds of wild life, for the record is consistent in that piecemeal protection, through private action and by law, was gradually extended to a variety of gound and water creatures, game and otherwise. None the less, even today, wild plants and many mammals are virtually defenceless in the open countryside—despite the passage of useful consolidating legislation since the last war, and the inauguration of a Government agency, the Nature Conservancy, in 1949 to aid wild life. One of the bugbears of statutory protection is complexity. Fish for example involve multiple controls (which vary between freshwater and sea fish, and are not identical in all parts of the United Kingdom) as to the issue of licences, close seasons, methods of catching, size limits of fish and netting, disease, pollution, poaching, etc. Clarity and consistency have never been hallmarks of man's attitude to Nature, and they are qualities more in demand than ever as our understanding grows.

Of course the law has never been the sole means of protection. Not only is personal responsibility essential in order to make legislation effective, but history shows that private enterprise will nearly always act first and explore ahead. This happened in the case of Nature Reserves, not only the specialised bird sanctuaries (for example those started by the R.S.P.B.), but the broader based areas where various forms of wild life—fauna and flora—might exist and develop in relation to each other: ecology, in fact, in practice. Organisation began comparatively late. The National Trust took steps to acquire Wicken Fen in 1899, and the Society for the Promotion of Nature Reserves (S.P.N.R.) did the same at Woodwalton Fen in Huntingdonshire in 1919. Wicken Fen (and other wild areas since acquired) was really incidental to the main purpose of the National Trust: in contrast to the activities of the S.P.N.R., created and inspired by the Hon. Charles Rothschild in 1912, with the objects inherent in its title. Rothschild was behind the plan to locate Nature Reserves all over the country, but times were unpropitious (1915), and nothing was done to implement his ideas on a national scale for over thirty years.

Meanwhile progress continued in the usual way, by stealth. Nature Reserves were created *in effect* after the First World War in many of the properties of the Forestry Commission, especially in the National Forest Parks, likewise in a number of private woodlands, and in the gathering grounds of the various water undertakings. But the most significant event between the wars was the formation in 1926 of the Norfolk Naturalists' Trust, with power to own or hold land for the purpose of Reserves. This was a pioneer step. No similar body was created until after the Second World War, Yorkshire following in 1946, but now County Trusts exist all over the country and are a vital element in the pattern of conservation. In contrast to the local natural history societies which foster observation and the recording of scientific information, the Trusts exist primarily to maintain Reserves (over 500 in 1970); but of course the functions are complementary and overlap.

The County Trust movement did not develop spontaneously. The way had been prepared by the spread of knowledge about ecology, difficult dogged work pursued by a handful of professional ecologists, notably Professor A. G. Tansley whose *magnum opus*, *The British Islands and their Vegetation* (C.U.P.), was published in 1939. Another influence was the incidence of war, when boredom, homesickness and the deprivations associated with Service life helped generate a remarkable revival of interest in the countryside. In such ways the ground was being got ready; but it was the S.P.N.R. which in 1941 once again took the lead by calling a conference and mobilising opinion in an effort to continue where Rothschild's First War plan had left off. This contributed both to the proliferation of County Trusts after the Second War and to the formation of the Council for Nature in 1958,[10] as the representative body at national level of most voluntary organisations concerned with the study and conservation of Nature. In education there also emerged out of the war the Field Studies Council, which had begun life in 1943 as the Committee for the Promotion of Field Studies. The aim of the Council was—as it is today—to 'encourage the pursuit of fieldwork and research in every branch of knowledge whose essential subject matter is out of doors'. This involved the acquisition of Field Centres in different parts of England and Wales, and the organisation of residential courses in environmental subjects for schoolchildren, students, and adults. Later, teachers in schools formed their own National Rural and Environmental Studies Association. Both these bodies have a common purpose in 'training members of the community . . . in the principles of conservation and proper use of the countryside'.[11]

*   *   *

Every account of the progress of an idea, its origin as a minority fad, its growth and gradual acceptance by the public—and wild life conservation is an outstanding example—reveals a familiar pattern, incorporating at least two strong strands. One is the foresight, devotion and persistence of a handful of men and women at the head of the movement, who may often approach their goal from different directions. Another is the way the volunteers and the civil servants make contact, and then eventually work together. In his *Nature Conservation in Britain*,[12] Sir Dudley Stamp gives an example of this. He relates how public opinion was being formed before the Second World War, and the way prepared for State intervention. But this was not a matter solely of conservation. The real issue was the need for national planning in order to make the best use of land, already disappearing under development at the rate of 100,000 acres a year. He refers to the Land Utilisation Survey carried out under his direction in 1931–3, which recorded 'with the help of thousands of volunteers, the then existing use (or non-use) of every acre of England, Wales and Scotland'. The Survey made possible three historic Government Reports, which in their turn fathered all the post-war planning legislation.

The first of these was the Barlow Report 1940,[13] from which emerged the general conclusion that there must be 'forward planning in the location of industry and that the days of *laissez-faire* producing a satisfactory answer were over'. The second was the Scott Report 1942[13] on Land Utilisation in Rural Areas, and the third was the Uthwatt Report 1942,[13] which dealt with the development value of land. Meantime central planning machinery was being set up, and a new Ministry of Town and Country Planning allotted functions previously exercised by the Ministry of Health and the Ministry of Works. Although it did not last long under that title, the M.T.C.P. brought into being the Town and Country Planning Act 1947, the real start of national land use control.

So far as the countryside was concerned, it was the Scott Report that set the pace, and Stamp himself who drafted the paragraphs that related to national recreation and Nature conservation. Thus Section 178 outlined the need for National Parks and other open spaces, the preservation of the coast, and the registration of common lands, their upkeep and use. Section 179 recommended that Nature Reserves (apart from those inherent in National Parks) should be defined and established as separate entities, including areas of geological interest. Another part of the Report referred to rights-of-way.

In each case further investigation followed. National Parks became the subject of the Dower Report[14] published in 1945, when various committees[15] under the chairmanship of Sir Arthur Hobhouse thought further about both National Parks and the knotty question of rights-of-way and public access. The fruits of this work were embodied in the National Parks and Access to the Countryside Act 1949.

Another committee, led by Sir Julian Huxley, concerned itself with wild life. Its report, *Conservation in England and Wales*,[16] and the corresponding document for Scotland, were paramount in persuading the Government to set up its own agency, the Nature Conservancy: first as a Research Council, and then reconstituted by Royal Charter in 1949 as a legal entity on its own. Its aims were:

> to provide scientific advice on the conservation and control of the natural flora and fauna of Great Britain; to establish, maintain and manage Nature reserves in Great Britain, including the maintenance of physical features of scientific interest; and to organise and develop the scientific services related thereto.

Once again it was the war that spurred a solution. Eighty years had passed since the passage of the Seabirds Protection Act, and since that date an incalculable amount of private and public effort had been expended in the cause of wild life conservation. 1949 was obviously not the end, but it was the end of unco-ordinated effort, and opened a new chapter of State and private individuals acting together.

The Idea of Pleasure

Falcon is poised over fell in the cool,
Salmon draws
Its lovely quarrons through the pool.

> A birthday, a birth
> On English earth
> Restores, restore will, has restored
> To England's story
> The directed calm, the actual glory.

Auden's lines,[17] written between the two World Wars when land-abuse was at its worst, strike the chord of resurrection, the restoration of refuge and wild life; but—for me at any rate—they also convey the idea that the countryside is not only a haven for creatures but a source of delight, to be enjoyed through the senses. Curiously enough, the sensuous—above all the visual—reaction to pioneer industry in the countryside was not at first unfavourable. One reason, as W. G. Hoskins explains,[18] was that the physical impact was slight.

In the early eighteenth century machinery was still being operated manually, or by horses, watermills, or windmills. Enterprises were small, run by craftsmen, many of them part-time farmers. Industrial areas in the midlands and the north were still predominantly rural—partially enclosed farmland, peppered with paddocks, pits and work-shops. Most manufacture was still being carried on in cottages as in the Middle Ages. Improved textile machinery, such as Arkwright's spinning jenny, merely expanded the industry *in situ* without altering its struc-ture; but water power heralded the concentration of labour in factories.

> The first true factory built in England was the silk mill built for John and Thomas Lombe at Derby in 1718–22. It was five or six storeys high, employed three hundred men, and was driven by the water-power of the river Derwent. It was, as Mantoux says, in every respect a modern factory, with automatic tools, continuous and unlimited production, and specialised functions for the operatives. Within fifty years there were several silk factories employing four hundred to eight hundred persons, but the silk industry was of secondary importance and did not initiate the Factory System. It was when Power reached the cotton, woollen, and iron industries that the face of the country really began to change on a large scale, and that was not until the 1770s.[19]

Water however had its limitations as a source of power. Flow was wayward, and the number of stream-side sites restricted. Although the steam engine had been invented by Thomas Newcomen early in the century, and several hundred machines manufactured by Boulton and Watt between 1775 and 1800, not until the early nineteenth century was steam-driven plant widely used. It was then that factories rapidly replaced cottages as places of manufacture, and that factory buildings were erected—no longer in remote dales, but on the edge of towns where labour was readily to hand. Men, women, and children crowded in to work—many of them displaced by enclosure of farmland and the destruction of peasant holdings—and went to live in drab streets of cheap terraced houses, devoid of sanitation and decencies, run up any-where and everywhere by the factory owners. The advent of steam power altered the nature and increased the scale of industrial enterprise, while canals and railways broke down the bonds of communication. It was then that the real assault upon the landscape began, and the term 'Black Country' became a reality.

A second reason why early industry made some appeal to poets and painters was the prevailing passion for the picturesque. Tall factory buildings, classically proportioned, were not unattractive in a rural setting—indeed some are now being preserved as monuments of industrial archaeology. A smoking furnace added lustre to the scene, while there was something grandly horrific about shift work, with the lights glittering all during the night, and the workers toiling like ants. But this veneer soon peeled off in the hard light of day. The real horror of it all beset William Blake, when in one context or another he referred repeatedly to 'satanic mills' and 'England's green and pleasant land'. Many other voices bewailed the loss of local beauty; while the sheer ugliness and human degradation have been recorded for ever in the novels of Charles Dickens. Wordsworth too commented unfavourably in platitudinous verse; on the other hand he was much more effective in sensing the need for conservation, particularly for National Parks. In 1835 he declared that 'the Lake District should be deemed a sort of National property in which every man has a right and interest who has an eye to perceive and a heart to enjoy'. Although his aim was that impossible thing, the preservation of the *status quo*, at least he looked ahead by emphasising the *public* interest in scenery, in contrast to the previous age when landowners laid out parks and contrived vistas purely for their *private* enjoyment.

The idea of pleasure, even when aroused by innocent landscapes, suffered severely from Victorian attitudes. As an argument on its own, beauty—natural or aesthetic—has never cut much ice in England; and in the nineteenth century particularly people felt it necessary to justify their feelings, if not conceal them totally. Morality was dragged in at every point. Pugin—that tyrant of mid-Victorian taste—laid down that Gothic was the only *Christian* style of architecture, and elaborate four-teenth-century Decorated at that. Ruskin championed beauty on grounds of goodness, while William Morris—another moralist, but a robust and satisfying artist—reacted against commercial ugliness and the Victorian passion for faking, by reviving handicrafts and practising guild socialism.[20]

The defence of beauty was most effective when allied to some cause that needed no excuse. Fortunately for the English countryside a saviour appeared—a subject about which there could in the end be no real argument—sanitation. Epidemics of cholera, typhus and typhoid proved great persuaders, and by the 1840s the fight was on for systematic sewerage, clean water, and the proper disposal of household rubbish—and of the dead. Public health became a crusade; and although for a time medical men resisted the discovery of bacteria and the necessity for antiseptic routines, and although the first effective Public Health Act had to wait until 1875, there could only be one outcome if the nation was to survive.

Health was respectable and had a large progeny. Better housing for the poor preceded town planning, while the literal letting-in of air to slums and noxious alleys fathered the wider conception of access to open spaces and opportunities for recreation. This subject had a lengthy and chequered history. Public parks in towns came first, but inevitably—as the urban population continued to multiply—attention was focused upon the surviving common lands that bordered upon towns. The problem was complicated by the natural desire of the owners of the soil to cash in on rising land values. The foundation of the Commons Preservation Society in 1865 has already been mentioned,[21] also the series of successful campaigns to save open spaces, especially those in the vicinity of London. Although the Society soon set about rescuing rural commons, the incentive was primarily urban, concerned more with the townsman's need for recreation than with the countryman's rights of husbandry. It was the fight for access that linked the two. Thus within a few years the same Society took up the cause of rights-of-way, and in 1899 it joined forces with the National Footpaths Preservation Society.

Those who directed the affairs of the C.P.S. were a remarkable band of expert, eminent and devoted men: including Sir Robert Hunter, one of the founders of the National Trust, Sir John Shaw-Lefevre (Viscount Eversley), responsible for framing the Ancient Monuments Act 1882, in association with Sir John Lubbock (Lord Avebury), naturalist, scholar, and the originator of Bank Holidays. The 1882 Act was a permissive measure, which enabled an owner to place a monument in the care of the State for protection and preservation; and many owners took advantage of it. Shaw-Lefevre was also instrumental in inserting clauses in the Local Government Act 1894, which defined the duties of parish rural district and county councils as to the maintenance of rights-of-way. Both Acts were landmarks in the history of amenity, yet neither proved adequate in the test case of Stonehenge and—as happens still—it had to be left to a voluntary society to take the action necessary for the public good. The story is striking.

*   *   *

In 1901, when the Army was setting up camps on Salisbury Plain, the owner of Stonehenge, Sir Edmund Antrobus, 'erected a substantial and unsightly barbed-wire fence round the Monument, enclosing a few acres, and an entrance fee of one shilling a head was charged to visitors'.[22] The effect was to rob Stonehenge of its peculiar character—'a strange relic of the twilight of the world, standing untouched through countless centuries, and to convert it into an antiquarian's specimen. It lost its solemnity, due to its loneliness in the vast plain. The inhabitants of the district, who could not afford to pay one shilling a head for entrance, had lost their accustomed right of access to it.'[22] Neither public indignation, nor protracted attempts by the Government and the C.P.S. to purchase the Monument for a reasonable price, had any effect. Sir Edmund wanted £50,000 or nothing. Nor would he have anything to do with the Ancient Monuments Act. So the C.P.S. went to law— and lost. In a complicated tangle of legalities, the judge clarified nothing except to demonstrate his bias in favour of the owner. He thought that 'the vulgar populace had, by their destructive propensities, disqualified themselves as visitors to a place of antiquarian interest',[22] and quoted Horace in support. He dismissed the evidence of fifteen witnesses, most of them carters, who had used the right-of-way for up to fifty years, as untrustworthy, in the sense that they were 'illiterate, obviously exaggerating, and inaccurate'.[22] After a hearing lasting seven days, the costs amounted to £4000, a large part falling on the C.P.S. and its personal guarantors. Although urged to appeal, the Society decided it could not afford to do so, and admitted defeat. It was a bad blow for amenity, but the case had its consequences in that it hastened more effective legislation and informed public opinion in a dramatic fashion of the issues at stake. Ultimately Stonehenge came under the care of the State, in conjunction with the National Trust which now owns Stonehenge Down.

*   *   *

The National Trust for Places of Historic Interest and Natural Beauty, founded in 1895, has been referred to in connection with the purchase of Wicken Fen. Its interest in wild life however was secondary, nor did it intend to forestall or duplicate the work of the S.P.N.R. As its title indicates, the three founders—Miss Octavia Hill, Sir Robert Hunter and Canon H. D. Rawnsley—were concerned fundamentally with the aesthetics of environment, i.e. man-made as well as natural beauty. They therefore aimed to acquire buildings as well as land, permit public access, encourage an atmosphere of appreciation, and ensure that their organisation had the means and the standing to pursue these aims in perpetuity. They and their successors have succeeded remarkably well. Although the Trust has come in for periodic criticism over the past seventy-five years, its achievements—however assessed—are of a high order; and, despite population and other pressures, have conformed remarkably closely to the founders' aims: namely, to own or act as the guardian of property in the national interest and for the benefit of posterity. At the same time standards of maintenance have been high, improvements imaginative, and access by the public well-managed.

So great was the value placed upon its work that as early as 1907, barely twelve years after its foundation, Parliament conferred upon the Trust the unique power to declare its properties inalienable: which meant that they could not be sold or mortgaged, nor compulsorily acquired, except by permission of Parliament, a dispensation hitherto exercised only once.[23] These safeguards stand today, together with certain easements and extensions (such as the power to preserve chattels), made possible by later legislation, and which have kept the Trust abreast of contemporary needs. As a result, the latest report lists about 370,000 acres owned outright by the Trust and some 70,000 acres protected by covenant, besides over 200 houses of architectural and historic interest. Its properties vary enormously: mountain and moorland, coastland and woods, commons and pastures, gardens, lakes, waterfalls, bridges and canals. Its buildings range from early remains to Regency mansions, often containing important collections of pictures, furniture and *objets d'art*, illustrating almost every facet of style and construction in the development of domestic life.

In essence therefore the Trust has always been—and tried to remain— a holding organisation: thus, in the field of recreation, a provider rather than a propagandist. It has not always been possible to stick exclusively to this role, for by its nature the Trust can never stand aside from publicity, nor expect that its work unaided will speak for itself. To be involved in amenity is a dynamic undertaking, especially as a pioneer, and as late as the 1930s the Trust was trying to 'maintain almost single-handed the struggle to protect the best of the countryside'.[24] In early days people applied to it from every side to save this or that 'heirloom', it attracted a long list of affiliated organisations, it acted as a general consultant, and it intervened frequently in cases of preservation not necessarily connected with its own properties or immediate interests. By the outbreak of the Second World War, this policy had already had to be modified. For one thing, a number of amenity organisations—of national standing such as the Council for the Preservation of Rural England, not to mention numerous local associations—had come into being for the express purpose of influencing public opinion. For another, the Government was beginning to move at last in matters of land use, planning control, and rural recreation. Besides this, the Trust was constantly negotiating with national and local authorities through its involvement in farming, forestry, access, and many other matters deriving from its ownership of property. It also had a special relationship with the Treasury, and depended greatly upon the exertions and interest of men in prominent positions. As a private organisation with public responsibility, it had to steer a delicate course in order to avoid becoming a State within a State. It decided therefore to concentrate more closely upon its original purpose of preservation: a policy that paid off in the various concessions secured through legislation and in other benefits that facilitated the natural extension of its work. Such were the Country House Scheme 1937,[25] the Gardens Scheme 1948,[26] a substantial contribution from the Exchequer to the Jubilee Appeal in 1945, the establishment of the National Land Fund in 1946,[27] and much else since that would have amazed and delighted the trinity that founded the Trust in 1895.

The Means of Leisure

The dilemma of the National Trust was the dilemma of organisation for amenity as a whole. Although difficult often in detail, the business of purchasing or protecting a country house, park, hill-top, or a piece of common land for public enjoyment was relatively straightforward. The parallel problem, often more difficult because more diffuse, was—while encouraging the public to appreciate these things—to make it possible for them to do so. Holidays, cheap transport, and the means of leisure were essential concomitants of amenity, but they did not arrive overnight. None the less this was an urban force of great magnitude that could not be denied. It was a great day when in 1850 Grey's Factory Act established a sixty-hour week, with compulsory closing at two p.m. on Saturday afternoons. Likewise Sir John Lubbock's Act of 1871, providing four statutory 'bank holidays' a year, was another important step forward. By the end of the century—though adequate holidays with pay were still exceptional—leisure was beginning to be seen as a necessary requirement for everyone.

As to means, the railways were first in the field with cheap fares and excursions, a development that took the ordinary man and his family into the countryside and popularised the seaside. However it was difficult to travel far outside the railway line, especially on a day's outing; but the possibilities were greatly extended by the 'safety' bicycle, introduced *c.* 1885–6, having chain transmission, ball bearings and pneumatic tyres—gears came later. This was a cheap and handy form of transport, for you could put your machine in the guard's van and start out from any station. It was a pleasant way of exploring the countryside, companionable (ladies clad in bloomers soon joined in), and carried few social distinctions, being as popular with the professional classes as with the artisans. Moreover the Cyclists' Touring Club, founded in 1878, gave cycling holidays a great impetus by supplying its members with maps and a list of recommended accommodation. The bicycle was at the height of its social popularity in the Edwardian era, before cars became common, and was the way for instance that most of H. G. Wells' heroes and heroines got about.

Other open-air organisations soon proliferated—for walking, camping, climbing, sailing, etc. The Ramblers' Association—to take one example—is recognised today as the national organisation for walkers, and is powerful and highly respected. Although adopting its present title as late as 1935, its origins lay in the Federation of Rambling Clubs founded in 1905 by Lawrence Chubb[28] to unite the activities of the many individual clubs that had come into being in the previous twenty-five years. Although the holiday business was growing rapidly, many problems remained. One was the restriction of access to privately owned land, especially moorland where game was reared for shooting, but also in more accessible cultivated districts where farmers were already being bothered by litter and damage, and actively resisting the intrusion of wandering townsmen. Another was the shortage of accommodation in remote and beautiful places visited by walkers, and to a less extent by cyclists. The ordinary farmhouse which took visitors in did not meet this need. Naturally the farmer's wife charged what she could in the summer, and catered principally for families who stayed at least a week. What really was wanted was a sequence of huts, strategically placed ten to twenty miles apart, equipped with bunks, mattresses, water, a cooking stove, and not much else, available for one or two nights only. In the ordinary way this was not a commercial proposition.

The problem was both economic and social, for it mostly affected young people, from school age upwards, who had little money but an overriding desire to get out into the open air and fend for themselves. The Boy Scouts Association, born in 1908, and later the Girl Guides, provided part of the solution; also the extraordinary energy of T. A. Leonard who founded the Co-operative Holidays Association in 1891 and the Holiday Fellowship in 1913; both of which offered simple accommodation in superb surroundings. A few other organisations followed suit after the First World War.

But the real solution came from Germany, where Richard Schirrmann, a schoolmaster, had launched the Youth Hostel movement by 1914, with 200 hostels and 21,000 overnights recorded in that year. After 1918 the idea spread like wildfire, fanned by the special circumstances of German life—the reaction against industrialism and militarism, the poverty induced by the inflation of the mark, and the characteristic the Germans have always had of romanticising the simple life. When the Nazis came to power in 1933, the movement was so well founded that —instead of abolishing it—they preferred to adapt it to their own political and offensive purposes. By then however other countries were making headway. In Britain the Youth Hostels Association (Y.H.A.) had started in 1930, the main object being 'to help all, but especially young people, to a greater knowledge, care and love of the countryside, particularly by the provision of hostels or other simple accommodation for them on their travels'.[29] Nine years later there were nearly 300 hostels and over 83,000 members. As costs were kept down to a minimum (overnight fee, one shilling), most of the support had to come from outside benefactions and willing work by volunteers; but that was an integral part of the impetus of the movement.

After the Second World War, the Y.H.A. and other open-air organisations entered a completely new phase of growth, challenged as they were by the massive demand for recreation in the countryside in an age of affluence. This involves appraisal (later, in this book) not merely of the means but of the kinds of leisure demanded and of their survival under the pressures put upon them. In these matters, of course, the motor car plays a vital part; but as it was already creating problems long before war broke out in September 1939, it is worth a word now.

Any account of the way people, living a confined urban life, have demanded and obtained opportunities for leisure in the countryside, reveals a pattern of conflict. At first the problem was relatively easy to control, for in the days of Victorian railways, the horse and the bicycle, mobility was obviously limited. People either congregated in resorts to which they had travelled by train, or spread out from the towns over surrounding territory in such numbers as could be absorbed without difficulty. Money too was unevenly distributed, and that put an additional brake on travelling and tourism. However, with the arrival of the motor car and the motor cycle and their rapid development between the wars, pressure built up fast. By comparison with today, the quantity of traffic on the roads, even by 1939, was modest; even so it engendered the same sort of troubles that beset us now, since many of the high-ways—but especially rural by-roads—had hardly altered in capacity since the Middle Ages, conforming rather to the vagaries of property boundaries than to serving the needs of traffic. Although, as early as the 1920s, large sums were being spent on widening, straightening and improving the surface of roads—even so the programme was inadequate. Moreover the idea of providing positively for the motorist was slow in coming—lay-bys, lavatories, caravan and camping sites, picnic areas, viewpoints, even good signposting, all common enough in countries such as Switzerland, which had long depended on visitors for an important part of their income.

Congestion on the roads was one thing, where to go was another. Cars and coaches were making available a whole range of outdoor pleasures—solitary as well as gregarious—that many people had not even been able to contemplate before. Just as remote parts of the country were becoming yearly more accessible, so too was the prospect of a break-through in family leisure at moderate cost. All combined to create a crisis at the root of the problem: in other words, the danger— by sheer weight of numbers—of destroying the source of leisure itself. In the 1930s saturation point was still far off, but already certain beauty spots were being suffocated at holiday time, litter left about in shoals, crops trampled, fences broken, and gates left open—all the out-come of human pressure and ignorance, itself the legacy of a century or more of urban seclusion, of man cut off from everyday contact with the countryside. Yet the very people who were invading the country in this way, even those who left it like a battlefield, were gradually becoming aware of the need to protect what they were trying to enjoy. The urge for access and recreation carried with it the seeds of care and responsi-bility, thus it was mainly townsmen who rallied first to the cause of amenity.

Planning for Amenity

The preliminaries of protection however were painfully slow and amateur. Although urban planning had at last been recognised by Parliament,[30] the idea of exercising control over the use of rural land was still regarded as heresy. The decade after the end of the First World War was probably the worst. Agriculture was in distress and farm land was cheap. The pent-up pressure for housing and industrial development swept away would-be planners in a flood. The result was a free-for-all, a rush to build what and where you wanted, restrained by nothing but myopic by-laws. Protests in defence of amenity were shouted down— dismissed as mere sentimentality or as interference with the sacred rights of the individual, the man with the money. It was the heyday of the by-pass villa and the pretentious bungalow, ribbon-built to save the cost of service roads and public utilities; of the drab, no less depressing, council house, regimented in one-class estates, segregated socially and physically from the rest of the community. Open country was particu-larly vulnerable, and long stretches of coastline were submerged in sporadic development. A classic case was that of Peacehaven, between Brighton and Newhaven, where a newspaper campaign, aimed ostensibly at hastening house building for men returned from the war, resulted in several square miles of man-made desolation among virgin downland. But there were numerous Peacehavens of varying scale about the country.

The prospect therefore was of subtopia unlimited, against which a mixed bag of preservation and naturalist societies were powerless, unless planning was extended—not only negatively to check land abuse, but to play a positive role in guiding development outside the immediate surrounding of towns. Public opinion however was not yet ready; and so once again it devolved upon private initiative to make a move, through the foundation in 1926 of the Council for the Preservation of Rural England (C.P.R.E.).[31] The weakest thing perhaps about the C.P.R.E. was its name. The term 'preservation' sounds negative and nostalgic, and implies resistance to change at all costs. In fact the Council erred remarkably little in this respect. What it aimed to do— and what it has done over the years with increasing success—was to rationalise protest and co-ordinate action among its constituent members, offer a central service of information and consultation, and ensure that amenity attain a status which Government departments, and private and corporate developers alike, could not easily overlook. It filled the gap, in fact, left open by the National Trust: namely, that it should act—not as the landlord or permanent guardian of historic properties and beauty spots—but as a pressure group committed to propagandising for amenity. It meant that, until the countryside came under effective planning, the C.P.R.E. was forced to assume a quasi-planning role which should have been played by a Ministry.

For instance the C.P.R.E. invited the Labour Government of 1929 to investigate the possibility of establishing National Parks—areas of fine landscape, rich in natural resources and wild life—where conservation and recreation and other apparently conflicting uses of land might none the less be successfully combined. The subject was by no means new. A Private Bill to permit access to mountains and moorland had first been introduced in 1884 by James (Lord) Bryce, another in 1888 by Thomas Ellis. Bryce returned with fresh Bills year after year, all without success, and was followed by C. P. (Sir Charles) Trevelyan in 1908, 1926, 1927 and 1928. Finally in September 1929 the Government appointed a Committee under the chairmanship of Dr Christopher Addison M.P. (Lord Addison), in direct response to the memorandum submitted by the C.P.R.E. The Committee reported in favour of the proposal, but by now the year was 1931 and the economic crisis postponed all action. Even so, the campaign continued. Fresh Bills were presented in 1930 and 1931. In 1935 the C.P.R.E. set up a Standing Committee on National Parks, and the Government was urged repeatedly to implement the Addison Report.

Paradoxically it was the Forestry Commission—already under fire for 'desecrating' the landscape with regiments of conifers—that responded first: by granting facilities to youth hostellers, and then by forming so-called National Forest Parks in Argyll (1936), Snowdonia (1937) and the Forest of Dean (1938). In these places, and in the New Forest in Hampshire (already popular with visitors), the public was given access and practical assistance for open-air recreation. The policy was extended after the war, and paid off handsomely. As Roger Miles writes:

> There is no doubt about the success of the forest park movement. Since 1960, well over a quarter of a million people have stayed overnight each year in the designated areas, apart from uncounted day-visitors, and the numbers continue to rise. Through the parks the Commissioners have managed to improve their relations with the public; while the public, subconsciously perhaps, has acquired some appreciation of the forester's skills and difficulties. Valuable

experience has been gained of the requirements of people on holiday in remote rural areas, including such diverse items as car parks, lavatories, camp sites, hostels, litter collection, the marking of forest trails, water points and picnic areas. The Commission has also set an exceptionally high standard in the production of guide books for the forest parks and other regions of special interest.[32]

In April 1932 the campaign was given an edge by militant action. Hikers organised mass trespass in the Peak District, and it was here that Tom Stephenson[33] conceived the idea of a long-distance footpath through disputed land over the Pennines. The Pennine Way became a rallying cry for the open-air movement, and Tom Stephenson himself—by his practical idealism and tough persistence—played a leading part in the fight for public access. But opposition was powerful, and preparations for war provided the Government with a ready-made excuse to do nothing. Eventually in 1938 Arthur Creech Jones presented a Bill that passed its second reading, but was so mutilated in committee that many of its supporters withdrew their backing. Although it reached the statute book as the Access to Mountains Act 1939, it was rendered inoperative by the outbreak of war, and in the end was repealed by post-war legislation.

However, what peace had failed to do, war accomplished. The need for National Parks was emphasised in the Scott Report 1942, and reiterated by Ministers at frequent intervals as the war went on. In 1944 it was announced that John Dower had been commissioned to undertake a fresh survey of the subject, his Report appearing in May 1945, just after the close of hostilities in Europe. May therefore was a historic month on both counts, for Dower's was a masterly document—imaginatively conceived and expertly presented, defining the scope and function of National Parks, suggesting suitable areas, outlining the administration, examining the problems—so that it is now acknowledged as the basic blueprint of recreational planning in the countryside. There was a family as well as a public interest in this work, for Dower was the son-in-law of Sir Charles Trevelyan,[34] who had fought so hard for public access in the past. Moreover, after Dower's early and untimely death, his widow, Pauline, served with distinction as Deputy Chairman of the National Parks Commission for some seventeen years; and their son Michael has since made a name for himself in the same field, through his work for the Civic Trust, and as Director of the Dartington Amenity Research Trust (D.A.R.T.).

I have related that, soon after the elections in 1945, a new Committee was set up (under Sir Arthur Hobhouse) to consider how the Dower Report should be applied; likewise to hammer out procedures for rights-of-way and access to the countryside generally. The Hobhouse findings were published in 1947, and in the main crystallised what

Dower had proposed: including the appointment of a National Parks Commission, an executive body with specific powers to acquire land and provide facilities, responsible to the Ministry of Town and Country Planning; the selection of National Park areas, each to be administered by a Committee (the planning authority for the Park), half its members to be nominated by the Commission, half by the local authorities on the spot; and a series of supporting suggestions as to areas of scenic value outside the Parks, publicity and finance. The latter was remarkably modest in scale—less than ten million pounds spread over ten years for capital requirements, and an annual sum of not more than £750,000 for running expenses—but it was backed by an offer from Dr Dalton, Chancellor of the Exchequer, to use the National Land Fund to support (among other causes) National Parks. To some extent the Hobhouse Report was anticipated by the Town and Country Planning Act 1947, especially as to land use and the control of development. Since however important matters, such as access and Nature conservation,[35] were either omitted or inadequately covered by this Act, further legislation was finally agreed and embodied in the National Parks and Access to the Countryside Act 1949.

In certain essentials the new Act proved a disappointment. The National Parks Commission was made advisory, not executive: so that at the very outset it was denied the status and ability to stand up to Ministries and other statutory agencies, which sought to make use of National Park land. Ten Parks were designated between 1950 and 1955, and in eight of them the administration was virtually handed over to their constituent County Councils. Only two (the Peak District and the Lake District) operated under Joint Boards and enjoyed any semblance of independence, and only the Peak had its own Planning Officer and staff. Support from the National Land Fund was withdrawn in 1957, and Government money was confined to percentage grants in respect of approved expenditure only. It is understandable that local planning authorities, constituted in 1947, should not wish to have their powers whittled away in 1949: hence the decision to make National Parks part of the structure of local government, with a minimum of interference from the centre. But the immediate result was to convert the Parks into Cinderellas and delay the arrival of Prince Charming. None the less the 1949 Act was a heartening step forward, coming as it did sixty-five years after James Bryce had presented his first Bill in 1884.

Amenity is Everywhere
In a brief historical essay such as this, it is all too easy to convey the impression that amenity is an extra, something which—though good to strive for—can be added to life on top of the real business of existence. This attitude, typical of urbanised countries and particularly true of this

one, is a heritage of the Industrial Revolution, which dehumanised work and divorced man from Nature.

No one denies of course that in earlier days, as well as in later ones, most people lived in what we should regard as squalid conditions, in which disease was rife and the expectation of life small. None the less whatever the economic miseries and social inequalities of pre-Industrial England, there was always compensation in the fact that a field lay beyond every doorstep, and that Nature—a beneficent mystery—was respected both as the source of life and as the end of it. Existence and environment were inextricable.

This explains why, once the damage done by industrialism had gone deep and man had become disorientated—say by the third quarter of the nineteenth century—the approach (or return) to amenity was so hesitant and piecemeal. Like a marriage, once broken, it is harder to repair than to make a fresh union. The whole movement, if such it can be called, was a series of actions and reactions, irregular in direction and pace, touching a variety of apparently disconnected subjects, from the protection of wild life to the betterment of housing. Yet in all this disparity, there was a common, though often undeclared theme: the desire for harmony and humanity, and to regain in contemporary form what had been taken for granted in the past. Amenity however was an elusive ideal; and owing to the seclusion of large populations in London and the large industrial towns, it seemed necessary at first to seek it *outside* everyday surroundings. In other words the environment of Victorian industry and urban life was often so depressing that it could best be mitigated by trying for a while to forget it altogether: hence the popularity of the seaside, sport, and all kinds of open-air recreation. The search for amenity became synonymous with escape: thus the need to conserve unspoiled areas of the countryside, together with the means of access, in order to be sure of having somewhere to escape to.

But in its essence amenity is not a haven, rural or otherwise, available only during the holidays or at other times away from residence or employment. It is a continuous and comprehensive state, inherent in the quality of living, as conveyed both by everyday environment and the circumstances of life. It affects the town therefore no less than the country; and is expressed for example in the design and structure of buildings; the standard of public services; the provision of shops, schools, institutions, and places of entertainment; communications; the control of noise and smells; conditions of employment; and much else. In short, as a basic human requirement, it lies at the heart of urban as well as of rural planning; or, as we now recognise, of planning as a whole.

Such concepts were however slow to evolve in the Victorian Age. The practical pioneers of planning were specialists, often people of great stature, but specialists none the less: men like Edwin Chadwick and Southwood Smith devoted to the cause of sanitation, or Florence

Nightingale to that of nursing. It was not for example until the 1870s that the links between poverty, education, housing and health[36] were beginning to be recognised; and longer still before the dissolution of the belief that poverty was an actual moral defect. The idea died hard too that the State was a necessary evil; that it should 'interfere' as little as possible with the private citizen, and confine itself to correcting abuses rather than initiating improvements.

It was not until 1919 that the Government made any comprehensive attempt to deal with the statutory business of amenity, however defined. The department set up, the Ministry of Health, was given far too many duties—a rag-bag of housing, health, water supply, sewerage, public assistance, and whatnot. It lacked the necessary cohesion of aim and organisation, because the relationship of the State to the private citizen had developed piecemeal, and the country was not yet prepared for the State to go any further. Thus it happened that physical planning and the control of land use were submerged in the post-war chaos of reconstruction, when development ran riot. A prime example was the shift of population towards London, the south midlands and the south-east, due to heavy unemployment in the traditional centres of industry: resulting in an appalling misuse of land, and in a wilderness of tasteless and sporadic building.

Although the first Town Planning Act had been passed in 1909, there was no statutory control of development in the countryside before the Town and Country Planning Act 1932 and the Restriction of Ribbon Development Act 1935; but these were half-hearted pieces of legislation. They did little to influence the siting of new factories or ensure the social success of housing that accompanied them. As the 1930s moved on, the situation was further confused by preparations for defence and the setting up of 'shadow' installations for war production. It was not until the Barlow Commission[37] recommended a central planning authority that the Government came round. By that time the Second World War had begun, and with it a completely new awareness of the need to control land use, as already described.

*   *   *

The story of amenity, in its intrinsic sense, is lightened from time to time by the efforts of outstanding individuals. If you leave aside the Utopian theorists of all ages and the private developers of the seventeenth and eighteenth centuries, however harmonious their works, the first name must certainly be that of Robert Owen, the genius of the mills at New Lanark, where he established housing and labour conditions far in advance of his time, and encouraged a progressive system of education. Yet his reputation rests more upon his social thinking than upon his various attempts to establish model communities in the United Kingdom and the United States, all of which failed. More relevant, though less comprehensive in aim and scope, were the housing and welfare schemes established by industrialists at Saltaire (1852), Bournville (1879) and Port Sunlight (1888), all of them designed as adjuncts to the enterprises concerned. The real founder of urban planning, in which the environment of labour and living was thought out from the start, was Ebenezer Howard. It was he who conceived the idea of the Garden City,[38] and in the following brief exposition I follow Sir Frederic Osborn in his latest assessment of Howard's work.[39]

Howard first put his finger on what had happened to town life in the nineteenth century. People had thronged into the towns to secure work, better wages, and better living. For this they had paid a price—overcrowding, inferior housing, pollution, and the loneliness of large amorphous communities. While recognising the disadvantages of country life, e.g. its poverty and lack of opportunity, Howard (no countryman himself) was in no doubt about the therapy of Nature and a rural environment. He wanted therefore a 'town in the country', and stated his case in simple uninhibited terms: 'How to restore the people to the land—that beautiful land of ours, with its canopy of sky, the air that blows upon it, the sun that warms it, the rain and dew that moisten it—the very embodiment of Divine love for man.'

His aim was neither negative nor nostalgic. He was equally uninterested in artificial home-made communities as in semi-urban estates populated by townsmen who—in their attempt to escape the town—had merely created a pale imitation of country life, while generating fresh problems of daily travel and social seclusion. Howard proposed a new town of 30,000 people, a balanced unit, sub-divided into neighbourhoods, representative of different classes and occupations, provided *in situ* with factories, offices, shops, schools, other necessary institutions, and internal open spaces. Houses would vary in size and character, but all would have gardens. The central area of the town would cover about 1000 acres, surrounded by 5000 acres of agricultural land or 'green-belt'. The whole area would rest in single ownership, but be leased out to the individual interests under control as to use, densities, and architectural character. No fringe development in the green-belt was permitted, but once the central area had been filled up, then expansion would take place by starting another town in similar circumstances beyond the agricultural periphery.

Such in short were the essentials of Howard's thinking, and applied first to Letchworth Garden City as from 1903, and then to Welwyn Garden City as from 1920. This is not the place to pursue the intricacies and adaptations of Howard's plans. The point is that Howard produced the first practical blueprint for urban environmental planning; and which, after many vicissitudes, led to the creation of New Towns following the Act of 1946; and this takes no account of the influence exerted by his work upon the re-development of existing towns. In pursuing a policy of 'decongestion and dispersal' in this manner, successive Governments have adopted Howard's central belief that town life should be humanised, basically by limiting size,[40] by ministering to social and economic needs on the spot, and by trying to relate urban and rural land use. Howard therefore passes into history as one of the great pioneers of amenity planning in this country, as applied to the town.

Whereas as a townsman Howard sought to integrate town and country, so as a countryman did Sir George Stapledon, though using different data and deploying different arguments. Both Howard and Stapledon accepted the benefits of Nature as an axiom, but while Howard took agriculture for granted, Stapledon did not. As an agricultural scientist, he was deeply troubled lest the technology of farming get out of hand: that, by merely intensifying the production of crops and stock in response to economic demand, it should deplete and pervert the resources of Nature, and end in the destruction of man. Above all, by restoring respect for the biological forces that govern the environment, he sought to renew the basis of our physical and psychological well-being: a subject which, in the context of amenity, he called 'human ecology'. For these reasons—re-stated in an essay by his biographer, Robert Waller, in the Appendix to this book—Stapledon preached integration as the only alternative to the suffocation of the countryside by the town.

B. DARTINGTON HALL: INTEGRATION IN PRACTICE
Why Dartington?
The account that follows finds a place in this book for three reasons. First, the formative years of the Dartington Hall Estate coincided with those in which English farming, forestry, and country life, were undergoing radical changes between the two World Wars and in the early 1950s. Secondly, although in one sense the Dartington enterprise is unique and therefore unrepeatable, in another—and in fact—it is such a wide-ranging and practical example of renewal in the countryside, that it has already proved itself in many of the activities it promotes, and shown the way forward for others. As to results it has not only brought employment and social benefits to its own and other areas in rural Devon, but has gone far towards solving some of the toughest problems of integration between town and country life at large. Lastly, since I spent fifteen years as a freelance historian attached part-time to the Estate, I was in a position enjoyed by no one else to record in detail and in depth

all that happened. I write therefore with intimate knowledge and from first-hand experience.

In 1951 my wife and I were up to our necks running a hilly 130-acre farm at Brushford on the edge of Exmoor. We had bought the place in 1947, and were still busy building up our stock of Guernsey cows and Wessex pigs, converting the solid stone shippons from beef to dairy, and reclaiming a lot of rough land—some of it water-logged clay pastures beside the Taunton–Barnstaple railway line, the rest steep scrubby cleeves hanging like a poncho over the shoulders of the holding. It was hard, tiring, and challenging work, very expensive, and we were soon heavily 'in the red'.

As an author however, I had a second string to my bow. I got busy with articles and books, lectures, and broadcasts for the B.B.C. West Region of Bristol, and so earned a second income. Moreover I was in excellent health, and young enough to sustain two demanding occupations.

Towards the end of 1950 it was suggested I should write a sixty-minute feature—it was all sound radio in those days of course—about Dartington Hall, near Totnes. It was a challenge and I jumped at it. The fact that I had never been there and knew nothing about it was no deterrent for a professional writer. That I should handle it, ignorant and unbiased, was a positive advantage; because of course I had *heard* of Dartington, who hadn't?

People had been saying saucy things about the place for a long time. Much was hearsay, and I soon formed the impression that if you talked to an agricultural scientist, or a forester, or perhaps an artist, someone in fact who had worked continuously in one of the departments, then you learned something constructive, though not necessarily wholly favourable to the Estate. As an outsider I myself had merely picked up some of the funny stories about the School, where the children were said to be allowed to do anything they liked; or I had heard some of the other horror tales about life at the Hall. Dartington, it seemed, was staffed by Moscow-trained Reds, yet sustained by a limitless flow of American money—a confusing combination, especially when coloured by references to naked sun-bathing parties and other unmentionable pastimes, practised in an environment of seductive beauty. Dartington was at the same time a Lotus land and a wart upon the fair face of Devon, but a happy hunting ground for all those who got inside.

It was hard not to allow this sort of nonsense to muddy one's mind before starting work; but it was exciting nonsense and gave an edge to every journey I was to make in the early days, each one a fifty-mile run south to Totnes from my farm at Brushford. But first I had to secure permission for the programme from the two Founder-Trustees, Leonard and Dorothy Elmhirst. I met them in an Exeter nursing-home, where Leonard was temporarily laid up with illness, and I remember the meeting vividly. Mainly I remember their reluctance. Dartington had been on the air before, and in other ways had had plenty of publicity, much of it carping and adverse, some of it uncritically fulsome–both equally unbalanced and damaging. I was to realise later that part of the fault lay with Dartington itself. Those in charge had never prepared a policy for publicity. They distrusted it, and Micawber-like hoped that the Estate would speak for itself. It did time and again in an anarchic and often injurious way, in that any Tom, Dick or Harry, who had spent a week (or even a weekend) at the Hall, or nursed a grudge of some kind (sacked, perhaps, for some good or bad reason), or who felt the urge to expound some private theory about what Dartington ought to be doing, was at complete liberty to speak out. The only sanction—that such statements were unofficial—was offset by the fact that the heads of departments, and the Trustees[1] themselves (the final authority at Dartington) preferred to say nothing at all.

There was another handicap, which I discovered at the very outset of my meeting with the Elmhirsts at Exeter: the extreme difficulty of saying anything simple about the aims and achievements of the Dartington enterprise. To my amazement, when I asked the obvious question, 'What is Dartington about?', neither Leonard nor Dorothy could give me a straight answer; and they even disagreed between themselves in the animated discussion that followed. This might have been fatal, for if the founders were not clear about their aims, who else could be? No wonder a cloud of mystery hung over the place, or that a hundred half-baked views had been expressed. Nor did it speak well for the serious intentions or efficiency of an organisation of such size and importance.

Yet the Elmhirsts did impress me at once by their sincerity, intelligence, and transparent idealism. Dorothy—tall, watchful, entrenched in her private serenity—said little, except to ask me one or two penetrating questions about my own qualifications. Leonard looked tired, indeed was ill at the time, but as the conversation developed he moved into his mental stride. I was able to exchange ideas with him about rural planning and land use, and I asked about the economics of the Trust, and how the social activities were paid for. It was then that he gave me an inkling of the extraordinary diversity of his interests, above all of the continuing duel between the heritage of thought and belief derived from his background, and the relentless probing of his intellect. The same was true in different circumstances of Dorothy. It was a duel that gave the clue to their creation of Dartington, and which generated so much fascination and fruitful difficulty.

Leonard's early life influenced all that followed. Son of a parson-landowner in the West Riding, where the family had been settled for more than 600 years, he was the second eldest of eight boys and a girl. He was brought up in orthodox fashion, and educated at Repton and Trinity College, Cambridge. His father had ceased to practise as a parson in middle life, and after about 1900 devoted all his time to looking after the Elmhirst property outside Barnsley. He treated his tenants and children alike with a mixture of feudal authority and personal affection. I had the impression that he was an austere man, who had discarded formal belief in the Church but retained an impregnable moral authority. The boys were brought up simply, learned self-reliance and handiness on the estate, and lived a relatively Spartan life. There was not much money about, and they were encouraged to fend for themselves. Leonard was instinctively at home in the countryside, loved Nature, and got on well with people. He was accessible, yet entirely independent, and ready to strike out on his own whatever the consequences. These qualities never changed. He also acquired a strong sense of history—it carried him away at times—and a deep respect for land as the source of physical existence and the basis of society. Land provided food, drink, wealth and power; and history explained what man did with these things.

Leonard spent all his early manhood looking for answers to the land. The search took him abroad to study rural problems at their opposite extremes: in India where a purely peasant society, complicated by caste and religious differences, was already breaking down under the impact of the West; and in the United States of America where land was treated primarily as a business. Both countries fascinated him, and their attitudes embodied lessons that he was determined somehow some day to apply in England. In India, during the First World War, he met Sam Higginbottom, the American farmer-missionary who had founded the Allahabad Agricultural Institute and was seeking to pull the peasant out of poverty by teaching him better farming. After the war Leonard worked his way as a ship's writer over to America, and graduated the hard way at Cornell for an agricultural degree in 1921. Soon afterwards he returned to India at the invitation of the poet, Rabindranath Tagore, who had recently founded his International University (Visva-Bharati) at Santiniketan in the province of Bengal. Tagore commissioned Leonard to found and develop a department of Rural Reconstruction at Sriniketan near by, to train students and carry out research: a pioneer undertaking that absorbed all Leonard's energies for the two years, 1922–4, when the department was finally handed over to an all-Indian staff. The story of Leonard's association with India is a long one, his friendship with Tagore and Nehru, and the services he rendered in subsequent years—all this has been related elsewhere.[2] In 1924 he left Sriniketan and in the following April married Dorothy Whitney Straight, whom he had first met during his time at Cornell.

Dorothy was the daughter of William C. Whitney, the American financier and statesman, who had died in 1904, leaving her at the age of seventeen with an immense fortune. Determined to use her wealth in a responsible manner, she was soon caught up in welfare work in New

York, and took an active part in political and social movements, notably the campaign for women's suffrage. In 1911 she married Willard Straight and accompanied him to China. where he was engaged in railroad building and industrial development, Willard died in France in 1918, and afterwards Dorothy immersed herself in a vortex of work, social, educational, and economic. She became well known for her liberal opinions at a time when America was entering a period of reaction and isolation. Among other ventures she supported *The New Republic*, a progressive weekly founded by her husband, and edited later by her son, Michael. In his will Willard had requested her to do something for Cornell, where he had been a student, 'to make it a more human place'. It was there that she met Leonard Elmhirst, and helped him first to salve the fortunes of a club[3] for foreign students. Later they co-operated in a plan to build Willard Straight Hall, which has since become a vital centre of student life.

Leonard and Dorothy Elmhirst combined in their ideas and activities during forty-three years of married life to form a partnership, outstanding in the quality of all they did. Agreed on fundamentals, they complemented each other in specific interests. For instance Leonard's concern for the land was reinforced by Dorothy's passion for the arts.[4] Both had advanced ideas about education—like everything else they put them into practice—and both were determined to justify their advantages of wealth and culture by applying them to help solve problems of the day. They had deep sympathies and a vast circle of friends, but they were not sentimental and were well aware of the designs of spongers. As I duly learned they could be unexpectedly tough.

When I left Exeter after that first meeting, I had no doubt about the Elmhirsts, but I was not much clearer about Dartington. I had their permission at any rate to go ahead with the B.B.C. programme, provided I played fair. This indeed I tried to do; but I am now well aware that, as broadcast in June 1951, it was a pedestrian piece—mainly because it did avoid snide and slant. To try to convey accurately and intelligibly all that had happened at Dartington in the previous twenty-five years, when most people (even the heads of departments) disagreed about the purpose of the Estate, was virtually an impossibility. Besides this, I hadn't the benefit of television. Dartington is *par excellence* a paradise for the camera. So I was confined to livening up the interviews with noises off—fading in machinery, farm work, music, etc.—which might have come from anywhere and which were the bread-and-butter of almost every feature programme in those days. The value of the programme lay in its authenticity, and in hearing the voices and opinions of people actually involved in the life of the Estate. That still stands as an historical record.

Far more important for me was the subsequent invitation by the Trustees to write the definitive history of the whole enterprise. I was talking idly to Leonard in his study, and we were looking out over the magnificent horse shoe of terraced lawns in the gardens below the Hall. Soon we were joined by Peter Sutcliffe, secretary of the Trust and managing director of Dartington Hall Ltd. I was not feeling well, but my slight indisposition soon vanished when I heard their proposal, large enough to excite any young writer and sweetened by a fee ten times anything I had ever received from the B.B.C., or for that matter from any publisher. After the initial euphoria, I asked some sobering questions. I was not the first to receive the invitation. My predecessors, like myself, had accepted with enthusiasm, but eventually all had sunk beneath the sheer weight of material and the complexity of the subject. I knew instinctively what the Elmhirsts were trying to do, but when it came down to dry definition and description it was all too easy to lose one's way in a maze of bold avenues, that soon deteriorated into forest paths or petered out altogether.

I asked how long the job would take. Six months was their estimate. Two years, I suggested cautiously, thinking of the farm at Brushford and of the prospect of grappling with Dartington in the early mornings when half-awake, or late evenings when half-asleep, and of the 100-mile drives to Totnes and back to collect material and see people. Neither side knew it, but this was the beginning of a fifteen-year stint, a totally absorbing commitment involving the sorting of several tons of papers, filing thousands of letters and documents—reports, minutes, financial accounts, many rescued at the eleventh hour from salvage. It involved the active help of two assistants[5] and the organisation of a Records Office for the deposit of all the selected material, published and unpublished, and adding to it an ancillary collection of maps, photographs, notices and programmes. Some of this matter related only indirectly to the Estate, for the Elmhirsts had a host of outside interests, while their private correspondence often gave the clue to their public actions. None of it therefore could be omitted in order to arrive at a full understanding. Out of it all emerged ultimately two reports: the first covering the period 1925–56 (the formative years), the second continuing until 1965, forty years in all. The final result was a mammoth history of more than 300,000 words, confidential in detail, unpublishable as a whole, of which only twelve duplicated copies exist.[6] The fact that I was able to publish in 1958 a book about Dartington,[7] founded on the first part of the private history, was a separate undertaking.

Essentially then, the commission given me by the Trustees in 1951, and conceived as a relatively short report, became in the end a continuing archival record, backed by original material stored on the spot and enlarged as departments transferred their past filing to the Records Office. When I left in 1966, my task finally complete, the plan was to maintain the record in the same form, and to employ an historian to bring it up to date at stated intervals. That plan holds good, although

Dartington is now developing so fast and in so many new directions that it may well take a team of researchers to do the job. For me it was a unique experience, a creative as well as a critical exercise, that I would not have missed for anything in the world.

Background

It would have been so easy to start a precious community, inward-looking, protected by money, and insulated from the harsh winds of the world. For a short time Dartington did indeed look like this, partly because it had to start from scratch in a neglected area, and because much of the initial effort had inevitably to come from family and friends.

The urge to retire from the world, to live alone as the ancient hermits did, or in a small, self-supporting, like-minded, group, has often found expression in the history of man. It is a natural and noble concept. One has only to think of the orders of monks and nuns, characteristic of many religions but particularly of Christianity, which actuated by a desire to serve God have also served man, and continue to do so. It was the Benedictine communities that saved Western civilisation in the Dark Ages; and it was the Benedictines and other orders that not only preserved learning in times of stress, but extended the frontiers of knowledge, taught the young, harboured the sick and the needy, and helped reclaim the wilderness. They provided missionaries as well as contemplatives, clerks, executives, and artisans; but their strength lay in their corporate organisation, inspired and cemented by their belief in God.

Similar motives, partly political but essentially religious, drove settlers from England and Europe—Dissenters of many shades—to pioneer the New World. They long held together as distinct communities, partly for self-protection and survival in hostile surroundings, but in their character religion remained the base. It was not until the nineteenth century that other motives—politics and commerce principally—took precedence among pioneers: by which time science and sophistication were altering the structure of society and ousting dogmatic belief. This new dynamic contributed simultaneously to the growth of towns and the decline of villages, and undermined the whole heritage of rural life, which was essentially one of intimate, self-contained, communities. As the countryside in England declined for both economic and social reasons, so in time did dependence on religion, whether expressed in loyalty to church or chapel, or informally in local arts and customs which had often originated in religious practice.

It was revolt against this process of disintegration, no less than a yearning for relief from the pressures of urban life, that gave such impetus to the amenity movements described in the previous chapter. With it came attempts here and there to return to some form of communal living. In a sense it was the Benedictine phenomenon all over again, though with one important difference. Whereas a number of recognisably religious communities have indeed been founded in the twentieth century, more or less collective in structure, others have taken different forms, though usually ethical in character or aim. Wherever a group has been launched without a compulsive ideal or a practical *raison d'être*, then usually it has failed. Escapism alone is not a working philosophy and it is expensive. Merely to seek the simple life as a substitute for everyday existence invites disaster. Before the war the hallmark was unmistakable.[8] It was the beardies and weirdies who wore peasant dress, abjured meat, and danced round the mulberry bush. All they succeeded in doing was to damage the cause of intrinsically good things, such as simple dress, good food, and home-made entertainment.

I mention this because Dartington was dogged by some of these people from the start, and was categorised as 'a community' in a disparaging sense that forty or more years have even now not quite removed. But additionally for the ordinary citizen, Dartington represented a fantasy world of rural simplicity, satisfying work, natural beauty, and ideal relationships. In other words he projected upon Dartington what he missed in his own life and deeply desired. He wanted Dartington to be that kind of place, hence the strength of the label, for it papered over a psychological vacuum in his own personality and circumstances. He both envied and resented it. The label conformed to the general sense of the Elmhirsts' aims; but how these were applied was another matter.

※　　　※　　　※

In September 1925 Leonard and Dorothy Elmhirst bought Dartington for £30,000. The core of the property was the Hall, a magnificent fourteenth-century country house, laid out with its attendant apartments in the form of a double quadrangle by John Holland, half-brother of Richard II. In the sixteenth century Dartington came into the hands of Sir Arthur Champernowne, whose successors kept it in the family for nearly 400 years, until 1925. Sir Arthur civilised Dartington, adapted Holland's great structures to more homely use, and made a pleasant house for himself out of the private rooms behind the Banqueting Hall. Many of the outer buildings were allowed to fall down, but in the eighteenth century further modernisation was carried out in the domestic quarters—e.g. the addition of windows, passages and internal staircases. A dividing wall was also built across the main courtyard, transforming the northern half into a farmstead, called the Barton; and it remained in farm use until the courtyard was restored in 1928. The Elmhirsts arrived just in time. As a safety precaution the roof had been taken off the Banqueting Hall a century earlier, but many other buildings were on the point of collapse. Fortunately there are photographs, fascinating examples of visual history, showing the extent of the decay. They place on record not only the material disintegration but the social as well. Once a great estate covering several parishes, Dartington had by 1925 been reduced to a mere 820 acres: consisting of two farms of some 600 acres, woodlands (with some splendid trees, planted by the Champernownes) of 190 acres; the buildings and the grounds accounting for the rest. The Hall itself had stood empty for four years.[9]

The Elmhirsts planned for rehabilitation in the broadest sense. First, physical reconstruction and re-development of all the resources of the Estate, in order to make it a paying concern. Secondly, as a result of modernisation, to provide everyone employed at Dartington with decent living conditions and scope for a satisfying life. Lastly, to publish—or at least communicate openly—how this was done; and so to make available the fruits of experience, mistakes included, to all who had the future of the countryside at heart. As was said time and again, it was not necessary to copy Dartington as a total enterprise but to extract from it what was relevant and useful. Dartington was a laboratory, but alive and actual, and not conducted in the refined atmosphere of academic research.

Looking back now, it is not difficult to disentangle events, and to see that most of the ventures launched before 1939 were in line with the aims. At the beginning however Dartington was confusing—it attracted, repelled, but above all it confused. One reason was that much happened in the first few years, and not all of it could be classified as 'rural reconstruction'. This was due to the vigour and variety of the Elmhirsts' interests, which extended far outside Dartington. In consequence they generated a number of activities barely connected with the purpose of the Estate, and for which the only positive link was a personal or administrative one.[10]

Simply stated, one thing led to another—as so often happens when a big venture gets under way. Due to its own momentum, Dartington launched into several undertakings not conceived at the outset, and only justified by a process of rationalisation after the event. Progress therefore was to a large degree pragmatic, although it would certainly have been stultifying to reject every opportunity that arose in this way. The critical factor in such situations is the extent to which control is exercised without stifling initiative, yet also without eroding or vitiating the essential aim. Only those in charge and on the spot can judge, and the Elmhirsts had to make—under pressure—many critical decisions of this nature between 1925 and 1939. In the 1930s, it seemed to the outsider that a whole lot of not wholly connected activities were going on at once, maintained not purely on practical grounds, but by a frightening mixture of faith and finance.

Like so many people with a mission, the Elmhirsts were in a hurry. Both were generous and apt to act on impulse, and both were inclined in the American fashion to 'buy the answer'. This happened for example if a likely personality came to their notice, or if a formula based on theoretical investigation or other plausible research proved convincing. Having agreed a plan and found the means, they would give the man his head or import an outside expert to see the business through, usually with a fixed timetable in mind, without adequate allowance for that kind of cautious, as opposed to empirical, growth, which is necessary to almost every new enterprise. By trying to force the pace in this way, the Elmhirsts found themselves again and again thrown back on hand-to-mouth measures, which discredited much of their planning. Most of the commercial departments at Dartington had teething troubles of this sort in the early years, and several went under as a result. Moreover the Estate was trying to establish itself in a period of slump, and to break into a fiercely competitive market that was contracting under exterior economic forces. In this way the organisation used up great quantities of capital which, despite Dorothy Elmhirst's fortune, placed it in real difficulty; and from which it was only saved by the seller's market of the war.

As to the non-commercial departments—the education, the research offices, the arts activities, etc.—all of them heavy financial burdens: here again the Elmhirsts had their hands forced by their hearts. One example was the generous and human manner in which they offered a home to an influx of refugee artists, mainly from Nazi Germany; and so involved themselves in costly unfamiliar undertakings, such as financing the Jooss Ballet, which no one had ever dreamed of doing at the outset. None the less, expensive though these experiences were, they enriched Dartington enormously in spirit and gave the lie to any idea that it was or should become an inward-looking community.

Business

Physical reconstruction at Dartington started in the autumn of 1925 with repairs to the private house, and continued virtually without stop until the outbreak of war. Early in 1926 responsibility for all the medieval buildings was placed in the hands of William Weir, an architect with intimate knowledge of historic restorations;[11] and for the next ten years or so no ancient structure was touched without his advice. The result—as everyone can see today—was gloriously successful. Weir stipulated at the outset that no attempt should be made to fake anything, so that whether by use of different materials or of contemporary techniques all new work should be seen for what it was. Likewise, if any old building was needed for some new use (as all were in time), then it should be boldly adapted for that purpose, albeit with a minimum of disturbance to the original work.

Reconstruction at Dartington was but one part of the massive and far-ranging programme of physical rehabilitation; but it was sufficient in itself to require an army of workmen and quantities of materials, especially timber—the one resource with which the Estate was well

Cotswold stone and timber cruck

RURAL HOUSING

Post-war cottages

Hedge-laying today

COUNTRY CRAFTS

Sawyers yesterday

endowed. In the first few years almost all the wood, both for the old buildings and the new, came from trees felled in the 190 acres of home plantations, and was carpentered on the spot: including the shaping and adzing of all the beams, collars, wall plates, purlins and rafters for the specialised re-roofing of the old Kitchens and the Banqueting Hall. Forestry therefore was the first of the Estate departments to be organised, and placed temporarily in the hands of Victor Elmhirst, one of Leonard's younger brothers. All the felling was done by John Tucker, a local woodman, and his two sons, while the sawing was contracted out. By the end of April 1926 however, sufficient staff and equipment had arrived for the Estate timber yard—long-hidden beneath brambles—to be opened up, so that by the autumn the infant department was turning out a creditable quantity of miscellaneous fencing, garden poles and fire-wood, as well as building timber. The department grew because it had to, no argument was needed, and this became a familiar pattern in the evolution of the Estate. But sheer pressure of day-to-day events often forced decisions that had later to be recanted or recast, and this was confusing and costly.

It was clear that, in forestry, the home supply of timber would soon be exhausted; thus Leonard was seeking suitable advice as early as the summer of 1926—no easy thing to find, for there was virtually no authoritative source of information between the Universities, which were concerned with the academic problems of silviculture, and the timber trade which minded most about quick profits from felling. The newly established Forestry Commission was not well disposed towards private landowners, and was concentrating all its efforts upon State forests. None the less Leonard secured the sympathetic interest of C. O. Hanson, the local Divisional Officer of the Commission, and good advice from W. E. Hiley (then lecturing in Forest Economics at Oxford), who recommended him to aim at approximately 2000 acres of trees, this being the minimum size for an economic forestry unit. A general plan was then drawn up, which in due course—after much tribulation—came to be realised with remarkable accuracy. Meantime, before the end of 1926, George Turner was brought in from the timber trade to run the department; and it was he who was instrumental in the purchase of large blocks of forestry property during 1928: 332 acres at Kingswood near Buckfastleigh, and 1100 acres from the Hambledon estate at Moretonhampstead. This represented Dartington's first major act of expansion from the original 820 acres, and towards the present round total of 4000 acres of farms, woodlands, buildings, amenity grounds, and other kinds of property.

Turner was primarily a buyer and a sawmiller. On his advice, a pro-fessional forester, Tom Brown, was recruited in 1929 to take charge of the woods. Although the two men co-operated well enough, it was becoming clear that—in the circumstances of Dartington—sawmilling

E

would have to be separated from the business of growing trees. The fact was that it would take many years and a heavy investment to make the new properties productive, so that the sawmill would have to buy in timber from the general market of the south-west in order to fulfil its orders and maintain its equilibrium. This was the next problem. It was realised before the end of 1929 that the existing mill and yard would soon prove inadequate. The decision was therefore taken to site a large new mill beside the Totnes–Plymouth road, some two miles from the Hall, and to construct an up-to-date plant. Plans were drafted and re-drafted, and modified up to the last minute, following a visit by Turner to the U.S.A. in 1931. Ultimately the new mill was formally opened, still incomplete, in April 1932, and given separate status from Woodlands as a subordinate unit within Dartington Hall Ltd., the overall organisation set up in July 1929 to control all the commercial activities on the Estate. The subsequent history of Dartington Sawmill, and the details of its structure, are not the concern of this chapter. Suffice it to say that as a hardwood mill, and in common with many other rural industries, it followed an irregular career of relative prosperity and absolute slump. This was due partly to distance from markets and sources of supply, and partly to over-dependence on too few sales outlets. It was rarely able to stand securely on its own feet, and in the absence of integration with Dartington Woodlands, it was eventually associated with a large firm of timber importers, handling both hard and softwoods over the whole territory of the south-west.

The Woodlands Department also started life in April 1932, under the direction of W. E. Hiley, who had been Leonard Elmhirst's first forestry adviser. Hiley was the leading forest economist in Britain, and his name will long be remembered as a pioneer and instructor in this field. He edited the *Quarterly Journal of Forestry* for many years, and was the author of a number of authoritative works on woodland management and finance.[12] In 1932 he lacked practical experience, but with Tom Brown[13] as his lieutenant it was hoped that the two men would complement each other, and combine to make a success of the department. The fact that they did so was not due to any personal affinity however. Their task was a formidable one. By 1932 the home woods were depleted, and since large areas of the new forest properties were covered with oak coppice or were otherwise semi-derelict, the amount of marketable timber was small. Clearance and replanting was therefore bound to be extensive and costly. It was this fact that decided Leonard and his colleagues to create and capitalise the Woodlands Department, according to a planned programme covering a long period of years, and to place the department directly under the Dartington Hall Trust rather than operate it as an ordinary commercial unit under Dartington Hall Ltd.

In the view of the Trustees there was a national need for research into both the economic and technical aspects of forestry; and so it was their wish that Woodlands should play a didactic as well as a commercial role. As Hiley expressed it later: 'My job was to improve the woodlands and make them pay for their improvement, and to keep records to show how this could be done.' He did not think as some did that, by its nature, forestry was an unprofitable undertaking and would never pay. On the contrary he argued that unless the department could be made economic, it would be of little use as a demonstration unit. He therefore reorganised the accounting system, and initiated a census and valuation of trees by woods and compartments in order, first to find a basis for a capital account, and secondly to be able to record changes in capital value through felling, planting and increment. In other respects the general organisation of the department was not altered, for this was largely determined by the location of the woods over a wide area, necessitating two service centres twenty-two miles apart: one at Dartington (Huxhams Cross), the other at Moretonhampstead. An annual planting programme of forty to fifty acres (mostly softwoods) was maintained, and the day-to-day business conducted smoothly and efficiently by Tom Brown. Hiley estimated that it would take not less than twenty years to make the department self-supporting, and forty to fifty years to establish a 'normal forest', i.e. one in which volume annually felled was balanced by annual increment. In the event he proved pessimistic, for despite—and because of—the war, which anticipated profits but reduced the stock of saleable timber, it was found possible to put the department on a paying basis as from January 1947.

Thereafter, for administrative purposes, the research activities of Woodlands were separated from the commercial, but Hiley continued to use the woods for a variety of economic and educational studies, many of which were published, notably the *Examination of Accounts*. In these annual or biennial publications, he disclosed the methods of costing and accountancy as applied to forestry operations at Dartington, and commented freely on the results. This was entirely in line with the brief drawn up for the department in 1932, and was perhaps the most striking example of the role that the Elmhirsts and their co-Trustees wanted Dartington to play.

✳   ✳   ✳

I have related forestry developments at Dartington in some detail, since they reveal many of the characteristics common to all the departments, but particularly those associated with the traditional employments of the land: the underlying purpose being, of course, to help provide an economic foundation for the Estate as a whole.

Farming, the other *primary* industry of the land, followed a not dissimilar course, although naturally the details differed.

Having had an agricultural training at Cornell, and finding at first small sympathy for his ideas among British agriculturalists, Leonard turned back to America for help. And it was through Cornell that he finally attracted a young Scotsman, J. R. (Jock) Currie, who had also been a student at that university, later completing his education at Glasgow and Oxford, to come to Dartington in 1927 to be his consultant and to remain as the resident agricultural economist. Although Jock Currie became a close friend and continued as Leonard's trusted adviser for over thirty years, he never regarded Dartington as a normal landed estate, whose first task was to exploit the resources of the land and show profitable returns, with research as a secondary obligation. While agreeing that the trading departments must justify themselves economically, he felt that too great a pressure for profits would prejudice the essentially educational purpose of the enterprise. In his view he was simply and solely a consultant. He took no responsibility for the commercial success or otherwise of the farms or any of the other departments. In theory this was an understandable position for a professional man to take; but in practice it proved embarrassing for it led to conflict with heads of departments, and revealed very clearly the dualism inherent in the whole conception of Dartington.

Again however these niceties did not prove insuperable in the urgent and exacting years before the Second World War, for events simply forced the pace. The farms had to be reorganised and got on to a paying basis, and an agricultural policy hammered out. The sitting tenants were soon paid off, and important additions made to the farm territory by purchase from neighbouring owners. In the end it was decided to run two principal farms, each of about 300 acres.

One, the Barton, was to retain its character as a mixed holding typical of the region but with an emphasis on dairying, based on a herd of South Devon cattle. Frank Crook, the previous tenant, agreed to stay on as manager. Hitherto the farmhouse and steading had been located in the Hall courtyard, but by 1930 the entire complex had been re-established on the rising ground just outside, including house, cowshed, dairy and certain buildings. Although by modern standards these were modest in cost and appearance, and recently have been totally replaced—Currie was particularly anxious to avoid any hint of a rich man's folly—they did good service. Although put up before the full possibilities of mechanisation had been grasped, they saved substantially on labour costs, and paid close attention to storage, manure handling, and the comfort and hygiene of the stock.

The other farm, the Old Parsonage, was conceived and run on totally different lines. An entirely new steading was erected on a virgin site, and the management entrusted to C. F. Nielsen, a Dane, who had an impressive background of agricultural experience acquired both in Denmark and the United Kingdom. His brief was to create a specialised dairy holding, and to aim at the highest standards of crop and stock husbandry, irrespective of local custom—an exciting prospect, but crammed with difficulties, both technical and personal. First, land had to be assembled from eight other properties, including a portion of the Estate, and welded into a homogenous unit. This was duly done with ruthless efficiency: two miles of overgrown Devon banks were removed to form large fields suitable for mechanical cultivation, a road was laid down, and extensive drainage carried out. Building was a problem on its own. In the absence of any generally accepted standards of farm construction, the new unit at Old Parsonage had to be evolved out of anxious consultation between Currie, Nielsen, and the architect, O. P. Milne. The entire installation was eventually put up in 1931–2 at a nett cost of approximately £8000, and incorporated many features well ahead of their time. For example, there was complete protection from the weather by continuous roofing over all the component parts of the steading, a carefully planned air circulation system with intake at ground level and extraction by roof ventilators, provision for mechanical handling and easy movement as between field, storage, animals, and disposal of milk and manure. Nielsen was an excellent judge of cattle, and like Crook chose the local South Devon breed for their high butter-fat and dual-purpose qualities; quite soon each farmer had built up an attested milk-recorded herd, producing tuberculin-tested milk.

One of the declared aims in having two types of dairy farm on the same estate was to compare the management, and draw lessons from the comparison. But it did not work out that way at all. Barton was a low-cost farm, where the land was already in fair heart. Old Parsonage, devoted to intensive milk production, operated at high cost; and, saddled at the start with a heavy burden of land clearance, took far longer to establish. Besides this, the two managers were as different as chalk and cheese. Crook, who had survived hard times in farming, was a skilled but cautious Devonian. Nielsen, a foreigner, was impatient to get on and prove himself. In the end Nielsen left Dartington to set up by himself, and both farms came under Crook who continued in charge until the end of the war. Profitability was reached after about ten years, but the Farms Department finally came into its own after the appointment of Ronald Hawtin in 1945. Hawtin had first worked as a tractor driver under Nielsen between 1931 and 1937. His abilities were soon recognised, and he was encouraged to take a farm institute course at Moulton in Northamptonshire, before gaining experience as a farm manager elsewhere. Ultimately the Trustees brought him back to reorganise and re-equip the Dartington farms, which had been run down during the war years. He accomplished a formidable task in very trying circumstances, and converted the department, soon extending to about 1000 acres of land, into a thriving concern. Under his management, all farm operations were so rationalised as to return healthy profits at a time when the Estate was emerging with some difficulty from the aftermath of the war. The Farms Department remains one of Dartington's best achievements, combining progress and professionalism in a complex and rapidly changing industry.

Other farm ventures were launched in the early days: a poultry unit that promised well but foundered, partly because the stock failed to stand up to intensive husbandry, and partly owing to the absence of adequate marketing and a level of guaranteed prices; a pig farm that made good progress until the war cut off sources of feeding-stuffs, but which recovered in peace-time as a small all-purpose holding based on milk and bacon: and an unsuccessful attempt on Dartmoor to raise high-quality wool and cheap mutton. In addition there was a considerable horticultural investment. One section concentrated on bulbs, harvesting daffodils and narcissi in the eight weeks between March and May. Dartington was well placed in terms of soil and climate for this crop; and the manager, Roger Morel, built up a thriving connection with Covent Garden. He had small success however with hard and soft fruit at Marley, four miles west of Dartington, which proved too wet and exposed. Excessive moisture promoted a rash of fungal diseases, while high winds unseated many of the young trees. Eventually the land was taken into the farms for more profitable use.

Lastly—gardens—a story on its own. The Hall gardens at Dartington are internationally famous for their architectural beauty, their marriage of historic features (principally the tiltyard or tournament ground and surrounding terraces) with fresh imaginative planting—surging spring colours and nostalgic autumn tints—and for their educational function in training young gardeners. Several minds have contributed to what amounts to an outstanding work of art, accomplished mainly under the direction of Dorothy Elmhirst herself. One man who played an important part in the 1930s was R. S. Lynch, who had spent many years working in gardens and landscape architects' offices in France. I mention him here however for another reason, for it was he who developed the four Estate nurseries, primarily for plants and shrubs for sale, and who founded a garden construction department. This was brought to a stop by the war, and Lynch himself was struck down by rheumatoid arthritis. The nurseries were switched to vegetable production, and after the war served as the main supplier to 'Greencrops', a horticultural marketing agency, set up by Dartington Hall Ltd. The new unit was efficiently handled, and did considerable business at a time when lack of imports offered a comparatively stable market for horticultural produce. Progress however was blocked, first by the refusal of planning permission for an up-to-date refrigeration plant and crop store, and secondly by the gradual return of speculative conditions in horticultural trading. Unlike farming there was no price guarantee system, and since most local suppliers only dealt in fruit and vegetables as a sideline, the natural tendency was to revert to the safer economy of agriculture proper. This was the pattern at Dartington too, and in the end the entire horticultural effort was closed down.

*   *   *

So much for the primary industries which, after nearly thirty years' expensive but highly informative experimentation, were consolidated into straight forestry and farming enterprises. In essence the same pattern of trial and evolution from small beginnings applied to the secondary industries, i.e. those engaged principally in the processing of primary products or providing other kinds of commercial services. These included sawmilling (with which were associated turnery and furniture-making), textiles, cider-making, building and glass-making. Sawmilling has already been mentioned. The textile department graduated from a single workshop in the courtyard to a new mill beside the river Bidwell on the Totnes–Plymouth road, and developed by painful stages into the present thriving concern, with one modern mill at Dartington and another at Kingsbridge, manufacturing tweeds and blankets. As for cider, the plant at Shinners Bridge was run in association with the orchards. Dartington cider and apple juice were quality products, and seemed so well established by 1945 that output was expanded. This proved fatal. By entering the mass market of cider and soft drinks, the department fell between two stools. It was able neither to compete with the big firms, nor to hold its own in selling a better and more expensive product. This was faulty management, for with an abundant supply of locally grown apples and sited in the heart of the cider country, the department had been well placed for survival. In building however, the right man was found at the right time. Having tried, without success, to conduct the construction programme of the Estate by direct labour, Leonard Elmhirst looked around for a qualified executive with commercial building and civil engineering experience, accustomed to working with architects and consultants, and sympathetic to progressive ideas. He persuaded A. E. Malbon, general manager of Welwyn Builders Ltd., to come to Dartington in 1930 and set up an independent company in order to complete all the construction planned over the next five years. This was the origin of Staverton Builders Ltd. which, now known as Staverton Contractors Ltd., has since become one of the biggest organisations of its kind in the south-west. Latterly Dartington has set up a factory at Torrington in north Devon for the production of decorative glass. This is of too recent origin for historical comment.

In analysing the commercial history of Dartington, one has of course to evaluate all the technical factors of supply, labour, production and marketing, trade by trade; and in this exercise the records kept at Dartington are invaluable, for they contain a wealth of statistics and other facts, without which any inquiry would be invalid. Of the utmost value are the lessons which apply to rural industry as a whole; and in order to sum up, I reproduce here some of the conclusions I reached in my original report to the Trustees in 1957–8. Time has overtaken some of the details, but not the main matter:

In primary industries, agriculture holds a unique position owing to the security it enjoys through price guarantees and other forms of Government aid. Horticulture, on the other hand, is dependent upon a combination of climatic, soil and geographical factors which, taken in conjunction with the vagaries of the market, make it a highly specialised and speculative industry. Private forestry falls somewhere between the two, in that it enjoys some Government assistance, notably in the establishment of plantations, but has no assured outlet as in agriculture.

Primary industries alone—however prosperous and efficient—are not a comprehensive solution to rural employment, for they can never employ more than, say, one-third of the working population of the countryside. There must be a diversity of industry if the exodus from the countryside is to be controlled. This means the encouragement of secondary industries, and it is here that the experience of Dartington is so valuable.

Briefly, there are two basic problems—the *size* of the unit, and its *location*. Most other problems are contingent upon these two.

The small rural unit has a number of inherent handicaps. It cannot, for instance, compete effectively in any market dominated by mass production. If it cannot sell its products locally, or competitively farther afield, then it is unlikely to be able to afford the sales organisation necessary to cover a wider territory. It must therefore depend either on quality, or special access to raw materials, or exceptionally able management. Alternatively it may have to enter into some contractual association with a larger urban enterprise (e.g. by making components)—a risky step because overdependence undermines independence, or at least lays the small firm open to market forces it cannot hope to control. Other factors may operate to its disadvantage—heavy transport costs and distance from markets, absence of cheap power, lack of processing or finishing services, above all a dearth of skilled labour.

All these have confronted Dartington, some of them in acute form, and a variety of solutions tried. In production the emphasis has been on quality rather than quantity, and a rapid move away from mainly manual processes towards mechanisation and technical efficiency. In sales—whereas agriculture presents few difficulties—other industries have fluctuated between all the media: direct retail sales, wholesaling and middlemen, and even a centralised sales office operating on behalf of all the departments. The latter proved a failure for several reasons, but basically because the diversity of goods made it impossible to market them successfully together. The advantages of centralisation lay rather at Board level, in financial and administrative services; and even in strengthening the link between employees and the Estate by means of housing and welfare, and by finding alternative employment when needed.

None the less there is the feeling that Dartington should have done far more in the field of co-operation, and to integrate production as well as administration, particularly in horticulture. In the early days Dartington Hall Ltd. was in too much of a hurry. Too many lines were tried, and expansion authorised on insufficient grounds. Integration comes both with forethought and cautious organic growth, not merely out of blueprint planning. Finally there is the human element. This is not only a question of pay and conditions of work, but of the quality of management at departmental level which, if of the right kind, can often overcome the inherent drawbacks of rural industry. Quite simply, Dartington did not in its first decade have enough good managers.

Research

When Leonard Elmhirst insisted from the first that every commercial department at Dartington should in some way act as a demonstration unit, and combine research with the normal task of balancing its books, what was the result? As it turned out, commercial research fell into two distinct categories. One comprised specific technical experiments, e.g. the artificial seasoning of timber (sawmill), dyeing (textiles), preservation of apple juice (cider house), and a variety of trials on the farms and in the woods. These were usually paid for, not by the individual departments or Dartington Hall Ltd., but by the Trust which maintained a laboratory, and whose other functions will be described shortly. The other category of research was covered by costings—using the accounts to guide development and assess the value of all the work being done. For this purpose Leonard called in Price, Waterhouse and Co., the well-known firm of chartered accountants, one of whose staff, E. S. Porter, entered the service of the Estate as Secretary of Dartington Hall Ltd. Under him and Dr. William Slater, the first managing director of the Company, a centralised organisation was built up, known as Central Office, to control administration and finance, and house the Estate Department for the maintenance of all the properties. Ultimately Central Office proved its worth, but it too had its teething troubles, following the tenets of Parkinson's law and becoming an empire on its own—an esoteric haven of administrators, protected by an appointments book, and embedded in a mass of figures, none of which seemed relevant to the Company's real situation or capable of keeping it out of deep water. After the war, and after the arrival of Peter Sutcliffe, the present overlord of Dartington's commercial and other interests, all this top hamper was cut down and the administration related more closely to reality.

I have devoted some space to Dartington's commercial history, because without an economic foundation—as Hiley pointed out in regard to forestry—Dartington would be of small value in any scheme of rural rehabilitation. Any rich man, buttressed by outside wealth, can spend money in the countryside, and spend it well, yet unless he creates a viable concern he solves little. This of course was an accusation long levelled at Dartington, and still is by those who have not grasped the fact that—after a generation of trial and growth—the Elmhirsts succeeded in their original aim, that of re-developing the resources of a large estate in the circumstances of modern life. By the late 1950s the commercial departments were yielding consistent profits, some of which were available for investment in the non-commercial enterprises. Since most people see or hear about this other complementary side of the Estate—its social, educational and cultural side—they assume it to be the whole of Dartington. In fact it is only half the story, though certainly an essential half.

Way of Life
The Elmhirsts always believed that, although economic problems must be faced first, it is equally necessary to provide the means for a full life. In other words a man must have a properly paid job, a house for his family, and all those facilities that permit a fair standard of living and adequate time for leisure. There must be access to amenities of one kind or another, in order that the leisure so gained may become a blessing and not a burden.

That briefly is the philosophy that accounts for the extraordinary variety of life at Dartington and the deliberate mixture of work, play and classroom: and why, now as in the past, you find the Barton Farm milking parlour within a stone's throw of the Barn Theatre; or, at one time, a vast dung heap at the Old Parsonage within sight and almost within smell of the kindergarten. In essence everything that goes on today was launched in the fifteen years before the war, though now there is more space and far better co-ordination both within and without the Estate. The fact that the Hall and other buildings have always been used by *outside* organisations for conferences and summer schools, or for festivals of several sorts,[14] may also have added to the confusion about Dartington—what it is, and what it does; yet the very existence of these functions, and the fact that they usually have been open to Estate people as well as to their own members, have helped make Dartington a cultural oasis in the wilderness of the south-west.

Never obtrusively the schoolmaster, yet Dartington has always been saturated with the importance of education and the arts, and it would not be the same without them. In the same way it has provided positively for sport and youth; and you only have to read the *Dartington Hall News*, the weekly newspaper (started as a single sheet in 1927), to realise how profuse the opportunities are for physical and mental relaxation, and how fully they are used. It is true that some members of the Estate have preferred to live outside all this. Notwithstanding, most people have been involved at some point and would tell you that, as a result, they have found life infinitely more enjoyable. The Elmhirsts said categorically that, if they did not make provision of this kind, they would not have got far with their programme of rehabilitation. Without it, the indigenous life of the area would have been limited to the traditional round of rural engagements. Not everyone however, not even every native-born countryman, wants or is able to go fishing, shooting or hunting; nor are he and his wife entirely satisfied with pub nights, whist drives, fêtes and jumble sales, or the present alternative of an evening with T.V. All these things flourish in and around Dartington but alone they could never supply the stimulus that has made the Estate a living entity within a rapidly changing countryside. It is the social opportunities at Dartington, as well as the outlets for employment, that have halted the drift into the local towns. In fact Dartington offers a more varied and interesting society, at all levels, than can be found anywhere south of Exeter (with its university, theatre, cathedral, and all the attractions of a county centre), and some would say, of Bristol.

Dartington is a honeypot. As a stately home, with a difference, it draws a summer flood of visitors, who come to see the Hall and the gardens before settling down to tea and spending in the shops.[15] This is run-of-the-mill tourism, common to many other places, and which if anything Dartington tries to play down. More important because rooted in the locality is the habit of participation in and patronage of plays, concerts, films, exhibitions; of classes in the arts and further education; of the youth centre and the sports clubs. Spoon-feeding? Members of the Estate, it is said, have had everything they wanted, and they have often neglected or abused what was offered them. That kind of criticism was certainly relevant in the late 1930s, when the artists from Germany and Russia set the pace, and by their very professionalism tended to discourage amateur effort; but they set artistic standards too. Before their time, and especially since, whether as audiences, administrators, or performers, Dartington people have combined more or less successfully these two aspects of involvement. It is not an easy balance, for while self-help is a necessity and a sign of vigour in the whole spectrum of human leisure, it can if unassisted soon slip into mediocrity or fade away altogether.

From the very beginning therefore, the Elmhirsts planned to create a kind of 'village college', with particular emphasis on the arts, and at a time when Henry Morris was pioneering a similar idea in the country-side of Cambridgeshire. In the 1920s and 1930s this was still a revolu-tionary step, and in a deeply conservative neighbourhood such as south Devon the goings-on at the Hall were much misunderstood and by some actively resented. It was perhaps the superficial things that gave most offence. Informality of dress (very mild compared with today's fashions), for instance, and above all of address. The fact that the Elmhirsts were 'Leonard' and 'Dorothy' to all and sundry horrified local society; and it is interesting that, once the novelty had worn off, many of the older employees reverted to 'Mr and Mrs Elmhirst', because they found it more seemly. In sum people were not ready for the com-mon touch of post-war democracy. They were even less ready for Dartington Hall School—but of that anon.

By its impact then, and because its objects were difficult to interpret and expensive to finance. Dartington required a strong hand at the out-set. It was forthcoming, and for many years both the Elmhirsts were intimately involved at every stage of development. Inevitably the aura they created was one of paternalism; but that was not resented. Leonard was the new squire and Dorothy the new lady of the manor: a tradi-tional situation in the countryside. What worried people was the appa-rent wish of the squire and his lady to divest themselves of the pre-rogatives of autocracy—not merely the formalities but certain realities as well: such as making decisions without telling people what they proposed to do, or footing the bill as a matter of course for every club and fund in the parish. The Elmhirsts disconcerted their neighbours by taking their employees into their confidence (often on matters that barely concerned them), and refusing to subsidise some ancient but anomalous charity. They dominated Dartington therefore, not so much by ownership and wealth as by personality and ideas. This remained true of Dorothy to the day of her death in December 1968, and of Leonard who in his late seventies is still the boss today.

*   *   *

As early as 1927 both the Elmhirsts realised that the scale and pace of progress at Dartington was such that it was becoming impossible—as well as undesirable—to continue to take personal responsibility for everything. Dartington was not just their private hobby, nor must it appear so. Some form of practical organisation was needed to control policy, conduct the everyday business of the Estate, and pay the bills. It was then that they turned for help, first to F. A. S. Gwatkin, partner in the London firm of solicitors of McKenna and Co.; and later to Leonard's youngest brother Alfred, who ran the family estate near Barnsley and also practised as a solicitor, to play the part of senior statesmen, valuable not only for their innate abilities and experience, but also for the fact that—not living at Dartington—they were always able to take a detached view of the aims and activities of the Estate.

The first practical step was taken in July 1929 with the establishment of Dartington Hall Ltd., a private limited liability company with an initial capital of £65,000, later raised to £125,000; its prime purpose being to control the majority of commercial operations and measure their efficiency. All the finance was provided by Dorothy Elmhirst, and in due course all the commercial enterprises[16] contributed by means of rent, loan interest, and dividends to the general income of the Estate.

In 1931–2 was set up the Dartington Hall Trust, in essence an educational foundation, charitable in status, and endowed with wide powers to foster what may be termed the 'Dartington idea'. In the Trust were invested all the land and properties, and all the shares of Dartington Hall Ltd. and later those of the other commercial concerns. The Trust was also buttressed by large investments outside Dartington, the income from which helped meet the heavy deficits incurred in the early years of development, as well as promote the non-commercial undertakings.[17] In addition therefore to the obligations of ownership, viz., the upkeep of grounds and buildings, the Trust assumed certain functions that gave it its special character. These included the maintenance of certain welfare services,[18] the promotion of education,[19] the encouragement of the arts,[20] and the support of research.[21] All these activities operated through Trustee departments, in parallel to those of the commercial organisation. In short the Trust acted simultaneously as the father-and-mother of the Estate as a whole, as well as nanny to its non-commercial —social, educational, cultural—children.

Since, in my book *Dartington Hall*, I have described the details of the upbringing and growth to manhood of these children, there is no need to repeat the story at length here. But it is right to reflect a little on this didactic aspect of Dartington. As for all children, leisure began within the intimate circle of their parents. So the earliest activities were those of a family and their friends: in this case the employees of Dartington, composing a complete cross-section of society. Interests ranged far and wide—tennis, cricket, gardening, exploration of the countryside, play-reading, music-making, painting, craft work, dancing, debates, and the like. Instead of church was held the Sunday Evening Meeting. This was an important weekly event, at which heads of departments talked about their work, or there was a general discussion of what Dartington was trying to do; or more often as time went on a talk or a performance by some person or group from outside the Estate.

In this way the horizon broadened rapidly, and by 1930 (or soon after) the lists record such items as lectures by Tagore, the Huxleys, King-Hall and Bertrand Russell; a poetry reading by Richard Church; a lieder recital by Sophie Wyss and a choral concert by The English Singers. Drama and dance-mime however, more than any other media, made the arts come alive to members of the Estate, for it was in the power of most to take part, and to treat performance as ordinary emotional discipline and a satisfying means of expression. In 1927 Maurice Browne came over from America with Ellen van Volkenburg—the historic occasion when Dorothy Elmhirst backed his production of R. C. Sherriff's *Journey's End*. Both helped produce an Estate performance of *Comus* in the Hall gardens in July 1929, and Ellen took charge of drama at Dartington for the next few years. Other artists were invited—a group of them from the Cornish School in Seattle, U.S.A.—but the most dynamic personality was the English expressionist dancer Margaret Barr, a pupil of Martha Graham. Her gifted and elemental character dominated the artistic life of the Estate between 1930 and 1934.

This was the period *par excellence* when, by persuading a handful of professionals to infuse their energies into the everyday existence of the Estate, the Elmhirsts almost succeeded in a remarkable experiment: namely, through art, to dissolve the discords of social inequality. The strongest opposition came, unexpectedly, not from the Philistines, but from the established educationists, particularly those concerned with adult or further education. Extension work had begun early at Dartington and was given every encouragement: five courses between 1928 and 1933 for rural head teachers, a two-year domestic science course, and any number of evening classes supported at the local evening institute in Totnes and on the Estate itself. These continued without break. When, however, a fresh young extra-mural tutor, F. G. Thomas, tried to introduce drama into the extension programme, he was resolutely opposed by his own colleagues; for official tradition had always laid great stress on university-type classes and vocational training. Thomas held on none the less and found a strong ally in Leonard, who insisted that the arts were the most powerful force in social education, since by reason of their universality they overstepped all intellectual and class barriers. Although it bore fruit in time by influencing opinion, this early experiment at Dartington did not succeed, partly because it was not allowed to work itself through to a conclusion. There are however members of the Estate today who recall the excitement of Margaret Barr's *Spring Festival* and her *Mystery of the Nativity* produced in Staverton Church in 1931, likewise Thomas's *Midsummer Night's Dream* staged with village players at Liverton. These and other productions were bold attempts at involvement, and their memory still enthuses and saddens those who took part in them.

In 1934 the existing structure of the arts suddenly collapsed. Margaret Barr was too turbulent to last, and by the end of the summer an entirely fresh phase in the artistic life of the Estate had begun. Thanks to Hitler's anti-semitic laws and his hatred of anyone who refused to conform to the Nazi conceptions of art, refugees began to pour out of Germany. To Dartington came Kurt Jooss and Sigurd

Leeder, with the dancers, musicians and designers of their Ballet School and Company from Essen. Other artists followed, including Willi Soukop, the sculptor, Hans Oppenheim from the Deutsche Musik Bühne, and—after severe trials in a concentration camp—Rudolf Laban, the choreographer. In 1936 came Michel Chekhov (nephew of the playwright) formerly of the Second Moscow Art Theatre, and a refugee from Russia since 1928. To cope with this influx, the building programme had to be extended and accelerated, and a formal arts department established under the able leadership of Christopher Martin. For five hectic years the Hall and its environs became a sector of Central Europe, an international centre, teeming with students and artists performing ballets, plays and operas, and creating these and other works of art. It was a period of enormous vitality and considerable artistic achievement—but primarily professional, and a highly expensive commitment for the Trustees. Most of the amateurs felt unable to compete. The standards set were too high. Besides this, local Devon people were literally unable to understand half of what the foreigners were saying or trying to do: they were beings apart. On their side the artists, already uprooted, turned inwards the more intensely to themselves and their work. All this created a division between them, and put an end to any attempt at continuing the earlier experiment of involvement.

This professional phase however was relatively short. The war dispersed all but a few of the foreigners, and Dartington was given a breathing-space in which to reflect, and plan for a new pattern of art and education after the war. What took place in the generation 1945–70 is too intricate to relate in detail here, but the Estate moved steadily towards accommodating local opinion and co-operating with local authority, while meeting a far readier response towards its own ideas and activities. Practical schemes have been worked out, in the main with Devon County Council (but also with other Local Education Authorities) and with Exeter University, which have gone far to solving those same problems that faced the Elmhirsts at the beginning. In short, to provide facilities for leisure, so broad that no one need feel excluded, yet encouraging high standards of achievement, particularly in the arts, in order to improve the quality of living.

The pattern has two motifs—academic (rather than strictly professional) and amateur. At the Hall an Arts College provides training in all the principal arts, mainly for teachers; while a Further Education Centre offers short residential courses in a whole range of extra-mural subjects. At Shinners Bridge an Adult Education Centre and a Social Club cater for the evening and other leisure-time activities of the neighbourhood. In addition an Arts Society has been formed, responsible for a varied programme of plays, concerts, and exhibitions throughout the year. Latterly a new centre has been started at Beaford to serve the interests of the 'lost country' of north and north-west Devon. Staff and facilities are, where practicable, interchangeable, so that any sense of division is diminished; and it is possible to attend a performance of a Brecht play one evening, sing in the St Matthew Passion the next, play for Dartington United on Saturday afternoon, and fish on the river Dart on Sunday.

No problem is finally solved, no aim finally achieved. Those in charge at Dartington have always been aware of this fact, and of the pressure of change. They have constantly re-thought the function and purpose of all their institutions. Indeed some are of the opinion that changes have been made too readily and that, despite the financial and administrative stability of the Estate, there is always a sense of unease at what may happen next. That may be. But in the final judgement no one will deny that Dartington has made a unique contribution towards restoring a depleted countryside, and is always ahead in the search to integrate the two civilisations of town and country.

The School

I have left to last what some people regard as the most significant, certainly the best known, of all the departments at Dartington, for since it got into its stride in the early 1930s, the school has hogged much of the publicity. For them Dartington means the school, and not much else. This is not to the advantage of the Estate, for however favourable or unfavourable the image created by the school, it does not reflect the enterprise as a whole. Yet, although its relationship to the Estate has always been ambiguous, the origins of the school are easy to explain.

When Dorothy Whitney Straight married Leonard Elmhirst in 1925, she bought with her from America her three young children—Whitney, Beatrice and Michael Straight. Her immediate concern was to continue their education, for hitherto they had been attending classes at the Lincoln School, New York, a 'progressive' and experimental school of a kind hardly known in England at the time. Indeed it was because she was unable to find a suitable English school, and because she and Leonard were committed to the concept of 'free education', that they decided to start a school of their own. Preparation took time, and it was not until September 1926 that a teaching staff had been assembled for a five-day discussion under Professor Eduard Lindemann, an American educationist from the School of Social Work in New York. At the end of the month the school was opened with about a dozen pupils, the majority of them boys, age-range seven to sixteen. During the next few years the numbers rose slowly, and never exceeded thirty before a fresh start was made under W. B. Curry in 1931.

Other than that it was co-educational and boarding, the distinctiveness of this early Dartington Hall School lay in the emphasis placed upon arts and crafts, upon projects and non-academic subjects, upon ideas about self-expression and self-government—above all upon participation in Estate affairs as a method of teaching.

> The Estate and its departments seem to us to offer an opportunity of restoring an education with some better balance between practice and theory, and of rendering available, as normal educational assets to boys and girls, the chances of all-round development that rural life can give.[22]

This early attempt to integrate school and Estate did not work; and the failure of this part of the curriculum was confirmed in a report on the school, which concluded that an enterprise of this kind required an exceptional standard of teaching, and that the use of Estate departments for occupational work was a mistake. Most commercial activity was exhausting, and quite simply above the heads of the children, especially the younger ones; moreover few of the managers made good teachers. What was needed was constructive training of a similar character, not necessarily needing prolonged attention, divorced from money, and designed solely as an outlet for the child itself.[23]

This report, which I suspect confirmed the Elmhirsts' own thoughts,[24] influenced the decision to start afresh: to separate the school from the Estate, erect a new set of buildings with their own grounds and facilities, and appoint a qualified staff.

Between 1928 and 1931 the new foundation gradually took shape. The school was to be divided into three sections—primary, junior and senior—and a new building to house the primary children was put up at Aller Park, about 400 yards north-east of the Hall. The main school building was to be sited at Foxhole, overlooking Shinners Bridge. This programme was well under way when W. B. Curry arrived as head-master in the summer of 1931.[25] Most of the pupils however could not be accommodated before the September term 1932, by which time Curry had himself managed to modify and alter some of the plans. I have no intention of writing a chapter about Dartington Hall School as an educational establishment. Curry put his own ideas and experiences into print, and there are other publications bearing on the subject.[26] What matters here is to define the impact of the school on the Estate, and its relevance to the Elmhirsts' plan for rural rehabilitation.

Curry was a brilliant individualist and a visionary schoolmaster. He attracted some excellent teachers and—backed by the Trustees who gave him all the facilities he needed—he created in the eight years before the war a school that undoubtedly led the field in progressive education. Many of his ideas are now accepted without question. He recruited about 150 pupils and was staunchly supported by the majority of the parents. Moreover, in the nature of things, he had to accept a number of children from broken homes or who for other reasons were psychologically upset, and he contended with this uninvited problem with remarkable success. Many who overcame their troubles at Dartington Hall School, owe Curry a great debt today: as do others who in all truth look back on their days at Dartington as 'the happiest time of their lives'. Proof of this lies in the number of Dartington pupils who later sent their own children to the school.

On the other hand, there is little doubt that in Curry's time the reputation of the school bore adversely on the Estate. Heads of departments complained bitterly. What the Estate was trying to do was controversial enough already; but with Curry's image as an advanced socialist, a pacifist, a close friend of Bertrand Russell (then widely regarded as a dangerous crank), atheist, and inconoclast; with his declared policy of mixing boys and girls in their living quarters so that they shared bathrooms and lavatories, and bathed in the swimming-pool in the nude; with his attitude towards freedom in sex relations publicly declared; all this, in the eyes of some, made nonsense of the serious intentions of the Estate and did positive damage. It became as difficult for the agricultural economist to be taken seriously by his colleagues in the profession, as for a salesman to sell Dartington furniture to a department store. The reaction was basically the same: 'I have nothing against you personally; but Dartington is a crazy place and I suspect its works in any form.' It took the war and the reorganisation that followed to exorcise this kind of blanket hostility.

Teaching apart, it must also be recorded that the school made an important contribution to the intellectual and artistic life of the Estate in general. In lectures and debates on Sunday evenings, in all the arts, and in many other functions, Curry and his staff and pupils were prominent both as performers and audience. Curry also attracted a galaxy of men and women prominent in public life to entertain and educate the school: so that the programmes of those days now read like star performances. The relationship of the school to the Estate then and later could be described, not as any attempt at integration academically or otherwise, but as cross-fertilisation.

The war hit the school hard. Like other institutions, it declined in numbers and lost some of its buildings to evacuees. After 1945 the excitement of the 1930s was never regained, and Curry seemed to lose heart. He retired in 1957 and died in 1962 as the result of an accident. His successors, Hubert and Lois Child, were faced with the formidable task of restoring morale without abandoning faith in the principles on which the school was founded. This they accomplished with such success that by the time they themselves came to retire twelve years later, the number of pupils exceeded 250, and the Trustees had embarked on a heavy programme of rebuilding and expansion. Today, under a new head, Royston Lambert, the school is again in the forefront as a pioneer, exchanging pupils and staff with State schools and seeking other means of breaking down barriers between the two systems of education. It may well be that with this, and with the general rapprochement of town and country—in which Dartington is playing such an important part—the school will indeed achieve integration with the Estate. In other words it will both serve as the Estate 'comprehensive' and, in line with other Dartington enterprises, be constantly re-thinking its role in society.

PART THREE

*The Countryman's Countryside since the
Second World War, and its Future*

The war ended in the summer of 1945. Soon afterwards a new Government was swept into power, and hopes were high that a new Britain would be born out of all the idealism of victory, and out of all the vigorous re-thinking that had been generated during the war years. Men hoped that the countryside would not only be protected from the selfish spoliation of the past, but that its inner vitality would be so renewed as to create afresh a virile civilisation of its own. Those who loved the land believed passionately that it should no longer be treated as a chattel, but as an irreplaceable capital asset—the source of food and raw materials, the harbour of wild life and natural beauty, our very living space. To respect land was not just a visionary dream but common sense. To waste it would be to destroy any hope of survival, not only of the countryside, but of the nation itself.

By 1950—despite acute difficulties of economy and employment—legislation had been passed that did promise to fulfil some of these hopes. The four main Acts concerned—the New Towns Act 1946, the Town and Country Planning Act 1947, the Agriculture Act 1947, and the National Parks and Access to the Countryside Act 1949—were all imaginative and far-seeing; and although errors and inadequacies duly became evident, without such action a great opportunity would have been lost. Even so subsequent events so forced the pace that, notwithstanding a plethora of further legislation, we are today confronted with a crisis of resources and controls. Unless we conserve our land and protect our environment, unless we master the dynamics of existence and harmonise the way we work and live in town and country, then indeed we shall be fortunate to survive. Our children and their children will stand in far greater danger than us.

All this is the product of a revolution in technology and social relationships, hardly acknowledged before it was well under way. Even had it been foreseen, it is unlikely that any Government could have carried the nation ahead of events. In a democracy, radical action is often only acceptable at a point when revolutionary changes are already far advanced. Those that overtook the countryside between 1945 and 1970 have however proved no more than introductory. The pace of change is quickening daily. It is vital that we gain control, and try at least to get a glimpse of our destination.

Population
Civilisation consumes land, and man's mere presence has caused the

countryside to contract ever since he began to settle it, although this was not a matter of any lasting consequence before the Industrial Revolution. During the nineteenth century the growing imbalance of land and population was tolerated, partly by importing an abundance of cheap food, partly by disregarding the implications of population growth. The argument was offered that Britain owed her 'superiority' to these very factors: that sprawling industry and teeming towns were a mark of progress, and to grow food was really the business of peasant communities and pioneer continents, both of them backward in the time-scale of human history.

Between 1801 and 1931 the population of Britain rose from about ten million to just under forty-five million, and the proportion of town dwellers from less than thirty per cent to eighty per cent. The initial momentum was over by 1911, thereafter the rate of increase declined, and in the 1930s the margin of births over deaths was barely adequate for replacement. Although this low spell proved temporary and the population curve soon began to move up again, the future was considered dark. On the basis of pre-war statistics, it was thought that the population of Britain might reach $47\frac{1}{2}$ million by 1951 and then decline. Later the estimate was revised, but it remained conservative, projecting a total of fifty-four million by the end of the century. All these calculations proved wrong. The 1951 Census returned a total of $50\frac{1}{4}$ million, and in 1971 it is expected to approach fifty-six million. A recent estimate for the year 2001 is of the order of sixty-eight to sixty-nine million—assuming no radical change in the trend of birth and death rates, and no cataclysm, natural or man-made—but again it may prove too low.[1]

It is impossible in this book to discuss in depth the reason for population growth, a highly speculative subject which exercises the attention of a variety of experts—demographers, physicians, biologists, sociologists, anthropologists, economists, *et al.*: not to mention politicians who seem the most helpless of all. The variety of disciplines is an indication of its complexity as well of its importance. Indeed population in its relation to land lies at the very foundation of our future, since it is the growing number of people—attended by a rising standard of living—that exerts ever more pressure upon our diminishing space and resources.

In his Presidential Address to the British Association in 1966, Sir Joseph Hutchinson said:

> Our difficulties in population control are social and emotional. In this country we have not yet accepted it that population pressure is an immediate concern of our own, and not just a vague menace in distant parts of Asia . . . I believe that this country is in fact over-populated now, and will inevitably be more heavily over-populated in the future, whatever we may decide to do about it. Over-population

means, in simple terms, too many people for the resources in land that are available to them.[2]

The discussion ranges—and rages—round a large area which includes, but is by no means confined to, the techniques and implications of family planning. Procreation calls in question moral and religious principles, economic incentives, and the criteria of human welfare. There is no simple explanation of population increase or decrease, but it can be said that it rests heavily upon one extremely elusive element—confidence in the future of society.

Professor Hutchinson is not alone in his beliefs. A growing body of experts is convinced that Britain is already over-populated and will become acutely so by the end of the century: specifically in relation to land space, natural resources, the disposal of wastes and other forms of pollution, and in terms of economic dependence upon imports of fuel, raw materials, and certain foods, of which the world may run short. Despite disagreement in detail, the overwhelming consensus of opinion among those experts who attended the Symposium held at the Royal Geographical Society on 25th–26th September 1969 was that 'the optimum population for Britain has already been exceeded'.[3]

Professor Hutchinson referred to the concept of 'critical population density',[4] i.e. 'the maximum population density that can be supported by a given agricultural system without progressive deterioration of the land'. He emphasised that this applied not only to primitive agricultural societies, but to all human communities, especially Britain and Western Europe, and that the condition of the environment supplied the key. In other words, the way we use our land is an indication of how well or ill we understand what is at stake in the matter of survival. The following sentences in Professor Hutchinson's Address, although they do not follow one another in the text, are telling and sequent in the development of his argument:

> We may reasonably hope that our resources in land will be sufficient, if wisely managed, to meet the needs of our expanding population for our lifetime. But even on the most optimistic forecast, that leaves us barely time to meet what we can foresee of the needs of the twenty-first century. . . . We have the knowledge and the technology for control, but we lack the vision to plan and initiate a programme that we know will take several human generations to bring to fruition. . . . We need a target figure [for the population of Britain]. I would like to set 40 millions, though I believe that, short of catastrophe, it would take two centuries to achieve it. Perhaps more important than a target figure, we need a social philosophy that will embrace the concepts and consequences of a stable population. . . . The ecological concept of the climax involves a stable popula-

tion, within which individuals grow and mature and die, while the community maintains its vigour and stability.

The heart of the whole matter is, of course, the birth rate. . . . For make no mistake, this country already carries a population as great as the environment can support without degeneration, and it will call for all the knowledge and skill we can command to prevent irreparable damage before we achieve a stable population, even if we set about stabilisation without delay.[5]

So much for the warning about people. We now have to look at some of the consequences for the countryside of a population increase of about eleven million over the next thirty years; and try to assess the capacity of the land to sustain us all.

Land

The Second World War was the watershed in the flow of opinion about land use. Because bombing had cleared the cities and made re-housing and re-development necessary on a massive scale, the need for control was accepted and planning legislation passed. The emphasis on urban renewal helped in a back-handed way to stem the demand for rural land, reinforced by the fact that food was still short and rationing extended into peace. But the restriction did not last. In the event no one anticipated the scale and pace of the post-war demand for land, its multiplicity and intensity, and the ways in which the various uses reacted upon one another, each one posing a fresh set of problems. So much so that, at least by 1960, the actual and potential consequences were generating a feeling of despair. How much of the countryside would be left by the year 2000?

How much land is there in Britain, and how is it used? Statistics are surprisingly fluid and, as with population, are subject to periodic re-calculation. The following estimate, adjusted as nearly as possibleto 1970, will act as a guide.

Land Area and Land Use (millions of acres)[6]

	England/Wales	Scotland/N. Ireland	United Kingdom
Agriculture	29·5	17·8	47·3
Woodland	2·5	2·0	4·5
Towns/Industry Communications }	4·0	0·7	4·7
Other Uses	1·0+	2·0+	3·0+
Totals	37·0+	22·5+	59·5+

A total of 59½ million acres of land for 56 million people in 1970 allows just over one acre per person. For a population of 67 million in the year 2000, the allowance will be reduced to approximately nine-tenths of an acre per person: that is, space for survival, lumping all kinds of land together. To accommodate the additional eleven million, and to provide for the appropriate expansion of towns, industry, roads, reservoirs, and other urban uses, will require—it is estimated—not less than two million acres: plus a further one million for the blighting of land in the vicinity of such expansion, the dereliction of pollution, and the damage done by the extraction of minerals. Finally forestry is planning to absorb two million acres on its own. At least five to six million acres therefore will have to be subtracted from the total stock of land—almost all of it from farming—over the next thirty years for these purposes alone. Whereas trees and reservoirs will generally find a place in the remoter, less vulnerable, areas of the countryside, urban and industrial development will absorb the more accessible space in the lowlands, mainly of England. This makes it inevitable, not only that much fertile food-producing land will be lost, but that the effect of the loss will be to intensify pressure to an unbearable degree upon the land that remains.

Estimates of land loss, however approximate, must precede any attempt to grasp what has been happening in the countryside in the past generation, as well as what is likely to happen in the next. The pattern is roughly consistent in that, so long as the population increases, fresh land is consumed for the purposes of existence. In the sense that land has to be lived *on*—for housing, industry, recreation, and the rest—such uses always come first, even though it may ultimately prove impossible to sustain the anticipated total of human beings in the available space. Where people disagree is in what is meant by 'sustaining'. In primitive terms it means of course the sheer physical requirements of food and drink, and by its nature that question has to be answered next. How much land, and what kind of land, can be conserved to meet that need? How far is it necessary to feed ourselves from our own resources in this way?

Food

History shows that to grow food is a primary function of man on the land. This is not a platitude, for in Britain we tried hard to disprove it. For nearly seventy years, from the 1870s until the 1930s, agriculture was regarded as uneconomic and therefore unnecessary. It paid better to neglect our fields, and import most of our food in exchange for industrial exports and mercantile services. Free Trade was the formula, and let the countryside go hang. The story is told in Part One. This concept broke down, temporarily in the First World War, but finally only when the terms of trade moved against us, and in the emergency of the Second

World War—although its complete disappearance should not be assumed even now. The change of attitude however was—to be fair—one of heart as well as of pocket, and it led to the legislation already referred to. The two Acts passed by Parliament in 1947, which bore directly upon the future of farming, illustrate this point.

The Town and Country Planning Act 1947 brought all land under statutory control for the purposes of development, and laid special emphasis on the reservation of land for farming. Influenced partly by economic difficulties (e.g. the shortage of foreign exchange) and partly by the Scott Report 1942, it shed an aura of sanctity over rural land which in the event proved impossible to maintain; at least the purism of Scott had quite soon to give way to overriding pressures. Inevitably large areas of farmland had to be appropriated for urban and industrial uses, in all at an average annual rate of forty to fifty thousand acres a year. Driven by immediate necessity, the Act fell far short of its strategic aim. There was no effective machinery for determining the priority of land by reference to the value of the soil; while State agencies were allowed to ride roughshod over accepted planning procedures. Even so the idea of controlling land use by statutory means had clearly come to stay; the worst offences of the past—such as buying farmland cheap for speculative building—were progressively discouraged; and subsequent legislation facilitated improvements in planning techniques. Although serious inroads continued to be made into the stock of valuable agricultural land, farmers were awarded—and largely retained—a privileged position.[7]

The Agriculture Act 1947 spelled out in practical terms how the Government proposed to encourage farming as an industry, and make it in peace as well as in war a permanent part of the national economy: 'producing such part of the nation's food and other agricultural produce in the U.K. . . . at minimum prices consistently with proper remuneration and living conditions for farmers and workers in agriculture and an adequate return on capital invested in the industry.'

Public money was made available in two main ways: first, by production grants—aimed partly at helping defray the cost of capital improvements on farms,[8] and partly at encouraging a higher standard of husbandry;[9] secondly, by guaranteeing the prices of farm products so that farmers could plan ahead with some assurance of financial security.[10] Grant aid and guarantees however did not add up to the whole bill. The existing structure of research, education, veterinary service, and farm advice was strengthened and extended. The National Agricultural Advisory Service (N.A.A.S.) will serve as one example. Before the war farmers had generally distrusted Government servants who offered them advice. During the war this feeling was aggravated by the fact that advisory officers were attached to the War Agricultural Executive Committees (W.A.E.C.s), which graded farms for efficiency and exercised disciplinary powers. In 1946 however N.A.A.S. was set up as a service in its own right, and in 1957 it became advisory in fact as well as in name. Over the years it won a high reputation, not only in specialist matters of husbandry, but also in the practical business of preparing farm budgets and management plans.[11]

There is no need, at this stage, to delve deeper into the means by which Parliament helped farming after the war: whether directly by means of finance and services, or indirectly through interest in marketing, or in the regulation of wages and conditions of employment. The point seems proved beyond doubt that, whichever political party was in power in the post-war years, agriculture was deliberately woven into the fabric of the national economy. Yet, as time went on, there were strains, and certainly a price to pay for State security. If you depend on the State for support, you depend on its willingness to support you; and so lay yourself open to dictation as to how you should conduct your business. Farming therefore felt the cross-winds of national economic policy and finance; and it transpired that, once food surpluses began to reappear—as they did in the 1950s—the Government was generally reluctant to offset low market prices by a corresponding increase in grants and guarantees.[12] The squeeze was on at both ends. Productivity began to operate in earnest in agriculture, as in industry, but with this difference. While making special provision for certain types of holdings (hill farms, and small farms with, roughly, less than 100 acres), the Government made use of the economic pressure to induce a revolution, not only in the organisation of farming as a whole, but in the essential techniques of husbandry: matters which have only become evident in the past ten to fifteen years. In a word agriculture is becoming industrialised wherever industrial methods can be practically applied; and even where they cannot, the attempt is being made.

CHANGES IN FARMING

The following paragraphs are brief and selective, but their purpose is to give an impression of the main trends of change in farm practice, and of some of the ways in which they are affecting the countryside.

Arable

What does industrialisation mean in farming? In its simplest terms it is synonymous with uniform layout, mechanisation of routine, and the reduction of labour, in order economically to achieve as high an output as possible per man, per acre, per unit of livestock. Almost all agricultural techniques are subsidiary to this aim; and the resulting pattern strikes the onlooker most forcibly wherever arable husbandry is general —with or without livestock. It comprises, in effect, all the lowlands and gently contoured territory east and south of a line drawn from the Bristol Channel to the mouth of the Tees. Apart from the sheep and cattle farms on the Yorkshire Moors in the north-eastern corner of the area, arable either predominates—for cash and feed crops or horticulture (as in the Fens or parts of Kent, in association with orcharding)—or it combines with stock rearing and dairying. There are of course pockets of intensive cultivation outside this area, and other arable as well; but the map on page 158 shows how the main part of arable agriculture in Britain is contained within this large segment of England.

Here the landscape is being remodelled at varying pace to facilitate the full application of what amounts to factory methods. Hedges and spinneys are being bulldozed out, and other field boundaries dispersed, in order to gain more land, permit the maximum use of mechanised husbandry, and form farm units suitable for large-scale management. Since wheeled tractors and track-layers of increasing power (drawing machinery of appropriate capacity) need as much space as possible to operate efficiently, 100-acre fields are already commonplace; there are many larger than that. Cultivation itself is being transformed. The plough—a prehistoric implement in origin—may quite soon become obsolete. The main object of ploughing—to bury weeds and aerate the soil—can, it is argued, be attained in other ways. Stubble straw is normally burned, weeds and pests are controlled by spraying, while the chemical destruction of the residue of one crop enables a new one to be injected into the soil without further preparation. After-cultivations present few problems. Top dressing and spraying can be done from the air, if not by tractor, and harvesting accomplished by ever larger and more sophisticated machines, supported by highly organised systems of crop collection and storage. Time is money.

Crop yields have increased astonishingly, thanks to the development of new strains, heavier application of fertiliser, and various forms of chemical control. The *average* yield of wheat, for example, rose from 22·4 cwt. per acre in 1949 to 32·2 cwt. in 1969; of potatoes from 6·6 tons to 10·1 tons. Rotations are being progressively simplified. If corn is the main product, a break may be made with grass leys grazed by stock; or roots (e.g. sugar beet) or pulses (e.g. beans) which are potentially more profitable and avoid the intrusion of stock altogether: thus far the concession to established farm practice and the maintenance of humus. In some instances the final corner has already been cut for continuous corn cropping. The cultivation of field vegetables—always expensive in labour and other treatments—has likewise made spectacular advances. Singling and hoeing are being replaced by spaced seeding, assisted by sprays to master weeds and pests; while the control of climate (hitherto restricted to horticultural glasshouses) is being managed in the fields by means of plastic igloos and air houses, and

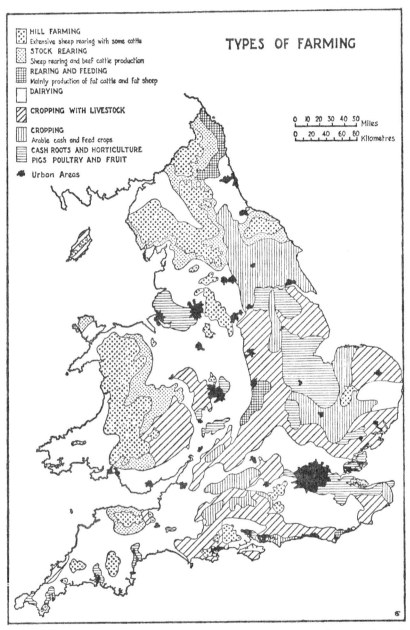

Adapted from the coloured map in the Association of Agriculture's handbook *Types of Farming in Britain*.

water provided by irrigation. There is no reason why many kinds of root vegetables, greenstuff and small fruit should not be raised intensively in this manner, and in mass quantity. Rhubarb and mushrooms have long been grown artificially, and field peas harvested, processed and packed mechanically in a tight time-schedule between field and factory. As things are going, the trend will accelerate.

Livestock

The clue to intensive livestock husbandry is 'controlled environment'. This means providing housing and other conditions which ostensibly combine the comfort of the animal with the convenience of the farmer: a practice that has aroused strong criticism on grounds of cruelty, none the less it is firmly established.

For some years after the war it was still common to see hens picking about the farmyard and messing in the machinery, laying their eggs where they liked. Traditionally both eggs and table birds provided pin money for the farmer's wife. By the early 1960s it had already become difficult to find any poultry in the open air at all, for this was the branch of farming that yielded quickest to factory methods—both birds and eggs. Chicken meat produced intensively soon proved popular and a cheap alternative to beef and mutton, a broiler being raised from day-old to four pounds liveweight in eight weeks. The birds stand on litter in semi-darkness, say 10,000 to a shed, in which the temperature is controlled and feed and water automatically supplied. Much research has gone into breeding and nutrition. Broiler production now exceeds thirty-five million head per year, and similar methods are being applied to turkeys and other forms of white meat. Egg production has moved through three main stages — traditional free range, deep litter (birds running free on litter indoors), and batteries (ranges of wire cages in a shed, with feed, water and manure disposal completely automated). Three-quarters of all the eggs laid now come from batteries where the laying average is approaching two hundred and twenty eggs per bird per year, and one poultryman can look after up to 50,000 birds. Almost the total requirement of eggs in Britain is now home produced.

All aspects of the poultry industry have now become big business and are concentrated in relatively few hands. Like industry proper it lends itself to rationalisation and integration. Thus the farmer—the man responsible for the broilers or the eggs—will be under contract with a firm or a co-operative from first to last. He can borrow capital to buy the poultry house and its equipment, which are supplied to him in the first place. He will buy his stock, feed, litter, etc., from or through a single source, and sell the finished product under contract. He is in fact simply a skilled processor, and about the only thing he is free to dispose of is the manure—a very valuable by-product, but also a problem, as will be shown. This is the logical pattern which has emerged after less than fifteen years.

Pigs are only a little less amenable to factory farming than poultry. Fattening for pork or bacon has long been conducted under cover, as the warmth and well-being of the animal are essential for rapid food conversion. Traditionally breeding and rearing to weaner stage is a separate business: the sows and litters allowed to run out, as they benefit from grazing and exercise, and their rootling can be a good preparation for cropping. However a modern 'controlled environment' house, fully automated, can take care of the entire life cycle of the pig with a minimum of attendance (e.g. one man to 3000–4000 pigs at fattening stage). Producing pig meat, as with broilers and eggs, can be solved by organisation. Although at present only one-third of the bacon in the shops is home produced, it could—subject to trade agreements—all be accounted for in this country. Pork is already. No need for markets, but a contractual system from start to finish, and like poultry virtually isolated from the main stream of farming. Even the buildings require comparatively little space; the stock of farmland would hardly be affected by them.

However the larger the animal the harder it becomes to apply factory techniques. Cattle have always played an intimate part in field management by grazing, or in winter by consuming fodder in yards, and returning fertility to the soil through manure. Yet, in the intensive areas, much has already been done towards altering even this time-honoured pattern. In short, whether for meat or milk, the beasts can be isolated from the fields; and if allowed out at all, only for a limited amount of exercise. Traditionally beef animals are born and reared in the hills, sold as stores to lowland farmers, who keep them in winter yards and on summer grass to killing weight at eighteen months to two years or longer. Nowadays the majority of beef calves derive from dairy herds. Friesians, the commonest breed, are genuinely dual-purpose. They milk well and they make good meat. Usually however a proportion of the cows and heifers are mated by artificial insemination to a beef bull (e.g. Hereford, Aberdeen Angus, Charolais, etc.). The calves are reared either naturally by multiple sucking, or artificially on milk substitutes and concentrates, or by a variation of both methods. In the ordinary way, as weaning goes on, the calves would be turned out to graze in the summer months. The intensive answer is to keep them continuously indoors, sometimes in very restricted conditions, and feed them on conserved grass or barley, until they reach eight to nine cwt. at twelve to fifteen months. Although the flesh may be pale (especially if barley-fed), the carcasses are lean and therefore popular with butchers and housewives. Latterly the fashion for 'barley beef' has received a check, mainly due to the rise in production costs; none the less intensive beef rearing by one means or another is unlikely to diminish, for this is

Farm wagon yesterday

COUNTRY CRAFTS

Basket-making today

Softwood plantations

FORESTRY

Hardwood husbandry

an economic answer to what, under industrial farming, is primarily regarded as an economic problem.

Finally we come to dairying, on which the majority of farmers depend for their living. Milk production is still the sheet anchor of agriculture, with a total of nearly three million cows yielding an average of 825 gallons per cow in 1970. Nurtured as a national commitment since the foundation of the Milk Marketing Board in 1934, it has ever since made remarkable progress in efficiency, however measured. The problems are formidable, and range over genetics, nutrition, field husbandry, crop storage, the design of buildings, the manufacture of a great variety of equipment, the control of disease, the analysis and recording of milk, and the collection, treatment, and disposal of a highly vulnerable product; though it is one which most householders take for granted, and complain if it is not delivered to them every day in the week. Dairy farms range from single holdings of fifty acres, to larger family concerns of 100–500 acres, and groups of farms extending over several thousand acres, centrally controlled. To secure acceptable standards and reasonable uniformity of practice within such a varied industry, would seem a superhuman achievement; yet economic pressures within and without have driven it inexorably forward.

Not long ago, for one man to milk thirty cows was considered a good ratio; now it is forty to fifty, rising in some cases to herds of 100 cows or more per milker. Milking techniques vary according to the nature of the land and the resources of the farmer: from outdoor bails that follow the cows round the fields, to old-fashioned fixed standings in the cowhouse, and parlours of various sorts; likewise after milking, if they are not being turned out to graze, the cows may stand around in yards and help themselves to silage, or lie down loose in cubicles. Such variations are likely to continue, so long as family-type farms survive. The number of individual dairy farmers is however declining, and industrial methods of management are coming in. Milking by contract is already well established, either as a permanent arrangement between owner and contractor, or on a temporary basis during illness and holidays. The 'cotel' has arrived. This is a large cowhouse complex for 300 or more head, milked by a team on a shift basis, the milkers working a five-day week. Herds of this size are not turned out for grazing. Instead grass and other fodder is brought in to them, and the animals take their exercise in a paddock near by. By such means it is possible to concentrate a far greater number of cows than is normally acceptable on a farm. Not only is there no question of driving them out to different fields each morning, and bringing them back in the afternoon, but it undermines the whole concept of carrying a herd to match the productive capacity of the farm in terms of grazing and winter feed. This has a number of implications. On the one hand it allows management to be much more intensive; it reduces labour and lifts wages (as in all types of industrial farming); it raises the ratio of cows per acre; and it opens up the prospect of growing more profitable arable crops, such as barley, to replace grass as the basic feed.

All this reflects a shift in the food market. Fresh milk is already at grips with 'long-life' milk and 'instant' milk powders, many of them imported. If full milk can be progressively conserved at a reasonable retail price, daily deliveries will come to an end, and the housewife will be able to buy at will from the supermarket or local store. Industrial dairying is already conforming to this pattern.

The Impact of Factory Farming

Factory farming signifies specialisation for an economic purpose. In husbandry it means divorce—separating one activity from another, when all have hitherto been regarded as interdependent. This has a variety of consequences, but here I wish by way of example to refer to a single problem of farm technique—the immediate outcome of the new methods—which demonstrates the problem most forcibly.

The heavy concentration of stock under cover, especially of cattle, raises in acute form the whole question of the disposal of 'farm waste'. With bedding (e.g. wood shavings for broilers, straw or sawdust for other stock), most of the dung and much of the urine is absorbed, and seepage is manageable. Where no bedding is used, then vast quantities of watery dung or slurry disappear down the drain. The flow will be swelled by gallons of water for swilling out dairy equipment, scrubbing down concrete, perhaps also by vegetable washing, seepage from silage clamps, etc. Most of this finds its way, directly or indirectly, into the nearest river; pollution follows and prosecution by the local River Authority. Now there is a hue and cry for safe methods of disposal, and fears that it will all cost a large amount of money.

Traditional farmers find this extraordinary, for with them there is no such problem. Farmyard manure is piled daily on to a heap, or at intervals dug out of yards, for spreading on the land: where it helps restore humus and improve the texture of the soil. Returning such manure to the fields, either directly or after composting, has always been regarded as a vital means of maintaining fertility. Indeed to sell manure off a general farm is considered bad practice and, along with hay, was often forbidden in farm leases in the past. Now manure has become a nuisance, and many modern farmers would gladly dismiss it from their minds. What was a side-issue has become a central difficulty, deriving directly from factory methods of stock husbandry. There is no need to discuss the techniques of disposal at present being explored,[13] but the following comment is revealing:

> In dairy farming, slurry is the maddest thing of all. Things have come to a fine pass when more work, worry and possible expense is

needed to handle the slurry than to produce the milk. So-called lagoons full of slurry have created more problems than they have solved. In desperation some farmers have connected their slurry effluent into council drains only to receive demands for up to £1000 per year. The position can possibly best be described by quoting from a Ministry of Agriculture statement: 'There does not appear to be an economic method whereby farm effluent can be purified sufficiently for discharge into a water course. The best advice that can be given at present is to treat manure so that it remains as solid as possible and to try to soak up the liquid portion with straw, sawdust, or any other absorbent material that may be available.' In other words, back to our old valuable tried farmyard manure. And a very expensive journey it has been.[14]

Regarded in isolation, the dilemma is this. Ordinary livestock husbandry produces less food, but at some immediate cost in handling it returns waste to and improves the soil. Factory methods produce more food and are economically attractive; but these advantages are countered by problems of pollution and by the cost of a system of disposal which, if it returns little or no waste to the land, impoverishes the soil.

Criticisms of factory farming are not of course confined to problems arising from the disposal of farm waste, although this is a practical and striking example. Objections generally are of two kinds—scientific and social. Scientific objections, mainly biological and ecological, extend beyond husbandry to the conservation of wild life and natural resources, and in a variety of ways, e.g. in the quality of food, bear upon human survival. This is discussed by Robert Waller in the Appendix. Social objections spring from the sense of loss by the destruction of landscape beauty, and by the break with rural tradition, whether it be the disappearing pattern of field and hedgerow or—at one remove—of village life itself. There is the added feeling that industrial agriculture will not only destroy the indigenous structure of the countryside, but will also prohibit access by townspeople who wish to enjoy fresh air and open spaces, a matter of great importance in an urbanised country such as England. Intensive farming cannot tolerate tourists, too much is at risk; it would be as unthinkable as letting a crowd of rubbernecks run riot in a power station. Perhaps the farmscape of the future will, in any event, be of a kind to repel visitors. Will there be any pleasure in walking or riding beside a prairie of young wheat, redolent of a hormone spray, without a tree or a bush in sight?

In these areas the buildings will also change, are changing fast. If not abandoned, many old farmhouses and cottages are becoming the homes of townsmen—commuters, retired people, or others who have business in the neighbourhood; barns too are being converted into dwellings. The new operative farmsteads will be fewer in number and far larger than their predecessors—factory-type complexes for stock, machinery, storage and administration. They will tend to be sited within strategic distance of their markets—not necessarily auction markets, for many of these may disappear—but processing and packing plants for vegetables, eggs, poultry, monster corn silos, abbatoirs and meat-packing stations; and the like. These in turn will be of easy access to conurbations or groups of towns, where the produce will be consumed. Farmers and farm workers, long declining in numbers, will continue to grow less. Not many will live beside their work. Most will have their homes in the nearest town or settlement, and come to work by car. This is less revolutionary than might appear. Farm people are already a minority in many parts of the countryside, and it is only a matter of time before most families own one or even two cars.

In some ways physical changes will be less striking than those which are overtaking the internal organisation of agriculture. Industrial farming responds to the industrial organisation of supply and sale, as it does in town industry. In the case of food it all starts with the housewife. Whether she intended it or not, she largely depends today—and will do so more than ever tomorrow—upon supermarkets and self-service stores, where she can buy standardised goods of known brand and quality: that is, mass-produced food, mass-processed and packed, all at tolerable prices. Her demands work back all the way along the line to the farmer. To satisfy her the food shop (of whatever kind or size) must have a reliable source of wholesale supply, and the wholesaler must be able to depend on producers. In these circumstances buying and selling in auction markets becomes increasingly hazardous. Instead, contracts are coming in at every stage, and it cannot be long before they replace markets, at any rate for large-scale dealing.

Contracting has obvious advantages. It ensures profit margins and offers security for capital investment; and industrial farming particularly needs an ample flow of capital to finance operations. The critical question is: who controls the market? Retailer, wholesaler (distributor) or producer? There is no clear answer at present, though much manoeuvring is taking place. Farmers however are rapidly becoming aware of the dangers and opportunities, and seem at last to be overcoming their innate disinclination to combine for trade. It is impossible to be precise about the pattern that will emerge, but the scale and cost of operations appear to point towards two main systems.

The first is *vertical integration*: that is, control of every stage of production and distribution by ownership or by contract between interdependent parties, one of whom will probably be dominant. The broiler trade already looks like this, and is steered by a handful of tycoon producers and distributors, from the breeding of the day-old chick to the delivery of the 'oven-ready' wrapped table bird to the shop, where it awaits the customer. The corn and feed trade, on the other hand, is fast falling into the hands of a few giant milling combines and merchants, who can dictate terms to both farmers and shopkeepers. On the whole the retailer seems disinclined to move back into production, although contact with the customer in the High Street is a potential weapon of great power, should it ever be wielded by a near-monopoly.

The second system is *horizontal integration*, whereby producers in the same line of business form a group for the collective buying of feedstuffs and other requisites, for the purchase and common use of machinery, and for the marketing of stock and crops—whether it be for any one or a combination of these purposes. Groups are a relatively recent development in farming, but one of great importance. In a pig production group, for example, one section will breed the piglets, and pass them when weaned to another section for fattening, all under contract between each other. The fatteners will sell to the processors or butchers and, operating from a position of strength as a single group, all members will benefit by the good prices gained. In general groups work well, wherever it is practicable to pool resources. This is not always a simple matter. In husbandry, for instance, owing to the vagaries of the climate, it is by no means straightforward to share the use, say, of harvesting machinery. In a catchy season everyone will want the combine on the same day; and that accounts partly for the over-capitalisation in machinery on farms, and partly for the success of independent contractors, whose business it is to get round the work as quickly as possible and satisfy everybody. None the less the group principle is sound, especially in farming where the union of individuals—too small to stand up to the big battalions on their own—obviously means strength, if the practical details can be worked out. And there is no reason why groups should not continue to extend their activities into all aspects of agriculture, so long as they retain their insistence upon quality and compulsory association under contract.[15]

It is these characteristics that distinguish a group from the traditional farmers' 'co-op', whose members are not compelled to trade solely with their own organisation, nor the 'co-op' with them. The lack of compulsion particularly—together with rather a rigid form of constitution inherited from the past—may account for the slow progress of this kind of organisation. However co-operation as such in farming is inevitable. It has been given active support by the National Farmers Union, and by the Government in the Agriculture Act 1967.[16] Had it come earlier, there might have been no need to set up the Milk and other Marketing Boards, which saved agriculture in the 1930s. Moreover it is likely that the major control of farming by producer organisations—even if Government support of agriculture continues indefinitely in some form —will arouse no desire on the part of Parliament to nationalise the industry. Not so, if the tune is to be called by massive combines of manufacturers and distributors or by finance houses, all with international affiliations. Agriculture and agribusiness may become synonymous in structure, but farming in its generic sense is a national interest. If it is to continue within the framework of free enterprise, it must stay—and be seen to stay—to a large extent in the hands of farmers.

Yet nationalisation may become inevitable in one essential—land ownership. Pressure upon space has so increased that the price of farmland has risen by over one hundred per cent in the last ten years. In 1960 the average price per acre was £123, in 1970 £256: well above this figure for the best land, and rarely less than £100 for the worst. At £200 per acre, the capital required to purchase a farm of, say 250 acres would be £50,000. At ten per cent interest the annual charge amounts to £5,000, less according to the proportion found by the farmer himself, though this takes no account of capital repayments.[17] But fixed capital is only one part of the bill. To stock and run the farm working capital is needed; and for a mixed dairy holding, carrying 100 or more milking cows, an additional £20,000 or so might be necessary: thus a total investment of around £70,000. The figure will rise with the fall in value of money and the decline in available farmland. Even to rent such a farm—should this be possible, for competition is intense—it would be necessary to pay say ten to twelve pounds per acre, or £2500–£3000 a year. But this is still a tolerable charge, while in the former case the burden on the owner-occupier is already almost unbearable. For owner-occupiers, only those who have inherited their land or purchased it in the past have any prospect, in the ordinary way of farming, of making sufficient margin both to live and keep the holding in good heart. State ownership of land may therefore be the eventual solution, with occupation by tenancy on terms equivalent to an additional form of Government subsidy. As things stand today however the rising price of farmland cannot fail to hasten the drive towards factory farming. It is a very simple equation. The high cost of land plus high overall operating costs have to be met by a high output from an integrated industry, composed in the main of large units capable of rationalisation. So long as the incentive is exclusively economic—in other words, farming reckoned as a business and nothing else—that must be the pattern. And that too will determine the pattern of a large part of the countryside and the nature of its farming population, indeed wherever intensive methods of husbandry can be applied.

Traditional Farming
There is of course another side to this story, wherein economics play a less dominant part; but before discussing other uses of the countryside, something must first be said about the kind of farming where, for various reasons, intensive methods are not possible or are hardly practised at all. This is a matter partly of topography. I am thinking principally

of the hill and upland country in the north and south-west of England, and in other parts of the United Kingdom, most of it lying outside the 'Hadrian's Wall' of agriculture (from the Bristol Channel to the mouth of the Tees), some of it within. It is also a matter of size—small farms which may be found anywhere in the country, but which are not capable of intensive output. In 1966 a Government survey revealed that about one-quarter of all home-produced food came from three-quarters of the nation's farms, and conversely that three-quarters of the food came from one-quarter of the farms.[18] The immediate inference is that the 'small' farm, whether it be a small-size farm or an extensive hill farm (both having small output), has no place in the structure of agriculture, and that it is a waste of manpower and money to keep it there. In fact the situation is less simple than it seems.

Hill farms, however assessed, are important for several reasons. They are responsible for about fourteen million acres of land, of which over eleven million are classified as rough grazing, most of it by definition difficult and demanding, thin soil, steep slopes, and often remote from the comforts of civilisation. Such farms are devoted largely, if not entirely, to the rearing of livestock, mostly sheep; and it requires a large number of animals—of the order of 500 breeding ewes—to make ends meet on a single holding. Mechanisation hardly applies; and although new techniques of sheep husbandry are being developed—e.g. more prolific breeding, wintering the flock under cover, artificial feeding of lambs, etc.—success still depends upon the personal skill, effort and endurance of the farmer, supported often only by his wife and family. These farms yield wool, and stock for breeding and fattening in the lowlands, an invaluable service which if withdrawn would seriously disrupt the cycle of livestock farming.[19] Successive Governments have recognised the value of the hills, and ever since the Hill Farming Act 1946 have provided special forms of assistance, additional to the normal run of support: viz., subsidies paid yearly on hill sheep and cattle, and high capital grants for the improvement of steadings and fields.[20] The fact that hill farmers earn small incomes—many in Wales, for example, earn less than an agricultural worker—is a tribute to their toughness and sense of devotion which cannot be measured solely in cash.

None the less it is good sense to try to improve the profitability of hill farming and to ensure that, if a farm cannot carry a certain minimum of breeding stock, changes should be made. That means amalgamation where appropriate, and the encouragement of other forms of income. This was a matter attempted in the Agriculture Act 1967, which empowered the establishment of Rural Development Boards to work out plans for the integration of farming, forestry and tourism: in order to help find a reasonable living for people who live and work in remote and difficult areas. The Act also offered grants for amalgamation and compensation to occupiers who were to be 'amalgamated'.[21] To sum up.

Since it depends on extensive grazing, a hill farm has to be of a certain size; it cannot be too small. However this fact—taken into consideration with the special forms of assistance and the possibility of integration with other kinds of land use—lifts the curtain on the future of farming in the hills. And it should act as a brake upon any attempt to intensify hill husbandry beyond an acceptable limit.

A small-size farm—not a hill farm—seems harder to justify, for it plays no vital part in the cycle of livestock breeding; and taken together such farms contribute only a small proportion of the nation's food. Yet there is a qualification at the outset. A number of small-size farms, ranging between five and 100 acres, are remarkably successful: those, for example, engaged in growing fruit and vegetables on highly fertile land (as in the Vale of Evesham), or the smallholdings of the Land Settlement Association, or the factory-type stock farmers producing bacon, broilers, or eggs in intensive housing. Most of these benefit by some form of co-operative trading, or are firmly secured by contract with sources of supply and outlets for sale. Such businesses pay well and hardly constitute a problem under this heading, nor do they fall within the lowest bracket of small producers in the Government survey of 1966, despite their lack of acres.[22]

The problem farms—that struggle to avoid bankruptcy (many do not succeed)—are those which for solid reasons cannot intensify their output beyond a certain point, or do not qualify for special assistance as hill farms. An example, of which I have intimate experience, is the seventy-five to 150-acre holding, sited on broken scrubby land in the south-west, where sharp short slopes limit mechanisation, the soil is poor and the climate wet, and the steading is endowed with massive stone shippons, difficult to adapt. Farms of this kind are family-run; and in the past they survived solely as near-subsistence enterprises, rearing beef and sheep. Much new money was invested in them in the 1950s, and all sorts of devices were resorted to for a higher income: conversion to milk (for the monthly cheque), a hen battery (if the farmer happened to be good at poultry—not all are), pigs, part-time contracting (with a hedge-trimmer or a land-drainer or a lorry for haulage), or taking in summer visitors (if the house was suitable and it was holiday country). Such manœuvres could be cited in variation in many other parts of the country, and reflect a problem as much social as economic. As in the hills, these small or marginal farmers work all hours in all conditions to keep afloat; and in many places, without their efforts, the land would have long fallen back to rush and scrub. Indeed much of the pleasant landscape that remains, prized for its typical English beauty, is due to them.

It was to benefit this kind of holding that the Small Farmers' Scheme was introduced in 1958. By means of special acreage and husbandry grants, it offered help for farms of between twenty and 100 acres where, on the advice of N.A.A.S., there seemed a reasonable chance of success.[23] In 1965 the Scheme was extended to farms of up to 125 acres; and it was calculated that altogether some 100,000 farmers might qualify. The Scheme undoubtedly had some success, and so long as the level of aid kept in step with rising costs, it did much to maintain the structure of family farming. It seems however that farms of less than fifty acres benefited least, and recently stronger inducements have been offered to extinguish such holdings.

> The gap between costs and living standards on the one hand and agricultural prices on the other has widened and will continue to do so. It is not that there is no place for small farms but that standards have altered and the minimum size of farm that can provide a living gradually becomes greater.[24]

The surprising thing is that there are so many small farms still operating.[25] They constitute by far the largest category of agricultural holding, of which only some 15,000 are provided by statutory authorities, and intended chiefly as a means of advancement for farm workers.[26] The inference is that the land always attracts some people who, however slender their resources, are determined to devote their energies to cultivating a few acres of soil or keeping a small head of stock. This is a social fact; and it is likely that even if statutory smallholdings disappear some day, and even if the Government withdraws support from holdings below a certain minimum of acreage or output, smallholders will yet continue. Nor is the part-time farmer to be despised.

'Many people like part-time farming and are not trying to earn large profits from it. It is a method by which leisure hours can be made to pay for themselves, it affords a weekend refuge from life in a town and it gives some social status.'[27]

The Price of Change

In this brief outline of farming since the war, it is only possible to give an indication of the main changes in the techniques of agriculture, and of the causes of change. It is all too easy to assume that such changes will continue to their inexorable end, indeed that some have already completed their course, or that they will occur everywhere. In fact, looking around the countryside as a whole, it is not always easy to discern what has been happening or to appreciate the significance of what you do notice. Memory is short so that the origin of events is easily extinguished. The most obvious alterations in the countryside are those that derive from the impact of town life—the raw scar of a motorway, the march of giant pylons, a nuclear power station, gravel lakes and clay tips, the clutter on the coast, new factories, and the general expansion of building. These developments cannot be missed. Not all are unpleasant and most are inevitable in some form, in fact if not in appearance. We have to accept the consequences of a swelling population and a rising standard of living; and our ability to handle these matters since the war through planning is not to be despised. But although urban interests ultimately determine what we do with our land, it is less easy to comprehend purely rural changes; and by rural I mean, first of all, farming—since, as I have said before, the production of food is the primary function of the land.

Farming is in transition, though still in the early stages of the process. A farmer who died in 1939, revived today, would notice much that was familiar, and he would approve in many instances. In many parts of the country the landscape is still well wooded, hedged or walled, albeit punctuated with much crude concrete post-and-wire fencing. Fields are bigger, some of them enormous, and the eastern counties would strike him as naked; but they always were, the Fens being particularly dreary in that respect. Chalk wolds and downs likewise remain open windy places, the most striking difference there being the increase of plough-land right over the slopes. The absence of farm horses would strike him at once, the prevalence of tractors, the large capacity of ploughs and cultivating tackle, and the appearance of strange new harvesting machinery. He would be horrified in August and September by the wasteful habit of burning stubble, and he would regret the loss of old-fashioned hay and corn ricks. The fields would seem emptier than in his day; plenty of sheep on the hills; but more stock kept indoors, while the popularity of the black-and-white Friesian dairy cattle could hardly be missed, herds and herds of them in yards or paddocks, or grazing the ground tight behind strands of electric fencing. He would be amazed by the better look of grass, the good management of pasture for grazing and mowing, the clean appearance of most arable crops, and the reduction of rabbits and weeds. At certain times of the year he would ask what the smell was; and when told it was a hormone spray, he would ask what that was. His farmhouse looked much the same, from the outside at any rate, but there were many changes in the farmyard: one silo for grass, another for grain, a battery-like building for pigs, another for hens, while his neighbour had erected a yard-and-parlour complex that looked like a palace. Most of the old buildings—those that had not been demolished—were being used for storage, with an extension for machinery. A Dutch barn was half-full of baled hay and straw.

He would notice many other things of course, as time went on. On the whole, although fond of the old ways, he had no happy recollection of the poverty on the land between the wars. He therefore approved of the mechanical aids, of the installation of electricity, of the great lessening in manual effort, of greater yields and better financial returns. Any farmer worth his salt—and he was one—wanted to see two blades of grass grow where one grew before, and if that meant a better life for the husbandman—however achieved—he rejoiced. The fact that the farm was in some respects an uglier place than in the past worried him not at all. He may not have noticed it—the criss-cross of electricity cables and telephone wires, the stark asbestos sheeting, the empty oil drums, the heap of junk and scatter of empty bags. Tidiness was not necessarily the same thing as profits, it never was. Yes, materially, things were much better all round. But where were the men?

The purpose of this fairy tale is to illustrate in a slight way some of the revolutionary changes that have overtaken farming in the past twenty to thirty years, and to suggest that twenty to thirty years hence the changes will be much more striking—should present trends continue. Indeed many of the changes that have been half-concealed—such as hedge and tree removal in the areas of traditional stock or mixed farming—will suddenly become apparent to even the most casual eye. In 1969 I believe that about 3000 hedge trees were cut down in Somerset alone. At that rate, although the county is tolerably well wooded especially at the western end, nakedness will not remain hidden for much longer.

By the same token, it is yearly becoming easier to descry the general shape that agriculture is assuming, a generation after the Second World War. At the risk of repetition it stems from the fact that an expanding urban economy has persuaded successive Governments to try to industrialise the land: in order to produce the requisite amount of food, within the framework of foreign trade and currency commitments. Roughly the message can be summed up as, 'If you farm efficiently, we will keep you in business.' Keeping in business means of course the whole structure of Government support—the basic grants and guarantees, the special forms of assistance, all the education, advice, research, and other agricultural services. In other words, by investing some of the nation's resources in farming the plan has been to kill two birds with one stone—to get a good business return and to stand by the promises made in the Agriculture Act 1947. It was a challenge, a combination of stick and carrot, which the farmers accepted and have made good by producing almost two-thirds of the nation's requirements in temperate foods and just over half the food programme as a whole. Technically this is a remarkable record: in the face of a rising demand for food, certain changes in diet (notably a higher demand for protein), a steady increase in fixed costs, less land and less labour. The pace of progress was such that already by the 1960s, the volume of agricultural output was almost double pre-war, and productivity rising at six per cent per year. That compared well with any other industry, and farming could hold its head high on economic grounds alone.[28] By 1970 however the stick had so dominated the carrot that the less 'industrial' farmers rebelled, and made militant protests at the Annual Price Review—deputations, processions, and a limited form of strike by withholding supplies from the market. The lesson of this situation was that, as a test of efficiency, sheer production has its limitations, and in accepting the test farmers had placed themselves in a vulnerable position.

Economics moreover is notorious as a subject that can be argued both ways; and farm critics have never been lacking. One economist[29] stated that the true cost of agricultural support was far higher than the gross total of £269 million conceded at the 1970 Price Review. Hidden items had to be added, e.g. the non-rating of farm buildings, the monopoly price of milk (since no liquid milk was imported), the cost to the consumer of quotas and restrictive import agreements. With these taken into account, the total bill to the tax payer was of the order of £450 million or more. This offset much of the vaunted saving in foreign food imports, and was equivalent to a tariff of twenty-five to thirty per cent, well above the average for other industry. He further discounted the productivity claim by referring to the heavy investment of capital constantly needed to maintain the efficiency of agriculture; and he argued that to expand home farming further would have an adverse effect on the currency position, since it would reduce the ability of foreign food-producing countries to purchase British manufactures, and divert capital at home from more profitable industrial investment. This echo of Free Trade sentiments sent a shiver down many farmers' spines, though counter-arguments were soon rushed up. It was protested, for example, that although a surplus of some kinds of food still existed in the western hemisphere, they would soon decline as developing countries became more populous and more capable of paying for their needs. In which case, why should Britain be favoured as a buyer? In any event the price of foreign food was bound to rise, so that in the future it might cost more to purchase even the same quantity as we imported today.[30] The most telling argument of all—rising above the daily to-and-fro of national housekeeping—was, and remains, that to feed a growing population (another eleven million by the year 2000) it would be the height of folly to rely too heavily on foreign imports. It would 'pay' best, whatever the financial cost, to maintain production in agriculture, and keep the traditional farmers going while inducing them by means of higher subsidies to extract ever more from their farms. It is argued furthermore that, once you undermine confidence in farming and land goes back, it costs infinitely more in the end to restore—let alone raise—output. And there are signs already, so it is said, that confidence is declining: not by protests and public meetings, but by the fact that farmers in several counties are cutting down on costs and output by reverting to 'dog and stick' husbandry, or in other ways are sitting tight till times improve.

If starvation is indeed the bogey, then the answer would seem to lie—in the short term at least—in the direction described. However this raises other questions, less easy to answer simply.

More Food from less Land?

Is it possible from a declining area of land to go on producing more and more food? Some experts say 'yes', and assert that agriculture could not only feed Britain in the years to come, but become an important export industry: indeed that it is already becoming so. In *Modern Agriculture and Rural Planning*,[31] John Weller writes:

> A decade ago ... the idea that agriculture might become an industry with large export outlets would have been considered ridiculous. Nevertheless food production today could be on the threshold of a new era, not only meeting most home requirements but having a surplus sought after by foreign trade. This new concept could change the basic pattern of land-use requirements, reversing the economic arguments for continued urban expansion at the expense of agriculture.

Weller refers to the buoyant exports of industries ancillary to agriculture, e.g. tractors, farm machinery, and fertilisers; drink, notably whisky; fish and fish preparations; even jams and marmalades. He continues:

> It is not however in these spheres that change has been dramatic in the last few years, but in the export of farm produce. Between 1960 and 1964, farm exports rose by 67% from £40m to £72m, including livestock, meat, dairy products, wool, hides, cereals and seeds. Though the average increase is over £6 million a year, the sharpest increase of £12m was between 1963 and 1964. In fact the value of all food exports rose by 50% from £100m to £150m.

It may seem contradictory for this country both to import and export food. In fact this is happening partly because of the tangle of trade agreements, and partly because with certain exceptions the categories of farm produce going out and coming in do not seriously overlap. In meat for example, while importing large quantities of mutton, lamb, bacon and ham, and relatively small amounts of beef and veal, our main export in this field is live cattle for breeding and for slaughter. There is likewise an upward trend in the sale abroad of British dairy products, eggs, malt from barley, wool, hides and skins. An Agricultural Export Council was created in 1966, and Weller foresees that the value of such exports will soon exceed £500 million yearly.[32] This figure, by the way, more or less leaves out of account the potentialities of frozen foods, pre-packed horticultural produce, and processed or 'long-life' milk.[33] The latter has already been referred to as a possible threat to home supplies of liquid milk, but the same writer comments:

> It is more than probable that, rather than milk imports destroying the British milk industry, the demand for milk will outstrip the

world capacity for production. . . . Milk consumption throughout much of the Middle East, Africa, India and Asia is abysmally low. . . . The opportunity for exporting milk is the biggest challenge facing British agriculture and dairies. If grasped, and Britain leads as pioneers in this field, it could transform the economics of United Kingdom agriculture.

So envisaged the future sounds comforting. What have we to worry about if, thanks to the ingenuities of science, the admirable know-how of our farmers, manufacturers, and agribusinessmen, backed by a far-seeing Government, we can have our cake and eat it: i.e. produce most of the food we need and export as well? If that were so, a subsidised intensive agriculture would be justified up to the hilt, and awkward criticisms from economists would cease.

THE TWO ASSUMPTIONS

This kind of appraisal however is based on two large assumptions. The first is that we shall retain an adequate supply of suitable land. The second is that such land can be induced to yield and sustain an output of up to, perhaps, twice as much food as now.

Enough Land?

Weller suggests that, by the end of the century, the amount of improved or cultivable land may have shrunk to about one-third of an acre per person. He adds:

> It would be prudent to husband the fertile land available for food production and sacrifice for urban needs only that land unsuitable for factory farming. Unfortunately there is a general national indifference to the use made of land; few people consider it not only to be the most important of all national assets but are also prepared to accept the sacrifice to individual liberty necessary to make the best use of the resources available.[34]

This is a solemn statement. How much agricultural land have we left today and of what quality? From the estimate on page 153, we know that in 1970 the calculation (in millions of acres) was:

	England/Wales	Scotland/N. Ireland	United Kingdom
Agriculture	29·5	17·8	47·3

These totals are based on the annual agricultural returns, completed by farmers for the Ministry of Agriculture, and may be broken down into two main categories:

	England/Wales	Scotland/N. Ireland	United Kingdom
Crops/Pasture (Improved Farmland)	24·5	5·8	30·3
Rough Grazing (Hills/Moors)	5·0	12·0	17·0

Such returns are useful in composing the general pattern of land use throughout the country, but for determining the quality of land they can only be a general guide. It is certain however that while some allowance must be made for upgrading rough grazing, our remaining stock of fertile land is contained by the thirty million acres of crops and pasture. But it is essential to define more closely than this, in order to locate and protect the best soils upon which our very survival depends.

Classifying soils and assessing their actual and potential fertility is a complex undertaking, and a lengthy one when applied to the whole country. Moreover the business started late, and has never been properly co-ordinated between the various organisations and authorities. concerned. Soil mapping was carried out intermittently before the war mostly by the staffs of agricultural colleges. This work continues—at a national level by the Agricultural Research Council, and by a separate department in Scotland; but the detailed results (on one inch to the mile maps) are unlikely to be completed for many years yet. In a more advanced state are the maps now being prepared and published by the Agricultural Land Service of the Ministry of Agriculture. These classify land in five grades and estimate values in terms of cash output.[35] The Ordnance Survey is also revising and re-issuing its maps, but these will not contribute much to information about soil quality.

Most of our present knowledge derives from the Land Utilisation Survey organised in the 1930s by Professor Sir Dudley Stamp, who published the fruits of his work in 1948 as *The Land of Britain: Its Use and Misuse*.[36] Stamp classified land under three general headings, and sub-divided them into a total of ten sub-classifications. Omitting Northern Ireland, he assigned nearly twenty-two million acres to Good Quality, nearly fifteen million acres to Medium Quality, eighteen and a half million acres to Poor Quality, and the balance of one and a quarter million acres to urban or 'closely built over' land. Historic as it was, his survey was soon outdated and in various respects found wanting. Development Plans, produced by planning authorities under the 1947 Act, yielded more accurate information about urban and industrial land; while fresh expertise was provided by R. H. Best and J. T. Coppock,[37] who have since worked over the whole field, checking data and statistical methods. As a result they arrived at a new classification of land use, which took into account multiple and special uses which overlapped both the agricultural and urban categories. Since however these studies were generally based on the earlier work, they are likely to be replaced by the Second Land Utilisation Survey, conducted since 1960 by Miss Alice Coleman, Reader in Geography at King's College, London. This employs a more detailed classification than the Stamp survey, particularly in the mapping of industrial land use and the vegetation of uncultivated land, such as heath, mountain and moorland.[38]

The foregoing gives some idea of the difficulty of securing accurate information. While more precise land-use statistics are gradually becoming available, our knowledge is still woefully incomplete. Not until we know much more about the structure of the land itself, the composition of the soil and subsoil, its mineral and organic content, and the influence of climate and environment—shall we arrive at an accurate assessment of the potential fertility of the farmland that remains. From present incomplete knowledge it is hazarded that, out of thirty million acres of improved farmland in Britain, only about twenty-six million are suitable for intensive or semi-intensive agriculture, and that this may be reduced to as little as twenty million acres or less, even assuming that urban and other development over the next thirty years is restricted to the less valuable areas.[39]

Time is running out, and I quote from Weller again:

> Not only is the land area unknown at the present time according to terrain and fertility, but also the amount of good land, suitable for intensive food production, being lost each year. Good land is being sacrificed recklessly for a multitude of projects. This is evident from a study of the national press. Seldom is the assessment of change in land-use ever made on the relevant issues of agricultural fertility, food production and national need. This must be so, due to present ignorance. Nevertheless a rational policy for land-use can only evolve if full studies are made of the basic, national resource—the land of Britain.[40]

All this renders it impossible to accept the first assumption—that we shall retain an adequate supply of suitable land—without deep doubts. It is in fact an open question with, in my view, the dice loaded against a favourable answer.

Can the Land Respond?

The second assumption is equally doubtful—that these best soils, and some of the less valuable land as well, can be made to yield and sustain an aggregate output of up to, perhaps, twice as much as now. Why twice? First we have to allow for a population increase of *c.* twenty per cent over the next thirty years, and for a simultaneous rise in the average standard of living of all the sixty-seven or more million people who are expected to inhabit these islands by the year 2000. If you add to this the export of surplus temperate foods and other agricultural products mentioned by Weller, it would not be difficult in theory to double the demand. This calculation is made on the assumption that we continue to import those foods we cannot produce, or do not find it convenient to produce, in the same proportion to our total food requirements as now. Should however it not prove possible to import on this scale, either because we cannot find the money, or because foreign food will simply not be available—then we should have to try to make good this deficiency as well. That would be a mammoth, probably impossible, task.

Some interesting exercises are being done in this area of speculation. If you leave aside the last point—inability to import—the general attitude of agricultural experts seems to be optimistic. Weller has already been referred to, and his book deserves the fullest attention for its comprehensive grasp and wealth of information, and because it expresses the advanced thinking of orthodox agriculturalists and economists concerned with the land. Another authority, Dr G. W. Cooke F.R.S. deputy director of Rothamsted, in a paper entitled 'The Carrying Capacity of the Land in the year 2000',[41] confirms what is basically a mechanical, organisational, approach to the problem. He is not, for example, too disturbed by the loss of land, which in his view can be made good by an increase in efficiency. This will mean a greater use of fertilisers, especially nitrogen to raise the stock-carrying capacity of grassland; more pesticides and herbicides, particularly to sustain continuous cereal cropping; more prolific plant strains, and the use of chemicals to alter the way plants grow, e.g. chlorocholine chloride (C.C.C.) which shortens straw and prevents lodging in wheat; and more mechanisation to offset the decline in labour. By these and other means he foresees the possibility of providing from home resources all the temperate foods needed by the *present* level of population, although he attempts no forecast should the level rise.

It is clear that, in general, orthodox agricultural opinion envisages taking factory farming to the limit, albeit with 'adequate' precautions about pollution—e.g. the run-off of nitrates into rivers, and the use of persistent biocides, a matter which we are assured the Government already has in hand. Otherwise it is not unduly apprehensive that the continuing intensification of husbandry will do any permanent damage to the structure and fertility of the soil, or to the natural and human environment. Other scientific, as well as amateur, opinion is by no means convinced.

A SEGREGATED COUNTRYSIDE?

There are of course strongly dissident views, within the farming world as well as outside it, about factory farming and what may be termed the engineering approach to agriculture. Some of these views are outlined in the Appendix, but first I want to consider one of the consequences barely mentioned so far, should the trend to factory farming take its logical course.

This is that the countryside, particularly that of England, will be divided into two parts: one where intensive husbandry is followed, one where it is not. The division will not be total; but at one extreme the land will be largely devoid of cover, the natural features ironed out, and the landscape an arable prairie without stock, empty of everything but occasional complexes of farm buildings, a glitter of machinery crawling over the land, spotted by a handful of human beings whose business it is to work there. At the other extreme, the countryside will become an immense playground, peppered with forests, Nature reserves, reservoirs and artificial lakes, lightly grazed or otherwise farmed at a minimum level in order to prevent the land reverting to wilderness. In this part the urban visitor will have broad licence for leisure—e.g. camping, climbing, rambling, horse riding, sailing, cycling, access by car, picnicking, and (within limits) the study of wild life: alongside restricted facilities for field sports, such as shooting, fishing, and—if it is allowed to continue—hunting. Between these two extremes there will be gradations of traditional or semi-intensive farmland, upon which urban expansion will probably press the hardest, and where in consequence there will be no clear division between town and country—a kind of half-hearted suburbia, if not whole-hearted.

Multiple use—a handy phrase that easily becomes a substitute for thinking—cannot with impunity be applied to the intensive areas, i.e. the twenty million acres to which good farmland may be reduced by the end of the century, apart from a few special uses—such as woods, reservoirs and reserves—that already exist there. Access other than for agriculture is detrimental to factory farming, and if intrusion does take place, the less capable will the land be to produce the food necessary for survival. If you accept this view, it follows that most other activities—especially leisure—will have to be confined to the remainder of the countryside—to the hills, moors, and sea coast, and those intermediate areas in competition with urban and industrial development. It is here that multiple use will apply with a vengeance: and where the other primary land uses of forestry, water storage and mineral extraction will jostle for a place in company with Nature conservation, field sports and public recreation.

Forestry

The post-war target of the Forestry Commission was five million acres of properly managed woodland, or 8·8 per cent of the surface area of Great Britain: not a large proportion by Continental standards, but a considerable increase by our own. Of this total two million acres were to consist of replanted woodland in the hands of private owners, and three million acres of fresh afforestation by the Commission. These plans roused resistance. Owners felt they were being given a bad deal because grant aid was insufficient, and there seemed little prospect of saving small plantations under the new rules. Likewise the massive substitution of conifers for broad-leaved trees, which would lead to a radical alteration of the landscape, was feared and disliked by naturalists and country lovers of all kinds. By 1960 however the Commission had managed to meet some of these objections.

Following the removal of most of the uncertainties about the Dedication Scheme, the annual rate of private planting rose steadily during the 'fifties. The Forestry Commissioners did much to help this renaissance. The Approved Woodlands Scheme was started and offered owners an alternative to Dedication. Financial grants under both these schemes, and for planting in small woods, were increased from time to time in tune with rising costs. Plants were supplied and special grants for thinning, scrub clearance and poplar planting were made available, as well as capital loans for private and co-operative ventures.[42]

Tax concessions followed and private owners were encouraged to set up their own body, the Timber Growers Organisation (T.G.O.) to represent their interests. This policy of conciliation produced positive results. Already by 1958 'over a million acres of privately owned land were under active forestry management', and the acreage has risen considerably since.

The revival of private forestry had occurred without the compulsion which had seemed to be threatened in the 'forties; instead, more and more concessions had been made to woodland owners, and the 'fifties were characterised by a strengthening of co-operation between owners and the Commission's officers.[43]

Meanwhile, although the fixed target of five million acres had been relaxed, the Commission was making rapid progress with its own programme. Already by 1970 it was managing three million acres,[44] two-thirds under trees or ear-marked for planting, the remaining land being used for ancillary works or too exposed or infertile for forestry use. In all it was estimated that, allowing for a further $1\frac{1}{2}$ million acres of scrub woodland and hedgerow timber, there were about $4\frac{1}{2}$ million acres of trees in the country by that date, and that forestry was absorbing farmland at the rate of 50,000 acres a year, roughly equivalent to the annual amount taken by towns and industry. The original target of five million acres of profitable trees remains therefore a real possibility.

This is an impressive record, and a meritorious one if you accept the necessity of softwoods. Not everyone does. It will be remembered that the Forestry Commission was founded in 1919 to grow trees for commercial use. That holds good, and explains why from the very start the Commission decided to plant conifers, which earn more money than deciduous trees and bring a much quicker return. Most mature softwood goes for building timber and pulpwood, the thinnings for fencing stakes and, to a lesser extent now, for pit props. Market considerations are controversial however. Britain spends *c*. £700 million a year on imported timber, and the declared aim of the Commission is to raise the contribution of home-grown trees from ten per cent to twenty per cent *by volume* of the nation's needs. The increase *by value* sounds less impressive when, as it is claimed, the corresponding figures work out at 0·7 per cent and 1·4 per cent of the total bill, at 1970 prices. This takes no account of course of the capital value of the growing trees, of which hitherto only a small proportion have been thinned or felled as mature timber. Thus the value to the nation would rise as the woods get older and yield more marketable timber; even so it is argued by the critics that the total anticipated return on all the softwood plantations would show a loss of about sixty pounds per acre. Moreover the calculation is made on the assumption that softwood will hold its own against competitors, e.g. a synthetic substitute for cellulose. The timber trade is well aware of the threat but contends that, in view of the size of present demand and a possible world shortage of timber, softwood will be in strong demand for many years to come: indeed that it would be criminal to deny ourselves the means of meeting at least a small part of our needs.[45]

The social justification of modern forestry is equally contested. The total labour force of the Forestry Commission is a little over 7000, and those engaged in private forestry is less: in all a very small total by comparison with the 726,000 men and women engaged in farming. But it is claimed that forestry finds jobs for many other workers in the timber trade at large, and that the Commission in particular has brought employment and social benefits to remote communities, which otherwise might die out completely. A stronger case is made out for combining forestry with agriculture, as explored by the Zuckerman Report of 1957.[46] *Prima facie* there are real possibilities here, especially in mid-Wales,[47] the western highlands of Scotland, and in northern England. The pattern to be evolved ranges from areas where trees play the principal role but allow for hill grazing, to those where farming comes first with substantial planting on steep slopes, to farms where trees are primarily grown for shelter and amenity.

Existing tenancies are respected whenever farms are taken over, and plans are worked out for the best possible subdivision, or integration, of the whole property as between farming and forestry. One of many sound arrangements—which naturally vary from one district to another—is the retention of the good 'bottom' land for farming or sheep wintering, while the highest land, above the planting limit, is used for the summer pasturage of the sheep stocks. Gaps are left in the long array of plantations so that the sheep can be driven down when needed, or may find their own way to a lower level when sudden blizzards strike the hills.[48]

Integrated developments of this kind are going ahead; and while a great deal needs yet to be learned and applied in the practicalities of integration—which stands or falls by the successful combination of sheep and trees—this seems to be the proper approach to land use in much of our hill country.

None of this has saved the Forestry Commission, or the private estate and forestry syndicates, from harsh words uttered by some naturalists, who attack softwood monoculture on ecological grounds;[49] or by those who value trees mainly for their contribution to the beauty of the landscape. Criticism, it will be recalled, began in the 1930s when it was rightly directed against unimaginative planting of conifers, drawn up in parade ground order, without regard to contours or any attempt to diversify species either for ecological or for aesthetic purposes. Some change of heart has however come about since then. The Forestry Act 1951 empowered the Commission for the first time to provide for amenity in its planting plans; while in the National Parks and similar areas planning authorities can exercise limited control through the medium of Tree Preservation Orders.[50] In fact the record is better than this, for much is being accomplished by voluntary means, through consultation between interested parties, both as to the conservation of wild life and the enhancement of the landscape, though the critics would say this is no more than lip service.

Defenders of conifers claim that, while monoculture does exclude other growth and wild life when the trees are young, it is no worse in this respect than many miles of boggy moorland: further, that by varying the softwood species and by planting some hardwood (ten per cent of all new planting, according to the Forestry Commission), and once thinning has started, then the new woods do attract a variety of wild animals (some of them near-extinct, such as the pine marten), birds, rare plants and microlife. It is pointed out that the Commission now works closely with the Nature Conservancy and many of the Naturalist Trusts and societies. It has established Nature Reserves and Nature Trails, and set up Forest Centres where visitors are encouraged to come and study wild life. Stretches of water, useful for fighting forest fires, are stocked with fish and attract wildfowl. At Grizedale in Westmorland, for instance, the greylag geese have come back, accompanied by mallard and tufted duck; and there is a popular deer museum.

In such places conservation overlaps recreation, and there are already severe problems in trying to combine the two. The growing pressure of people, who at present enjoy these facilities without payment, will have to be carefully controlled, if the wild life now being nurtured is not to be driven out again or destroyed. Ironically the Forestry Commission is being enmeshed in a difficulty of its own making, though all is being done with the best intentions. The idea of Forest Parks, started in the 1930s, preceded that of National Parks; and in 1966 the policy was extended to other 'open forests', to which the public are given access. In a letter to the *Observer* of 9th August, 1970, Lord Taylor of Gryfe, Chairman of the Commission, reported that:

> ... this year some 15 million day visits will be made to our woodlands, and some one million camping nights spent in them. Also our new directory of the Commission's many and varied forest recreational facilities has been applied for by some 40,000 people since its publication in March.

The Commission is thus as deeply committed to recreation as to conservation, and it has to try to combine these commitments with its main business of timber production. The problem will worsen as the population rises, and as more people want to get out into the country for fresh air and relaxation. It follows that recreation will add to the arguments about amenity, particularly those levelled against the Commission for altering and degrading the character of the landscape. Ultimately beauty is a matter of opinion. Continental forests do not affront Continentals, but it is certainly true that England is the home of the hardwood. It would be a tragedy, should the countryside be deprived of all the oak spinneys, beech clumps, and other native trees in woods and hedgerows, which afford a natural habitat of great value and beauty, characteristic of our landscape.

This brings us back to the relationship of forestry and planning where statutory control is strictly limited. Miles writes:

> Forestry is an important land-use and the requirements of the industry have to be studied carefully within the main framework of development plans. Amenity values in the countryside depend frequently upon the presence or absence of trees, and the planner cannot do justice to this aspect of his work if there are no means of knowing about proposals for felling, replanting, or the afforestation of fresh land.[51]

The Forestry Commission has recently taken steps to train its staff in landscape husbandry, and in 1963 it appointed Sylvia Crowe as its consultant. As the author of *Forestry in the Landscape*, published in 1966,[52] she expressed ideas, already practised by Miles for some years, that are bound to have an important influence on future forestry operations: e.g. fitting planting into the landscape; the design of plantations; marrying their edges sympathetically with surrounding land; felling without leaving stark areas looking like battlefields; paying strict attention to the visual and practical aspects of car parks, picnic places and camping sites; choosing viewpoints, extending footpaths, and planning rides and roads with an eye for contour; above all wherever possible choosing species that benefit the land. Since these are the very things that critics say are absent from modern forestry, much will depend on the ability both of the Commission and of private owners to incorporate them in their future plans and actions. As most trees have to be grown for sale, there is a strong case—on technical and economic grounds—for keeping forestry out of planning; but if amenity interests become too strong, and especially if the market for timber undergoes any radical change, then forestry is likely to come under planning like most other kinds of development.

Water

Until recently water, like land, was taken for granted. Its very abundance obscured the fundamental fact that it is indispensable. Without water a human being would die within a few days. It is as vital as food and air. Only in the last 150 years has it been necessary, under the pressure of population and industrial use, to collect and store water artificially: by way of supplementing the natural pattern of rivers, lakes and pools; and only a few years ago was it agreed to treat it comprehensively as a national need, nationally controlled. Furthermore since so many interests are affected, it is almost impossible—where water is concerned—to avoid conflict.

Space for the storage of water is not an overwhelming problem when related to the total supply of land. The principal reservoirs of England and Wales occupy *c.* 38,000 acres; and it is estimated that in future no more than 15,000 acres will be needed every ten years, or some 45,000 acres by the end of the century: thus less than 100,000 acres in all, although the catchment areas contingent upon stored water are of a far greater extent. None the less this compares favourably with 50,000 acres now absorbed by building *every year.*[53]

Reservoirs rouse emotion by the nature of their impact rather than by crude requirements of space. They take land out of farming; alter the character of the landscape; influence the ecology of their surroundings in ways not yet fully understood; restrict access to many of their gathering grounds; and by concentration in hilly areas, notably in Wales, generate antagonism on the basis that they serve interests, not of the locality, but of distant users in large midland and other industrial towns.

As in other matters touching the well-being of the countryside, immediate problems are so pressing that it is difficult to select the right solution, which may be long-term and dependent on new techniques yet to be developed. At present the average daily demand for water for all purposes is in the region of 15,000 million gallons. About one-half of this total is used by the Central Electricity Generating Board (C.E.G.B.) for cooling or raising steam. Of the remainder, part is handled by the public water supply, part by independent sources, providing industry and commerce with *c.* 4000 million gallons and homes and gardens with *c.* 2000 million gallons.[54] Farming is a relatively small user, though the increase in irrigation may lead to a substantial rise in agricultural demand. The forecast is that the present total of all requirements will be doubled by the year 2000. How will this affect the countryside?

Water reaches the earth by precipitation from the atmosphere as rain, hail, sleet or snow: and so far it is not in man's power to increase the quantity *in toto*. Fortunately Britain is well supplied and, after allowing for evaporation and transpiration, there is an overall or residual abundance from natural sources. The problem therefore is not one of original supply, but of storage and distribution, and in this matter geography is unfavourable. The heaviest rainfall occurs in the emptiest regions—the hills of the north and west, where 100 inches a year are not uncommon. The heaviest demand stretches down from the north to the midlands and south-east, where annual rainfall may be as little as twenty inches. It follows that most water is stored in the hill basins, near the sources of the rivers, and has then to be transferred—sometimes for long distances—to users elsewhere.

Until the last war, water was provided piecemeal. However since the Water Act 1945, and particularly since the Water Resources Act 1963, the business has been largely rationalised. At present we have a Water Resources Board which plans water strategy and guides the twenty-nine River Authorities of England and Wales. Each of these Authorities[55] is allotted a territory in which it controls catchment and water-courses, and exercises wider powers over contingent matters, such as abstraction, land drainage pollution, and fisheries. Then there are the 400 or more Water Undertakers (public bodies or statutory companies) which actually supply and sell water to the users, and who of necessity (though not always successfully) collaborate with the River Authorities to secure the water they need.

The Water Resources Board is currently engaged in regional surveys of supply and demand. Reports have already been issued for the south-east and the north (north of a line from the Mersey to the Humber), and a third is in preparation for Wales and the midlands. It is evident from all this and other work that water can be conserved in a variety of ways, some of them by startling new techniques, as the following brief notes make clear.

Surface Reservoirs. These are of two kinds: the traditional *impounding* reservoir (e.g. Elan in mid-Wales), from which water is piped direct to the consuming area; and the *regulating* reservoir, which releases water via rivers and water-courses for abstraction lower down, when and where needed. This has the added potential of controlling floods and topping up flow during dry times. Also by using rivers as aqueducts in this way, it is possible to benefit fishing, recreation and amenity. Most modern reservoirs are of this type, including the controversial Cow Green on the Tees, and Clwyedog on the Severn.

Ground Water. This refers principally to natural underground reservoirs or aquifers, as are known to exist for example in the chalk downs at the western end of the Thames Valley. Water has long been abstracted from such sources by digging wells, but plans are now in hand to tap very large quantities by pumping, and to re-charge these natural reserves if necessary. In any event water can be transferred from one area to another by pumping from rivers, and this is already under consideration by the Essex River Authority in connection with the Great Ouse.

Tidal Barrages. Research is well advanced into the possibility of constructing barrages in Solway Firth, Morecambe Bay, the estuary of the Dee, and the Wash. These are massive measures fraught with difficulty. In the words of Sir William Goode, Chairman of the Water Resources Board:

> Barrage schemes involve a host of complicated problems more difficult to resolve than the engineering aspects. We need to know what will be the effects of changing a salt water environment into a freshwater environment; the effects on plants, on birds, on fish, especially migratory fish, on land drainage and from silting; what benefits can be expected from road communications, land reclamation, industrial development and recreation and amenity attractions. All these things have to be assessed and evaluated in order to reach a properly based conclusion.[56]

Desalination. This is an equally controversial proposal, and involves the extraction of salt from sea water by various artificial means. At present the strongest objection is one of cost—almost double, it seems that of ordinary water—but there is a firm indication that in time desalination could prove the most efficient of all methods. In theory therefore it might replace all other systems of water conservation and make virtually no demands upon land space at all.

In the immediate future however it is certain that we shall have to rely on adding to the surface storage of water; in other words, a number of new reservoirs, presumably of the regulating type, will have to be constructed. Seven new sites, for example, have been suggested for the north of England alone, all but one of which—it is claimed—could be sited outside National Parks. But is this an advantage? If factory farmland has to be segregated, then new reservoirs would where possible be confined either to playground areas or those intermediate sections of the countryside, where farming competes with other uses of the land. The former offer obvious advantages, and that is why reservoirs tend to congregate in them, particularly in National Parks. There are the geographical advantages of hills and headwaters, seclusion from urban pollution, and opportunities for public access and recreation under reasonable control. Less certain, but potentially important, are other benefits, some of them mutual. They concern hydro-electric development; agriculture (flood control and land drainage); forestry (although some water is lost by the transpiration of trees, plantations of the right diversity can help stabilise upland soils, and through foliage and undergrowth disperse the force of rain and run-off); wild life, especially water life; above all landscape husbandry which, in its widest sense, unites all the activities of man and Nature in the interests of conservation and beauty. So conceived, reservoirs play a far greater role than that of merely supplying water. They are instruments of multiple use in the most positive, beneficial, meaning; and they enhance the countryside by their presence.

If however farming in the future takes a different course, and as suggested in the Appendix turns more and more towards organic practice, the need for segregation will diminish. Farmland will then require to be integrated with, not divorced from, its environment. It will benefit from trees and other planting (though not necessarily in the forms familiar now), and from stretches of water; and so—geography apart—there may yet be sound conservational reasons for constructing and siting reservoirs in widely differing sectors of the countryside. And this may, in turn, affect any decision to develop alternative forms of water supply. Ultimately all the techniques may have to be brought into play —reservoirs, barrages, ground water schemes, desalination, and a great increase in the re-use of water by cleansing it of industrial and domestic effluent, in order to meet rising demand and benefit our health and environment. The purification of rivers, a problem high-lighted by the gross pollution following the strike of Local Authority employees in the autumn of 1970, is making people aware of larger issues: not only of cleaning water for re-use, but of recovering the human and other wastes which now run into the sea, and of returning to the land much of the fertility which intensive farming affects to discount, or claims can be replaced in other ways. Water, sewerage, and the prevention of pollution are not different subjects but one inter-related subject, which bears directly upon survival. Recently the Central Advisory Committee was re-constituted to consider this very matter. Thus fundamental thinking about water may help to alter fundamental thinking about land.

Holes in the Ground, and Desolation above it

Just as the countryside is the cradle of food, water and timber, so it is the mother of a mass of minerals that man must have. There is no getting away from this. Mining and quarrying are facts of life, and without them we should be a very poor country indeed. Coal and iron helped lay the foundations of our industrial wealth, and they are still important elements in our economy today. China clay in Cornwall is a thriving export, potash in Yorkshire may become so, and almost everywhere in Britain we draw upon abundant deposits of sand, gravel, brick clay, chalk, limestone, etc., for building, road construction, and other uses. The list is remarkably varied, and no one seriously suggests that we should fail to exploit these resources to our advantage. Extraction is a legitimate land use.

Destruction however is not, and the overriding problem today is to restore the land after extraction and other forms of industrial use, whether this took place in the past, is happening now, or is projected in the years ahead. The legacy left by the past is appalling: at least 130,000 acres in England and Wales, plus 15,000 acres in Scotland, of 'land so damaged by industrial or other development that it is incapable of beneficial use without treatment', to quote official terminology. But this is putting things at their lowest, merely minimising the scale. A more realistic estimation is of the order of 250,000 acres of industrial dereliction and blight. All this stems from the selfishness of our forebears, whose only concern was to get everything they could out of the land—whether they mined it, polluted it, built over it and then abandoned their buildings, or wasted it in other ways—on the grounds that possession gave them the right to do what they liked—and hang the consequences. Why should they be saddled with the cost of restoring dirt? This attitude, though not unknown in pre-industrial days—for example in the way Englishmen depleted their oak forests for ship building and iron smelting—became, with the march of industry, universal rather than exceptional. It was symptomatic of the new urban civilisation, and of the divorce of Nature and man; and its impact was infinitely more damaging than at any time in previous history. It is still with us today, though often wrapped up in less forceful language.

There is no need to dwell unduly upon the desolation of scrap heaps and subsidence; abandoned coal and iron mines in the midlands and north of England, in south Scotland and south Wales; potbanks in Staffordshire; brickfields round Peterborough; hill-and-dale ironstone workings in the east midlands; the sterilisation of land in the Lower Swansea Valley; oil shale 'bings' in the Scottish lowlands; the moonscape of Cornwall with its dead tin mines and current holes and hills of china clay; and literally thousands of gashes gouged out of the ground by quarrying of one sort or another all over the country. These are just the raw reminders of what *has* happened; and if that were all the situation would be almost tolerable. Indeed the statistics can be quite comforting. A quarter of a million acres of badlands represents only about 0·5 per cent of the total area of Great Britain: little more than twice the area to be absorbed by reservoirs by the year 2000. This is not serious in terms of land space, although the comparison stops there: for whereas reservoirs serve a continuing and useful purpose and may benefit the environment in ways already described, badlands benefit no one unless remedial treatment is put in hand, and this costs a great deal of money without obvious economic return. None the less one authority suggested in 1969 that about thirty million pounds would suffice to restore most of the dereliction we have inherited.[57] Nor would the sheer physical difficulties defeat the ingenuity of modern technology; indeed it is just the kind of challenge that scientists and engineers enjoy.

There is however a much more intractable problem. Dereliction grows, at a rate calculated at between 2000 and 4000 acres a year, the result of new mining and quarrying, new tipping, the pollution of chemical industry, and the frantic search to find new places to dump all the wastes of 'civilised' life today; and this is a figure arrived at after allowing for reclamation, now in hand or projected. The way things are going this is likely to be an under-estimate; and during the next thirty years—unless corrective action is taken—the present total of 250,000 acres of blighted land might well rise to half a million.

Again the problem is not so much one of technique as of will. There is already heartening evidence of what can be done, despite limited resources and the discouragements of finance. As early as the 1950s the county authority of Lancashire—one of the birth-places of the Industrial Revolution—began removing spoil heaps and dealing with pits and industrial junk in places like North Makerfield, Whalley's Basin (near Wigan), Bryn Hill and elsewhere; and the work continues although the scale of expenditure is pathetically small. In the east midlands, thanks to the Ironstone Restoration Fund[58] to which producers and the Exchequer make contributions on the basis of each ton extracted, restoration follows automatically on the heels of extraction; while the local authority has also begun to rehabilitate the awful wilderness of the past. The Central Electricity Generating Board is now engaged in a mammoth scheme to fill up 1000 acres of brick fields round Peterborough with pulverised fuel ash from its Trent Valley coal-fired power stations, and will spread valuable top soil accumulated by the sugar beet factories. The National Coal Board has a fine record of restoring its opencast sites—about 100,000 acres since 1952— though deep mining will continue to bury the land with large quantities of spoil. The N.C.B. already has 2000 tips covering 26,000 acres, while alas a further 37,000 acres are to be set aside for future tipping. A bold start has been made in the Potteries with the creation of Hanley Forest

Park; and there are a number of other examples of reclamation, most of them in the Black Country which, as the name implies, is a gigantic offence against 'England's green and pleasant land'.

The most visionary project of all is that of the Lower Swansea Valley, 1200 acres of extreme industrial dereliction, the aftermath of the high days of copper smelting, zinc, steel, tinplate and coal operations, now virtually dead. The effects were literally lethal.

The continuous envelopment of the valley in fume for nearly a hundred years resulted in almost a complete destruction of its vegetation. The indigenous sessile oak and birch woodland of Kilvey Hill and all grass and heather in the area disappeared. The topsoil, no longer held by plant roots, was washed off the valley sides leaving the subsoil to be eroded into gullies. The area became a virtual desert.[59]

Nothing effective was done until 1960, when a fresh investigation was started, thanks largely to the initiative of Robin Huws Jones, then a don at the University College of Swansea. Research and planning proceeded, leading to the publication in 1967 of a comprehensive report covering all aspects of rehabilitation—physical, economic and social. By then reclamation had already begun; and although progress is slow and much hindered, there are strong hopes that in time the ultimate end will be attained. Swansea is remarkable for the worst that the past can do, and for what the future can put right if there is the vision and determination to do it.

It is difficult not to read too much into these few successes, for they *are* few, and reclamation so far has been piecemeal and isolated. Means are inadequate because Parliament is half-hearted, which implies that our nation is still unaware and indifferent. This is all part of the legacy of *laissez-faire* and long years of conditioning to dereliction. It takes an Aberfan to rouse emotion, and even then feelings were outraged by human loss rather than by murder committed upon the land itself. Nor does the solution lie in emergency operations to prevent future trage-dies, but in thought-out and deeply felt planning, which will take account of the intrinsic value of land as a source of fertility and beauty as well as of economic use.

It needs therefore an emotional awareness on the part of the whole electorate, if the future is to be safeguarded and past mistakes made good. Emotion means money, much more than has been made available by the most recent legislation. At present, under the Industrial Develop-ment Act 1966, grant-aid of eighty-five per cent can be obtained for reclamation schemes approved by the Board of Trade, where industry can be re-developed. Outside these areas fifty per cent aid is offered by the Local Government Act of the same year. Latterly the scope of

Government aid has been increased under the Local Employment Act 1970, and in the financial year 1969–70 over three million of grant-aid was approved for reclamation. But this is still a long way off the thirty million pounds estimated for obliterating the past, or the sum needed to keep future dereliction in check.[60]

In his book, *Derelict Britain*, John Barr provides a masterly survey of the whole field of dereliction and reclamation, and I am indebted to him for much of the information in these paragraphs. He views the future in these terms:

What is required first is legislation to end the pollution of the land, along the lines of the laws we already have on pollution of the air and the water. Ideally, a Clean Land Act would create a strong national land-reclamation agency with a fixed budget, sufficiently generous and guaranteed on a long-term basis. The act's goal should be a ten-, or, at most, twenty-year campaign as determinedly organised as a military operation. Local planning authorities should prominently participate in the organisation and for a start should be required by the act accurately to survey all—not simply 'official'—dereliction within their boundaries. These surveys would include abandoned military lands and disused railways; land now being damaged by 'development' (such as waste tipping) which escapes planning control; land now in industrial use which does not have to be restored when use ceases; and land on which planning conditions imposed in the past have been inadequate or incapable of fulfilment. This means that a Clean Land Act will establish at the outset a realistic definition of derelict land.[61]

In Barr's view, planning authorities should be required to include reclamation in their development plans, and deal effectively with bad-lands according to a timed schedule. In future the best way of eliminating waste through extraction would be to apply the principle of the Ironstone Restoration Fund to all extractive industries, by levying a contribution 'per ton or cubic yard or other suitable unit' on the developers, supplemented by a statutory grant. The same principle could be adjusted to apply to any operation which destroys or pollutes land for industrial purposes, and the necessary techniques developed and paid for by the same means.

Not all reclamation can or ought to be left to commercial undertakings or statutory authorities. Voluntary effort by members of the Civic Trust, National Trust, British Trust of Conservation Volunteers,[62] County Naturalist Trusts, Inland Waterways Association, and other organisations, and by countless students, school pupils, and 'unorganised' individuals, have already proved of immense value. This is a matter not merely of spreading effort and cost, but of satisfying a human need, especially among young people, for doing something for the common good without pay, and for creating beauty in place of ugliness and degradation. Restoration is both a moral act and a work of art. These things are not to be measured solely by economic returns, although there is no doubt whatever that dereliction is inefficient and uneconomic, and that restoration earns many dividends.

*   *   *

So far in this part of the book I have been writing about the primary uses of the countryside in the past twenty-five years—farming, forestry, water management, and the extraction of minerals—and looking at some of the implications for the future. Can it be said—despite all the effort and initiative that has been expended since 1945—that the ultimate attitude has altered? Is not the paradox the same as it always has been, since the very beginning of the Industrial Revolution, that the closer man comes to the land—and there is nothing closer than tending soil and water and digging out deposits—the less value is placed upon it in terms of monetary reward? In other words 'land' work is still the worst paid, and often the least regarded. If this is true of the primary occupations, what of other rural employments? Or does it mean that country life—if the term is to retain any recognisable sense—will have to be detached from commerce altogether? But, first, a brief glance into the immediate past.

LIFE IN THE COUNTRYSIDE

I was born in Kent and spent my early childhood in Berkshire, at Greenham just outside Newbury. Greenham was deep country then. My father was away in the army in France, and almost my earliest recollection was looking out of the window at a fall of snow in the winter of 1916–17 soon after the ghastly battle of the Somme had ground half a million men into the grave. I knew little of that of course. Nor did anyone else in Greenham, unless it was a soldier home on leave or a family mourning their dead. Father came back occasionally. I remember sleeping in his dressing-room when he slept with my mother. I remember the smelly margarine at table, sago pudding and endless stewed apple. And I remember Armistice Day on 11th November, 1918, when half a platoon marched up from Newbury and presented arms outside Greenham school. Our house was just opposite, across the village green. In 1919, when I was six, father was posted to Constantinople to command an infantry battalion in the Occupation Force, and he took my mother with him. I was adopted for a time by the Vicar of Greenham and his family, who lived in a neo-Gothic barn of a house, right beside the Common. It was a gloomy place, laurels outside, damp darkness within. A heavy Morris wallpaper lined the high hall that reeked of a slow-burning stove in winter. The study smelled too, and we inhaled the odour of old books and clotted pipes as we kneeled at hard chairs with the servants at family prayers.

The Reverend J. N. Blagden—Mr Blagden or 'Blags' to my parents —was a parson of the old sort. A good man, formidable through deafness, so that his wife and two daughters had to shout to make him hear. My voice was less penetrating and I was inclined to dream. But Blags was a kindly man, devoted to his calling. Those were the days when the parson was priest, welfare officer, and father figure, all in one. There was no real squire, though a rich family lived in the big house and gave garden fêtes now and then. In a dying order of country life, Blags served his scattered parish with regularity, realism and affection. Visiting was the secret of his success. Every afternoon he mounted his bicycle (kept in the porch)—literally mounted by placing his left foot on the step, free-wheeled and then humped on to the saddle—and set off to see old Mrs Rawlings at the Lodge, or a girl in trouble at Berry's Bank, or down Pyle Hill to comfort any number of poverty-stricken arthritics in the semi-slums at Stroud Green. He baptised, confirmed, married and buried almost every man, woman and child for miles round—even the Methodists were friends—and on Sundays, when the ugly church overlooking the race-course was packed in strict hierarchical order with the poor at the back, he recited the service in a voice of resounding authority.

Blags was the kind of man who was able to hold a community together, long past the time when new forces were busily breaking up the foundations of village life. The war accelerated what had been begun before 1914, and we wrongly assumed that the miracles of wartime would vanish with the return of peace—the monoplane we had gaped at in 1918, and the tank that had trundled over the heather towards the firing butts and trenches near Brimpton. As a child I saw the tail-end of a way of life still in working order; but within a few years everything was disintegrating. A motor bus replaced the carrier's cart in the run to Kingsclere, and private cars and vans at forty miles an hour churned up the dust in the long straight stretch towards the golf course. Even Mrs Blagden was driving a car by 1925, though never Blags. The Common, the haunt of snakes and butterflies, roving gypsies and the occasional squatter, became ever more accessible and popular for Sunday walks and picnics; and in the Second World War it was converted into an airfield for American bombers. Heaven knows what has happened to the Common now. I haven't been back to look and I don't want to know. But I do know that inevitably Greenham has become a suburb of Newbury, and that my nostalgic memories are as unproductive as Canute's attempt to stem the tide. He knew, of course, as well as I do, the uselessness of demonstration without conviction.

The rape of the countryside between the wars was due as much to the loss of faith in the old order as to enthusiasm for the new. There *was* no

Converted railway track—the Tissington Trail

LEISURE USE OF LAND

Converted gravel pits—the Cotswold Water Park

Goyt Valley, before . . .

LEISURE USE OF LAND

. . . and after traffic control

new order, only abandonment of the old. The traditions of the land and the tenacity of village institutions survived as long as they did, because of the length and depth of their roots. You cannot totally eradicate a thousand years of habits and beliefs in a decade, unless you introduce a substitute of overwhelming power and purpose. Urban growth between the wars was vigorous but aimless, and it benefited only part of the population. Like a self-sown forest, it abandoned the old stumps and let the young plants take root where they could. There was no philosophy of existence in settlements of 'spec' or Council housing. Homes were spawned wherever people drifted; and drift depended upon the whim of private enterprise, which made its own rules and followed its own nose. It was not until the Second World War gave us the breathing space to look back at the mess we had created, and the desire to look forward to something better, that the nation began to formulate plans for the future. Then came the chance to give the countryside a new start—to find work for people living on the land, and to give them sound reasons for staying there.

Work as the Foundation
This was no easy matter for as I have explained the land has been steadily losing its power to employ. The more efficient its use, the fewer jobs it has to offer: efficiency measured economically, for that is still the yardstick however we trim it to social and other needs. The result is that the number of people now employed, as it were, first-hand on the land—which means all the jobs that can conceivably be defined as primary occupations[63]—is less than one million: or barely five per cent of the total of employed persons in the U.K., and the figure is declining. This is the logic of industrialisation, which either mechanises land work to the point of extinction, or by-passes it: so that, unless a new or counter-revolution revises our values—and this may happen through the threat of starvation or the dangerous depletion of the sources of power, such as gas and oil—we cannot hope to expand primary employment on the land; at best we may be able to stabilise it at something less than the present level.

The need therefore to create new jobs in the countryside has become more necessary than ever: a fact long recognised and advocated by experts such as the late Dr C. S. Orwin, head of the Oxford Institute of Agricultural Economics, and other investigators, and by the Elmhirsts who have shown what can be done at Dartington. I have pointed out earlier in this book that the Industrial Revolution not only changed the face of farming, but by displacing many of the alternative employments in the countryside—mainly crafts and cottage industries—it undermined the economic base upon which rural society rested. These foundations have never been replaced. Although small industries and workshops never vanished from the land—never indeed in the semi-countryside

ᴏ

within the periphery of industrial regions—their loss in the countryside proper was not made good; and this helped more than anything to upset the balance and diversity of country life as it used to be.

It is true that other forms of secondary employment have been introduced into many villages in the course of time; but this has been a haphazard development, dependent often upon chance colonisation by urban residents and commuters, or upon the seasonal vagaries of the holiday trade. Yet in essence this is the right answer if ways can be found to combine what might be called the peripatetic use of villages with the renewal of indigenous employments that serve contemporary needs. No community can prosper if it is regarded either as a place to get out to, or as one to get away from. The idea of self-sufficiency in the countryside has gone for ever, and the ideal is neither desirable nor attainable. But what can be done is to provide a core of permanent employment in a rural area—a group of villages and hamlets—where regular jobs are available for at least half the working population within a radius of five to ten[64] miles of their homes. Paradoxically the improvement in communications, which formerly helped to empty the countryside, is now well on the way to reversing the process. Ownership of cars and motor cycles is fast replacing the use of buses and trains for local transport, while the construction of motorways and the widening of major roads are aiding the decentralisation of industry. Congestion on the roads, as in the streets, is a problem not so much of the technique of communication, as of the pressure of population upon the available space, a complex conundrum of frightening proportions, evident in almost every aspect of our society today, and which—unless controlled at source—will overwhelm any attempt to solve it by treating its surface symptoms. Yet these same difficulties do not invalidate the fact that, if used aright, better communications and increased mobility can help renew country life, and not suffocate it.

What kind of work can be introduced into the countryside to give it new life? Rural industry is a convenient title and it will serve, but the term is misleading. It has misled some people into thinking that industry in the countryside has to be *rural* in character. But what does *rural* mean? Use of local raw materials? Handicrafts? A minimum of machinery and repetitive processes? Is a country garage servicing tractors and cars less rural than a sawyard? Dartington has demonstrated—and there is plenty of evidence from small-scale industries in practically every county—that size is a critical factor, in association with location and the nature of the trade.[65] This is confirmed by the experience of the Rural Industries Bureau (R.I.B.) which, since 1968, has significantly been renamed and reshaped as the Council for Small Industries in Rural Areas (CoSIRA).

The Rural Industries Bureau was originally founded to salve and re-animate the traditional crafts of the countryside—thatching, blacksmithing, saddlery, pottery, woodworking, *et al.*—and there is no doubt that, but for the technical, financial and other services of the R.I.B., some of these occupations would have died out. Their support and continuing re-alignment to modern markets remain an important part of CoSIRA's work; but in aggregate their number is small, and changing circumstances have altered activities as well as name. Although CoSIRA restricts itself to helping firms employing not more than twenty skilled operatives and ancillary staff, it now offers assistance to a remarkably wide range of manufacturing and servicing enterprises, including engineering, textiles, plastics, construction and a multitude of repair shops. The volume and variety of its work show that a surprising number of trades are viable in small units, whether for technical or managerial reasons. Good communications can offset distance from markets or sources of supply, while location in a village offers two-way advantages—jobs for locals (if only for the unskilled and semi-skilled, but including part-time work for women), and homes close by in pleasant surroundings.

A number of enterprises have survived or sprung up in the countryside—just too large or otherwise beyond the scope of CoSIRA—but which also qualify as 'rural'. These may be independent units or offshoots of larger firms, most of them 'light industry'. Some are aided by Government agencies, notably those induced to settle in mid-Wales or the highlands and islands of Scotland where new jobs are urgently needed to halt depopulation; or they have been persuaded by the Board of Trade and local authorities to go to selected country towns, where labour and housing are available and facilities for expansion exist. This is sound policy: namely to develop a small town or large village as a centre both for employment and for local administration and higher education. But the pattern is uneven. Technical objections apart, not every entrepreneur finds the countryside attractive for work, nor out of conservatism do all countrymen want light industry, although in the same breath they may complain at the lack of opportunities. Yet for reasons of scale and diversity, a range of small industries offer the best hope of rural revival. They are more certain of providing that core of permanent employment upon which other trades, shops and services depend, and which—if sufficient in number—impart that vital sense of identity so often absent in what passes for country life today.[66]

Exceptionally, a large-scale industry will move into the open countryside. If this happens, it is due to overriding economic or technical reasons, as in the case of the oil refineries at Fawley and Milford Haven, or the new electricity generating stations. Although under planning such invasions are infinitely better controlled than in the past, and close attention is paid to amenity so far as this is compatible with the sheer scale of development, no casuistry can obscure the consequences. In short, the impact will be that of imposing a town upon virgin territory, or at least of transforming local towns and settlements in size and character, and generally urbanising that part of the countryside. This may be—and obviously often is—necessary, and it has to be accepted; but it is an extension of town life, not a development of country life, and in no sense a contribution to solving the problems of rural society. This is a plain fact, and it is dishonest to try and explain it away in other terms.[67]

The Village as an Idea

There is no blinking the fact that, in the countryside as in the town, remunerative work is still the source of social vitality, and that it is economic weakness that has undermined rural life over the past hundred years. It has hardened the conviction that there are no jobs or social opportunities comparable with those in the town. Unless he has land or money or some kind of privileged employment, the ordinary countryman is a nice chap but, in truth, a second-class citizen. If not, why is he content to bury himself in the bush and earn a good deal less than the rest of us, who toil away in the town, chasing buses and undergrounds, but enjoying all the pleasures of being at the centre of things? Professionally it is 'square' to talk of 'village life'. People pity or patronise you if you do so, or simply do not take you seriously. Planners and sociologists insist in their obscure jargon that the phrase means nothing any more, and that you are out of touch if you use it.

Who is out of touch? To condemn the countryside because, having been deprived of its power to offer employment and opportunities for better living, it then loses its vitality and, for example, fails to hold its young people who stream into the towns for higher wages and bright lights, is begging the question in a big way. Let us not be squeamish with comparisons. During the last war, as a matter of deliberate policy, the Nazis starved and dehumanised their Russian prisoners to the extent that some of them practised cannibalism. 'That,' said the official spokesman, 'proves they are sub-human (*Untermenschen*). They do not deserve civilised treatment.'

Village life survives—infinite gradations of it—because wherever people congregate there must be a community of a kind. Naturally appearances have changed profoundly. The old social hierarchy has vanished, and with it the sense of in-bred exclusiveness common to older country-people. The most striking changes derive from the advent of the motor car, the motor cycle and the lorry; from the spread of sophisticated education and entertainment; from the immediacy of information about the world at large through the Press, telecommunications, and the popularity of travel; and from the acceptance of urban forms and values, whether it be in local government[68] or in any other aspect of everyday business and administration. And yet a core of country character remains. Where, by proximity or ease of access, the

Pony trekking

LEISURE USE OF LAND

Returning to kennel

Tactical tree planting against the wind

LAND USE IN THE UPLANDS

Reservoir construction

town presses the hardest, there naturally you find urban influence dominant and undigested; and very large sectors of the English country-side are now conditioned in this way, since they lie within commuter or city regions. Even so here, but even more in the remoter places, the residues of rural civilisation are not merely discernible but retain force for the future: evident in the continuity of families whose names you find on the latest electoral register as on the tombstones; but evident too in the names of new people who have come to the neighbourhood to teach, to do business, or to retire, but who play a positive part in society as well—by serving on a council or a committee, joining the Women's Institute, supporting church or chapel, attending a class at the secondary school turned further education college in the evening, or simply by patronising the pub. Such people are seeking a quality in living so often absent in the town—a feeling of permanence, some element of solitude and self-reliance, contact with soil and green fields, and the chance to live as a person at your own pace—in a word, a sense of identity.

If this is escape, then clearly escapism has become necessary as an antidote to the pressures of life elsewhere. It is not therefore a term of opprobrium, except as a comment upon the nature of urbanised existence. We cannot of course all live in villages, there are too many of us. Nor ultimately can we survive by escaping. But we can salve what country life has to offer and apply the lessons to the future—to create in our conurbations (as attempted in the Garden Cities and New Towns) that quality we now seek by taking refuge in the country.

There is therefore a place for the village—I use the word in the abstract as well as in the concrete—economically, socially, emotionally; and a very large place in its influence upon our thinking about life itself. Integration—in what manner and how successfully we combine country and town beneath the burden of a top-heavy population—is the cause-way to salvation. Unless we begin to build that with the materials of amenity, there will be no future. Earlier I defined amenity as 'the enhancement of life through the agency of environment and by the creative use of that environment', and 'in its essence amenity is not a haven, but a continuous and comprehensive state, inherent in the quality of living'. I return to these definitions in the light of two subjects which contribute to, and sometimes conflict with, the concept of amenity as applied to the countryside. These are leisure and Nature conservation.

*   *   *

The literature of leisure, as of Nature conservation, is immense, and it proliferates week by week. Since both subjects range so far in scope, and delve so deeply into the essentials of existence, they demand the attention of numerous experts within a variety of disciplines. This is evident not only in the volume and diversity of all that is being published and broadcast, but also in the multiplication of societies and groups generally concerned with the environment, and in the frequency of debates and meetings held up and down the country, consolidated at intervals by the 'Countryside in 1970' conferences, of which the latest took place in October of that year. My comments therefore are strictly limited in scope, and bear upon attitudes rather than events.

Leisure

The surge into the countryside for recreation is a post-war phenomenon of explosive force; and it will gather momentum in the years ahead with rising incomes, a shorter working week, and longer annual holidays with pay. For most townsmen the countryside is still primarily a playground, and they are coming to regard access to it as a matter of right. Since the reins and resources of government rest largely in their hands, there is little doubt that they will get what they want.

Carefully handled, this phenomenon can be turned, in part, to good account in the countryside: since in round terms the best opportunities for leisure occur where farming pays worst, viz., on the hills and moors and along parts of the coast. Tourism is already an important industry, and a rural region such as the south-west leans heavily upon it, despite its seasonal nature and the brevity of the season. It is for these reasons however that tourism—and open-air recreation generally—is difficult to absorb into the ordinary pattern of country life. Unlike rural industry or forestry or farming, it does not provide regular or permanent employment, except for a few. Out of season many hotels, restaurants and boarding houses in, for example, a seaside town are shut, and the place goes dead. In season it will be overwhelmed with visitors, and there will be a large intake of temporary workers. This is hardly a basis for rural revival. Indeed it is the custom of farmers and their wives, and other country-people who minister to the holiday trade, to look on the summer months as a period of additional—almost fortuitous—activity and income, rather like drilling and harvesting an extra cash crop. If it comes off, well and good; if not, they are not defeated.

But this attitude is already altering, for two reasons. One is the changing pattern of leisure, which makes light of seasons and so tends to iron out periodicity. For example, in the short term, it may take the form of a day or weekend trip during a fine winter spell. Or—in the case of a middle-class family with even a moderate income—it may be the acquisition of a second home, to which parents and children will go every available weekend as well as for holidays. The husband will leave his wife and offspring there for weeks at a time, while he works from a *pied-à-terre* in town. All this is made possible by car ownership and the new motorways; and the more road construction, the farther the country home can be from the town one; indeed the role of home may at some stage be reversed. Obviously a trend of this kind will have a profound effect upon some kinds of country business which, while just able to keep open for local trade in the winter, yet depend on the summer for their profitability. Continuous leisure or extended commuting—the boundary is hard to determine—could contribute materially to the economics of a rural region, mainly of villages and small towns.

The other reason is related to the hard fact that hill and marginal farming, especially on small-size farms, is becoming ever less remunerative, so that visitors' money is already an important, if not indispensable, element of income. So much so that in some instances farming is being pursued principally to keep the land clean and in good heart, and moorland grazed to prevent deterioration into wilderness; otherwise the countryside will fail to attract. The implications are as important for conservation as for leisure. Keeping fields fit for purposes other than commercial husbandry is a revolutionary idea in this country, though not abroad, and it sounds like prostitution to some countrymen. What is land for, they ask? Well, the reality will not be unpalatable, if it is a choice between having to do that or getting out. Apart from earning money by taking visitors into his home, or charging them for camping or picnicking or riding his horses, a farmer may qualify to benefit—as I shall explain—from the invisible advantages of amenity use. In return for abiding by traditional farm practice, and for allowing public access to his land, he will receive payment—probably in the form of an annual rent and related to the difference in income between customary and intensive husbandry.[69] This will be for the best in the long run, for traditional methods are intrinsically conservational, producing a natural ground cover protective to thin soil and exposed slopes, which is both attractive to wild life and the human eye, especially if aided by tree planting. Such should be the case in a great deal of playground territory, i.e. in National Parks and other kinds of protected land, where the exploitive incentives of farming, and to some extent of forestry, will have to be curbed and conditioned in the interests of amenity. In such instances the requirements of leisure and conservation will coincide.

I was involved first-hand in this controversy when it first blew up over Exmoor a few years ago, and when we found that over a period of eight years, 1957–65, open wild land—hill farmed and the very essence of Exmoor—was vanishing before plough and fence at an average rate of over 1000 acres a year. It fell to me as Chairman of the Exmoor Society (as also to my predecessors John Coleman-Cooke and John Goodland, and to my successor, S. H. Burton) to play a prominent part in this business willy-nilly. However what began as a hot dispute between conservationists, who argued for ecology and beauty, and farmers and landowners, who stood by their rights to make the most out of their land, sobered down into a civilised dialogue between the National Park Authority (which adopted the main points of the Society's case) and representatives of the N.F.U. and C.L.A. The magic solvent was provided by a fact-finding exercise: namely, a survey of the vegetation of Exmoor, conducted by Geoffrey Sinclair, who recorded his findings on a Land-Use Map, which the Society then made public, in association with a pamphlet, *Can Exmoor Survive?*, written by Sinclair and myself.[70] In this we published the statistics of acreage and types of ground cover as revealed by the map, summarised the main points of the controversy, and argued the case for conservational husbandry and recreational use in the vulnerable areas. Once facts had replaced feelings as the basis of discussion, solid progress was made towards relating the claims of amenity to those of occupation and ownership. Although these areas have yet to be finally fixed, agreement is very near (1971); and—most important—the crisis persuaded the Government of the day to introduce certain sections into the Countryside Act 1968, by which machinery is now available to safeguard similar types of land. Obviously this is a matter of national interest.

Leisure and conservation do not often make a comfortable marriage however. Their association can be destructive, and amenity suffers in consequence. In his historic study, first published in 1965, Michael Dower wrote:

> Three great waves have broken across the face of Britain since 1800. First, the sudden growth of dark industrial towns. Second, the thrusting movement along far-flung railways. Third, the sprawl of car-based suburbs. Now we see, under the guise of a modest word, the surge of a fourth wave which could be more powerful than all the others. The modest word is *leisure*.[71]

Assessment of leisure by the end of the century allows for a basic working week of thirty hours, the circulation of thirty million cars, and twelve million people over retirement age out of a total population of nearly seventy million. What this means for the countryside can barely be imagined when, after a weekend of motoring in the summer or a holiday on the coast, one sees what is happening now: traffic congestion, fouling of lay-bys, erosion of beaches and beauty spots, litter by the ton. All this will be enormously magnified. The mind reels; yet in itself the demand for open air, for active sports and leisurely pastimes in pleasant country, or simple family excursions, cannot be denied. It would be impossible, as well as morally wrong, to try to restrict these opportunities to those few who happen to have money or own large properties, where they can barricade themselves in to shoot pheasants or fish a well-stocked lake. Until the pressure of people is relaxed, and some solution found permanently to relate the size of the population to the capacity of our country, we have—through organisation—to contain leisure; and by containment I mean, not only accommodating sheer numbers of human beings and their equipment, but controlling their

impact so that the countryside itself—and all that is meant by amenity—
is not destroyed in the process. I attempt a brief survey of this problem
in the following paragraphs.

The Impact of Leisure

Broadly the use of land for leisure falls into two main categories. One is
the enjoyment of the indigenous pleasures of the countryside. The other
is the growth of essentially urban recreations in a rural setting. Many of
these activities overlap each other, and almost all bear the imprint of
mass requirements.

In the first category you find field sports such as shooting, fishing and
hunting, each of which has certain in-built limitations due to cost, the
operation of rights and licensing, and the amount of game available.
Shooting is expensive. You have to be licensed, guns and cartridges cost
a lot of money, and if you are a townsman you will probably belong to
a syndicate and pay heavily to do so. Fishing is less costly; none the less
you have to have a licence and pay for your water—and although coarse
fishing for roach, perch, pike, etc., has wider scope and is much more
popular than game fishing for salmon and trout, the number of anglers
is automatically limited by the stock of fish available in rivers and still
waters. Hunting, once the preserve of the wealthy, is no longer so. No
licence is required. Hiring a horse and paying a day's fee or 'cap' is not
prohibitive; but apart from that there is no need to ride to enjoy hunting. Very many people follow the hounds on foot or in cars: to the
extent that in some districts hunting is endangered by over-popularity.
Its followers far outnumber those who actively oppose the sport on
moral grounds, and as yet there seems no lack of foxes, deer or hares to
chase.

It is a simple step from field sports to the less 'sporting' pleasures of
riding or pony trekking, rambling on foot or by bicycle, caving, sea
cliff or rock climbing, camping, etc.; gardening, a national ploy served
by a huge industry, which for many people is the only way of making
contact with Nature; and thence to bird watching, plant recording, and
the whole range of Nature observation—whether practised as a personal
hobby or as a group exercise, such as constructing and enjoying a
Nature trail. All such activities—the majority already have a mass
following and the horizon is nowhere in sight—may be described as
'indigenous' in that in some degree each is allied to the life of the land.
And it is reasonable to regard the traditional amusements of village life
in the same light, however sophisticated they may appear now. Cricket,
football, fêtes, gymkhanas—all spring from the background of custom
and seasonal celebration, characteristic of small communities in the
countryside.

In the second category—the division is bound to be arbitrary—you
find a variety of recreations, all more or less urban. That is, they have

little or no intrinsic connection with country life; they involve a high degree of organisation and investment; their use of space may be intensive or extensive—but essentially they bring people and equipment into the countryside in such a way and on such a scale as to impose the town upon it. One obvious example is the addiction to water sports—bathing, rowing, sailing, canoeing, power boating, water skiing, etc.— whether at the seaside or on inland waters. Canal cruising, though hardly a water sport, is another form of water recreation greatly gaining in popularity. In general the cost of equipment, availability of accommodation, and means of travel, are limiting factors, but not yet to the extent of deterring a vast and growing number of enthusiasts for all such ploys. Other examples of active recreations within this general category include motor sports, gliding, winter skiing, golf, and all the team games and amusements associated with holiday and sports centres. Equally important is the passive enjoyment of the countryside by car or coach. It might be a party trip touring the highlands, with visits to stately homes and public gardens; or a caravan holiday pulling in to farmers' fields or centred on official sites; or simply a family outing on a Sunday afternoon to the nearest common or open space, where you can draw off the road, play ball with the children, and turn on the transistor.

Planners believe they know the kinds of recreation that people want in the countryside; they have some idea of the scale of demand; but there is still much to be learned about the amount and type of land needed, and what proportion can be put to multiple use. Intensity is a useful starting-point. In one sense the more intensive the use, the less disruption is caused to the countryside, although the associated problems of traffic and accommodation may be fierce, and actual physical erosion may occur on the site. At Northam Burrows, for example on the north coast of Devon, people and cars have so churned up the sand and the dunes, that wind and water are busily completing the work of destruction. However wherever crowds congregate control becomes more clear cut, and it is often possible to provide alternative amusements and activities. The seaside is especially favourable for spreading the load in this way. Inland centres, such as Woburn and Longleat play a similar role: each a stately home combining the functions of a museum, picture gallery, pleasure park, picnic site, 'lion reserve', and much else.

But there are limits to absorption in any one place, and it is necessary to multiply the number and vary the character of such 'honeypots' all over the country. One solution is the 'country park', introduced by the Countryside Act 1968: an area of land (or land and water), not smaller than twenty-five acres in extent, designed to offer opportunities for leisure in the open air, and located within easy distance of a town. Its purpose is to 'mop up' many people who would normally add to the congestion of the roads in their search for a suitable spot, protect farmers' fields from casual and careless use, and ease the pressure on remoter places. Official picnic sites serve a comparable purpose for travellers.

The same basic idea is expressed in certain regional parks, now being planned or constructed. A well-known example is that of the Lea Valley, formally constituted in January 1967, twenty-three miles in length and 10,000 acres in extent, running from rural Hertfordshire right into London. This is a long rasher of riverside land, some of it under horticulture, some of it pleasant though unremarkable farm and woodland, but spotted with reservoirs, sewage plants, and industrial development, and damaged by water pollution, gravel diggings, and other forms of dereliction. The plan is to create a multi-purpose recreational area by cleaning up the waterways, controlling industrial intrusion, softening the scars, and providing a variety of recreations including playing fields and sports centres, golf courses and facilities for swimming, fishing, rowing, riding and walking. Lea Valley is large and a model of its kind, since it is intended to serve the northern environs of London; but the same principle applies to other smaller projects in different parts of the country, especially where industrial dereliction and disuse can be turned to good recreational account. Another interesting project is the Cotswold Water Park which, over a period of years, will reclaim extensive gravel excavation for the pleasure of water sportsmen and naturalists between Cirencester and Swindon, serving a future population of some two millions within a radius of twenty-five miles.

Recreation varies of course both in intensity and kind. At the opposite extreme to Blackpool seafront or even the Lea Valley, the ecological and scenic qualities of an area of great landscape beauty and natural importance have to take precedence over public enjoyment. Some protection may be afforded by the sheer size of the place—though individual beauty spots or reserves are always vulnerable—and remoteness may also act as a deterrent. Automatic safeguards of this nature are however bound to decline in efficacy, due to increasing mobility and the rise of the number of families with cars. The ten National Parks, the A.O.N.B.s and other special areas, daily demonstrate the difficulties of satisfying both protection and use. Building and industrial development apart, the facts of the situation point inevitably to compromise. From the start National Parks have had to serve several purposes—conservation of beauty and wild life, public access and enjoyment, and (because most of the land is privately owned) the encouragement of farming, forestry and other local employments. Several Parks too have been invaded by State agencies for the purposes of power stations, reservoirs and defence. There is a constant struggle to fit everything in, and to make each part fit without damaging the whole. This requires the combined efforts of statutory and voluntary organisations, working in close collaboration. So far as leisure is concerned, one can point to heartening examples of enterprise, small as they may be in relation to the problem overall. Such are, selectively, the launching of Enterprise Neptune by the National Trust to save the coast; the conversion of disused railway lines in the Peak, the Wirral, Exmoor (the proposed Greenway), and other districts for walking, riding and Nature study; the protection of the Goyt Valley in Derbyshire from cars; the revival of a derelict port at Morwellham in south Devon as a centre for recreation, the study of wild life and industrial archaeology; the restoration of certain canals for cruising; and the registration of the remaining common lands for recreation among other uses, involving perhaps one million acres.

These are but samples—though notable ones—of public and private enterprise in the field of recreation: additional to the regular provision made in National Parks, State Forests, Nature Reserves and other places to cater positively for those who seek their leisure in the country-side. Impressive as this list may seem, in fact the sum of effort is pathetically small when related to the total impact that leisure is already making—and has yet to make—upon our countryside. Despite increased powers, the Countryside Commission spent barely more than one million pounds in 1970–1 on grant-aid and other tasks; and since it is ultimately finance that calls the tune, whoever spends it, this is an indication of how far we have to go. Properly provided, leisure costs a great deal of money; it will cost a great deal more in terms of conflict and disruption, if skimped.

Nature Conservation

Not all open-air activities can be channelled into designated areas. Even allowing for the full development of parks and picnic sites and 'honey-pots' of every sort, and for the most imaginative and extensive reclamation of derelict land for recreational use—a process that in any event will take many years to work out—it is unlikely that the leisure impulse of a whole nation can be so totally directed and confined.

A partial solution is offered by the services of Nature conservation: specifically by reserves and similar areas, whether under the aegis of the Nature Conservancy,[72] R.S.P.B., S.P.N.R., county trusts, or other naturalist organisations. The primary purpose of these places is not of course public enjoyment, which is potentially harmful, but the protection of wild life and, by extension, the responsible management of natural resources as a whole.[73] None the less leisure imposes multiple use upon conservation, as it does upon farming and forestry in National Parks and State Forests; and it is due to positive measures, e.g. information centres, observation hides, Nature trails, etc., that these vulnerable sites are in fact being turned to public advantage, i.e. for recreation. Moreover by encouraging voluntary effort, especially among young people, to help construct and maintain them, much is being done to educate the human attitude to Nature.

In the final analysis however it amounts yet again to 'enjoyment by

Milton Abbey, Dorset

IN STEP

Angling, Ullswater

The Soil Association, Suffolk

RURAL REHABILITATION

Dartington Hall, Devon

control'—which might possibly be justified if the number of reserves[74] and other protected sites, when added to the playground areas proper, were sufficient to satisfy the demand; but they are not. Inevitably pressure will continue to build up against the ordinary countryside— undesignated and unprotected for any purpose but farming—and this bears both upon access for leisure and upon the true role of conservation which, as I have made clear, range in their full significance far beyond the confines of this book. Control can however be extended even here and become acceptable, if applied to the whole country and be seen to work.

At present, to get out into familiar fields and woods requires either permission from the owner, or more practically many more footpaths and bridlepaths, well used and properly defined, than we have now. The 1949 Act—and subsequent legislation—recognised the need, but the business of mapping and making rights-of-way effective has been long drawn-out and is still incomplete. Even now there are several counties where it is almost impossible to walk or ride in the open countryside as of right; and had it not been for the watchful persistence of the Ramblers Association, the Commons Society and its affiliated bodies, and much private initiative, the situation would be much worse than it is.[75] Some populated districts—the Chilterns for instance—are exemplary in the provision of rights-of-way; likewise certain National Parks, A.O.N.B.s, and other areas where the pressure of people is producing results. Waymarking and signposting, urban though they seem to some, are necessary aids both to protect the farmer and to guide the user; and they are bound to become general practice, for it is the townsman who walks and rides for pleasure nowadays and so needs to be directed, whereas the countryman—if he moves off his own land—does so for another purpose and usually takes his car. Eventually no doubt we shall have an adequate rights-of-way system over the whole country—a complex of local and long-distance routes—and this will certainly open up far more country than could ever be done by restriction to playground areas and Nature reserves.

The problem of misuse of the countryside by townspeople—litter, damage to property, and the rest—serious as it seems, is superficial when compared to the crimes now being committed by pollution against air, land and water. Education of schoolchildren, the patient propaganda of the Country Code, all the admirable efforts of the Countryside Commission,[76] the National Park authorities, N.E.R.C., CoEnCo,[77] and all the environmental organisations, will be to no avail, so long as conservation is regarded simply as an aspect of behaviour, like putting on party manners. Conservation is not a gimmick, and it concerns country-people just as much as visitors from the town. This is where rights-of-way may well play a vital role in revealing to the townsman what is really happening to the land.

Freer access will bring many more people up against the territory of intensive husbandry, where further progress will be barred: not because an innocent walker might disturb a habitat, but because Nature as well as man must be kept out. For factory farmers too much is at stake to allow casual intrusion by the public, which is still unaware of the lengths to which man will go to dominate the forces of Nature and extract the utmost out of the land. There is some comfort in the watch being kept on the toxicity and persistence of some pesticides, and in the recent ban placed upon specific organo-chlorines, but this is only the tip of the trouble. It is not generally realised that, through effluent disposal and fertiliser run-off, agriculture can be as serious a source of pollution as industry; and that, if you accept only some of the arguments deployed in the Appendix, modern farm practice is playing fast and loose with soil fertility and plant and animal health, and thereby human health as well.

However farm opinion is becoming increasingly aware of conservational criticism. In an atmosphere of good will and good intentions, a conference took place at Silsoe in Bedfordshire in July 1969 at which an exercise was carried out to see what practical concessions a farm could make to conservation, while remaining a viable and profitable concern. The results have been published in a booklet, *Farming and Wildlife*, edited by Derek Barber, and published in 1970 by R.S.P.B.: together with a free leaflet summarising the conclusions. It would be ungenerous to minimise the importance of this undertaking, for Silsoe may become an historic event in the annals of agriculture, and it has already provoked further exercises. Moreover it undoubtedly influenced a thoughtful, perhaps too comforting, statement by Mr Cledwyn Hughes, Minister of Agriculture, in January 1970—since confirmed by his Conservative successor—promising Government support for co-operative action between farmers and naturalists. Yet the Silsoe conclusions were modest indeed: mainly an exhortation to farmers to save certain hedges and trees, spare an awkward corner in a field, and leave the odd pond and wet place intact, as habitats for wild life—especially for game which through sporting rights and rents could yield a financial return.

So far—even if for so short a distance—so good; and better still that we now have a Minister of Cabinet rank, responsible for environmental problems as a whole. Yet for the countryside the real question remains unanswered—that conservation cannot be imposed from the outside. Like art, it is not an extra to life but an inner part of it, an attitude rather than an additive. If man is to survive as a species, conservation begins with the land upon which he stands and from which he lives. This is the 'organic answer', which Robert Waller outlines in the Appendix. Conservation is survival.

Postscript

Anyone who writes a topical book engages in a race with events; and no race is swifter or more deadly than the one now being run by humanity in its sprint for survival. The purpose of it all—the prize, if you like—is not the glory of winning, but the relief of not losing; and the irony is that, though involuntary, the contest has been forced upon us by ourselves. Our devil is pressure. Pressure by people upon space for living, and upon natural resources which are the means for existence: be they reserves of minerals and fossil fuels, earth, water, wild life, the very air we breathe. Out of this situation springs the corollary, obvious enough, which is the uttermost necessity, not only to modify that pressure, but so to sustain the environment in all its manifestations that we may survive, and that our successors may have lives to live. The alternative is oblivion.

In this book however I am not attempting a study of the environment at large—a subject of vast magnitude and complexity beyond my powers—but to reduce the scale to one of local proportions and seek a solution through the medium of the English countryside, what it is, has been, and may become. History is the guide and it leads to a source of understanding which, for me, encloses all other explanations: namely, husbandry. While land is the capital of civilisation, husbandry is both a technique and an article of faith, for the way we use our land is a reflection of the quality of that civilisation.

Husbandry is the prime use of land; and so in this concluding essay I propose to comment upon recent critical events in farming, as they occurred between the completion of my manuscript in the autumn of 1970 and the correction of the proof in the early spring of 1971. The coincidence in time was fortuitous, but the significance does not of course lie there. During this period there has been a radical change in the attitude of Government to agriculture, no less momentous because the policy was openly declared beforehand. It amounts to this: that the era of 'cheap food' is over, and that cheapness will not come back either through unrestricted imports from abroad as in the halcyon days of Free Trade, or through the mechanics of Protection as enshrined in the Agriculture Act 1947. In reality food has not been cheap for a long time, though thanks to local surpluses and economic expedients it may have seemed so at times. Ultimately price is settled by supply and demand, and in a world of exploding populations and diminishing natural resources, the point is inevitably reached where manœuvring can no longer mask the true position. That point has arrived now, propelled by a meteoric rise in farming costs during 1970–1. In response the Government decided on two apparently contradictory courses of action. First, under the reigning system of deficiency payments and guarantees, it found £138 million to offset the rise in farm expediture. Secondly, it announced the introduction of a new system (to be phased in over a period of three years) by which farmers in future will 'get their price from the market'. This means that the price of food will rise to its real or market level, and that a levy will be imposed on any imported food that falls below that level. Thus the need for price support at home will disappear, and it seems likely that by the time the three years are up (if not before), the need for import levies will have vanished too.[1] Indeed the high cost of food in Continental countries, and the fact that Britain would have to conform to the price structure if it joined the Common Market, is one of the chief problems under discussion as I write. What it means, whether we join or not, is that the housewife will have to pay more for food—she will in fact have to pay the real not the subsidised price.

The abandonment of Protection does not mean that the Government will cease to sustain farming by means of capital and other grants and by the maintenance of its advisory, educational, and other services. The annual cost of agriculture to the taxpayer will however be less than in the past, partly because price support will have gone, and partly because the Government intends to 'encourage farming to stand on its own feet': which means, for example, that farmers will have to find the cost of certain marketing and research services[2] out of their own pockets and commit themselves—so is my belief—without reserve to co-operative buying and selling throughout the whole industry. Besides this State aid will be tied ever tighter to profitability. Already a variety of grant-aid arrangements have been revised and consolidated under the Farm Capital Grant Scheme (as from January 1971), and inducements made more attractive to amalgamate small farms and persuade small farmers to get out. The declared purpose of these changes is to secure higher efficiency in agriculture, at lower cost to the Exchequer, and—despite the inevitable rise in the cost of living—to enable farmers to produce yet more food for our expanding population.

But how will this affect husbandry? I fear that it will affect it adversely, for the motive is par excellence political and economic. It will encourage the intensification of output—as always from a diminishing area of land—and will therefore put a premium on factory farming. So it is relevant to turn briefly to a subject which lies outside the prime consideration of price, but which lies none the less at the very foundation of the science of agriculture. *Modern Farming and the Soil*,[3] an investigation of soil structure and soil fertility by the Agricultural Advisory Council, was published in January 1971 and is a disturbing document. The very fact of publication indicated that something has gone seriously wrong with contemporary farm practice, yet the Council was strangely guarded in its conclusions. Breakdown in soil strucure was ascribed to the use of heavy machinery and untimely cultivations, to inadequate drainage, and to other mainly mechanical causes. Depletion of the organic content of the soil by continuous arable cropping was played down. 'There is no evidence to show that the disappearance of livestock from certain areas and the replacement of ley-farming and farmyard manure by chemical fertilisers has led to any loss of inherent fertility.' Critics have hastened to contradict this statement, asserting that intensive cultivation, divorced from livestock and a balanced system of rotation, is indeed the main source of trouble, and that both the structure and the fertility of the soil are affected thereby. The official view seems to be that if we alter 'modern farming', then we shall be unable to produce the food we need, either at the right price or in sufficient quantity, to help fill the mouths of fifty-six million people today or sixty-seven million people tomorrow in this overcrowded island.

This then is the dilemma of survival—short-term production or long-term husbandry. In either case we are being pushed towards the precipice by population; and as I said at the beginning of this book, time is running out.

Appendix

THE ORGANIC ANSWER

by

Robert Waller, editor of *The Soil Association Journal* in consultation with
Harry Walters, F.I.Biol., F.I.F.S.T., F.R.S.H., scientific consultant to
the Soil Association.

Bio-philosophy

'Organic' can mean quite contrary things to different people. The word
has a long history going back to the Greeks when *organon* meant a 'tool' or
'instrument', and *organikos* was equivalent to our 'mechanical'. Yet
today the organic school use it to mean the opposite of mechanical.
How has this happened? If the tool or instrument is a living structure,
such as the eye, then the eye can be considered an instrument for seeing,
the organ of sight. By this shift of meaning from the mechanical to the
functional, organic has gradually become associated with living things.
In the sixteenth century mechanical and organical were synonymous, but
in the eighteenth century the physical and biological references predominated. Burke and Coleridge began to use the word as the opposite
of artificial or mechanical, a now familiar contrast. Organic became a
word of praise implying natural, not planned, growth: something cultivated, not fabricated.

Organic has now become a popular word with many writers, who
recognise the need to shift our sights from the physical and chemical to
the living and biological, if we are to solve many baffling problems of
life. Organic stresses the idea of wholeness and growth. Organic
thinkers reject mechanistic and materialist explanations. They believe
in natural growth, in slow change and adaptation: that progress can
only last if it is in tune with natural processes.

On the Continent biological husbandry means the same thing as
organic husbandry does here. *Bios*—the Greek word for 'way of life'—
has now become bastardised everywhere and used as a publicity catch-
word. 'Bio' suggests links with a living function. At one end biochemistry seeks to reduce life to a series of linked chemical processes,
while at the other extreme it integrates the chemical functions into a
biological system. Where life begins and ends is not easy to define, yet

everybody can see the difference between a dead dog and a living one. When life goes, obviously some vital organising force has departed and chemical forces have taken over, starting the decomposition of the body —a process known as bio-degradation. This decomposition reduces the once living body to substances that feed the earth, and which provide nutrients for vegetation growing in the place where the animal died. This vegetation will feed another generation of animals. This bio-cycle of life-death-life is a cardinal element in organic thinking.

In Nature there is never final death, since the living soil—as Lady Eve Balfour emphasises in her book of that name[1]—always maintains a living micro- and macroflora regardless of season. The manner in which sunlight, rain, climate, and the whole active environment convert a seed into a full-grown plant, has been a wonder appreciated by man from ancient times; and it is expressed in the creation stories. To modern man it is the foundation of bio-philosophy, described for example by Harry Walters in his book, *The Living Rocks*.[2]

The confusion that derives from the use of the word 'organic' stems not only from historical changes of meaning, but also from the intrinsic difference between 'organism' and 'organisation'. The distinction is subtle but of the utmost importance. Man is an organism, and when he dies he can no longer continue his living functions, although his body is still there. He too begins to decompose like the dog and returns to the dust whence he came. Biochemistry gives way to chemistry, so to speak—a process we understand and accept. The organisation of life however cannot be explained. The organising force—which we call Nature—is a mystery but exists none the less, though some scientists affect to deny it because they cannot find an explanation.

Organic thinkers take this mystery seriously. They study how to give it the maximum freedom of operation, and they criticise modern husbandry because it interferes with natural processes. Man too is a great organiser. He plans, but his planning often acts in opposition to organic growth, although the two activities can be reconciled by allowing one to encourage the other. The power of thought is man's special gift. Nature organises spontaneously by laws inherent in soil, plant, animal and man—so far as man is simply a part of Nature—but the mind of man enables him to make a deliberate study of how organisms work. He can thus teach himself how to co-operate with the organising powers of Nature, so as to allow them the maximum creative opportunity. That in a few words is the basic principle of bio-philosophy, whether in agriculture, or medicine, or society.

There is a danger, however, latent in the idea of the organic when it is used metaphorically, as when we say that society or the earth or the universe is really one organism. What we mean is that it behaves like an organism. If society were only an organism, men would lose their freedom, for each part would simply serve the dictates of the whole. In fact every man is an individual with a personality that transcends organisms as such. All the parts of his physical being in some way serve that same personality, and his creativeness is an attribute of it. Likewise, if society were considered solely as an organism, we would end up with totalitarianism—the central government being the brain, sending out explicit directives to all the parts.

Diversity and Freedom

In practice the organic or biological philosophers of this country have always stressed individuality; they have opposed standardisation and central directives; they have insisted that every blade of grass is different to the next, and that the genius of plant breeding, for example, is to recognise difference and exploit it. Excellence in agricultural production has always been associated with locality—as with wines, cheeses, breeds of farm animals, etc. Every locality has its own soil and its variations of climate, and these exert influence on its character. Thus quality and distinction reside in making best use of the genius of locality.

Diversity allows for an infinity of ways of doing things. It keeps in the background (even in the gene pool of all life's variegated creatures) endless reserves of capacity that can take over when the current life-form or pattern is threatened or breaks down—as we have seen in the case of insects which become immune to D.D.T. If man—for his own ends and in order to save expense—over-simplifies the natural scene and makes it conform to a single pattern, he is inviting his own destruction. He will have no reserve capacity and no alternatives when his totalitarian scheme of living fails to function.

Thinking about the earth organically warns us against making drastic changes in one part of Nature, without considering repercussions on other parts. We talk nowadays of the 'spaceship earth' and of the finite character of our natural resources. This is one of the unexpected consequences of putting men on the moon. These men have been able to see the earth revolving in space relative to the rest of the universe. The difference between our earth and the moon—and probably other planets too—has struck them—and us—with wonder and with a feeling of reverence towards this planet. This difference is 'life'—the beautiful green mantle of vegetation and the fresh air that we breathe, which is but a thin envelope enclosing our world as it revolves in space. This same difference between the earth and the rest of creation, so far as we have been able to observe it, has increased our respect for life. It has also filled us with alarm, when we think of how easily our world might become a 'sterile and rocky promontory' like the moon. Organic philosophers have always been imbued with this feeling about life, its miracle and its frailty. They did not need to go to the moon to experience it; they experienced it within themselves and the world about them.

In our thinking about Nature, therefore, we must learn how to reconcile organism with freedom: by organising life (through know-ledge) in order to liberate organic growth. The organic thinker works in terms of freedom, persuasion and consent, not only when dealing with other human beings, but with plants and animals as well. His husbandry is firmly based upon observation of the individual and herd life of animals. He organises for his own benefit what animals are seen to do of their own accord, when living in conditions that favour their growth: similarly with plants. The soil and its invisible population, plants, animals and man himself—all are inter-related and serve each other so as to conserve both their individuality and their part in the whole. Unless this is so, the creativeness of the earth, which they nourish, dries up; and the function of its subordinate organisms become valueless. In recent years a new word has emerged which expresses the inter-related-ness of everything in Nature, and which allows us to speak of the earth as if it were one collective organism. This word is 'ecology', from *ekos*, the Greek word for 'home'. Ecology is the study of the relationship between organisms and their environment, always remembering that each organism is itself the environment of other organisms.

Husbandry

It is helpful therefore to talk of ecological husbandry in order to stress this inter-relatedness. But whether we talk of organic, biological, or ecological husbandry, what we mean is that we cannot have *good husbandry* unless we take into account what every one of these words implies about the functions of Nature. We are reminded that Nature is not a mere mechanism; above all it is not a factory. Growing things have to be cultivated, not fabricated. Farming is both a business and an art—agri—culture.

Much modern farming ignores this truth. It is factory farming in name and fact. To change the metaphor—it treats plants as if they were thirsty schoolchildren sucking up mineral waters through straws—the straws being the roots, and the mineral waters being the dissolved inorganic fertilisers. The soil is regarded as neutral, a medium for nutrients, and a convenient anchor for plant roots. Assaulting this plant factory are greedy birds and insects, that have to be eliminated to prevent them consuming the products before they reach the market. Besides this, the factory floor itself is alive with innumerable pests that nibble at the roots or cause diseases. They must be purged like beetles in roof timbers. If Nature could be rendered sterile, and inert farming carried on as extensive hydroponics,[3] control would be complete. Luckily logic of this kind is not only insane but impracticable. The world cannot be fed by such means, if only because there would not be enough water or nutrient substances available for production on such a scale. Nor can outdoor factory methods, as now practised, sustain the world in the long run. It would be impossible to keep the soil and surrounding countryside insulated from all the dangerous enemies of the kind described. Nature is not a machine powered by chemicals and maintenanced by toxic sprays. The only safe method of management is that which studies the immense diversity of Nature, and seeks to preserve the balance that it has itself created.

The art of agriculture lies in working with, not dominating Nature's diversity. The grass mixtures used by the orthodox farmer are far simpler and more selective than those favoured by the organic farmer. Moreover heavy treatments with fertiliser encourage rank growth of a few grasses and suppresses many others; yet the suppressed grasses and herbs all serve useful nutritional purposes, and reach maturity at different times of the year. If animals are allowed to choose between complex, un-fertilised, pastures and the more simplified but fertilised sward, they will nearly always choose the first.

The wise farmer does not regard his holding solely as a business. Farming for him is an art and a challenge, and it affords him pleasure as a result. He enjoys using his wits to follow the processes of Nature, as they unfold on his land. In that way he learns how to make Nature work for him. Each farm must be considered in its individual context as a part of the surrounding landscape, shaped by climate, history and society. The individuality of place and the significance of tradition are two elements that must be taken into serious account before policy is decided. It may well be that both these elements have been mismanaged in the past: in which case husbandry must begin with diagnosis. What has been done? How does this accord with what the land can do best?

If agriculture is to be regarded both as an art and as a business, it has to balance the claims of culture against those of civilisation: the latter being interpreted as a combination of external forces such as economics, taxation, and other expressions of the law of the land, which may impose restrictions upon the freedom of the individual. No doubt civilisation and culture (in this case, good husbandry) ought to be in harmony, but in our century they are not. For two hundred years now civilisation has been reducing culture to the status of a servant. Culture comes from within; but when the individual is compelled to conform to external forces, his inner or artistic judgment is slowly destroyed. In this country the growth of monopoly capitalism is having this effect on agriculture. Small family farms are being swallowed up by larger units, which are themselves dependent on integrated combines, controlling products from the soil to the supermarket, directing which crops, which fertilisers, which machines, and which sprays the farmer shall use. This may work for a time; but by destroying the artist in man and by taking away his mental freedom and enterprise, it must ultimately lead to the servile state—as certain to collapse in our own day as in former days, since it deprives man of the pleasure of being himself and turns him into a machine, just as it has already turned farm animals into machines. Man becomes 'organisation man'.

For these reasons the wise farmer is opposed to large, impersonal, agricultural units and seeks ways of conserving the smaller, humanly manageable unit—whether family farm or partnership—within a co-operative organisation: following the model of Nature, wherein a multitude of organisms operate individually and in association with each other, within a framework of order.

Land and Fertility

The wise farmer thinks first of his land. This is obvious, yet the techniques of intensive agriculture concentrate on feeding the crop at the expense of the soil. If the soil is fed and kept fertile, the crop will fundamentally look after itself. Of course different crops take different nutrients out of the soil, so that feeding the soil means replacing the lost nutrients, and making available those which are otherwise absent. The fertiliser theory recognises this one law, but imperfectly, since it places far too much emphasis upon three ingredients—nitrogen, phosphate and potash (N.P.K.) which until recently were sold as a complete fertiliser. This inadequate theory of plant nutrition has been supported for a number of years by an all-powerful N.P.K. Club, to which many of the leading figures in Government and commerce belong. The Club has dominated official policy to the extent of subsidising inorganic to the exclusion of organic fertilisers.

In reality plants feed on a diversity of nutrients too great to be analysed in full here. Overstressing three of these—because they force growth—leads to imbalance. It upsets the different ratios of nutrients in both soil and plant—e.g. the nitrogen/carbon ratio. The plant heavily fed with nitrogen has to put out more leaf in order to increase the photosynthetic process—absorb the rays of the sun—and synthesise more carbon. This forced growth weakens cellular structure and opens the door to pathogens. The nutrient value of the plant is inferior to that produced by slower growth and a more balanced feed. Worst of all, while N.P.K. feeds—or overfeeds—the plant, it fails to feed the soil. Soil health requires a high humus content. There is no biological value in N.P.K. The notion that three per cent of humus is sufficient in soil—the official dogma of N.A.A.S.—allows no reserve for exceptional climatic conditions. Eight per cent is nearer the minimum, particularly when allowance has to be made for compaction by heavy machinery. The stress under which land and man both exist today, emphasises the need to strengthen structure by means of adequate diet. Stress always searches out weakness.

The dangers deriving from the over-use of nitrogen have been documented by Harry Walters in his paper on *Nitrate in Soils, Plants and Animals*.[4] He supports his case with nearly 200 references in scientific literature. Yet fertiliser firms and official spokesmen have continually urged farmers to increase their use of nitrogen as a sure means to higher profits. The motive is not to improve quality but expand output, and to make this—the economic—the yardstick.

Land—not technology—is the real capital of civilisation. Ultimately everything comes out of it, and everything goes back into it. Land yields all the mineral resources, which are both feed for vegetation and raw material for industry. It bears the mantle of soil without which life could not exist; and we need to remember that man is the parasite of plants, for whereas plants can exist without him, he cannot exist without plants. All of man's constructions—his cities and his roads—rest on the ground, and life passes from the ground up. For these reasons we speak metaphorically of 'Mother Earth'. And although this phrase now sounds too anthropomorphic for the strict objective logic of a scientific genera-tion, it reminds us of our dependence on the land. Moreover this metaphorical form of thought is accompanied by important emotions—those of love and respect, which lead us to conserve the land and its products. The scientific conscience which persuades us to sweep away these symbols needs itself to be re-examined. It may be destroying a way of thinking and imagining necessary to our survival. It may well be a lethal example of over-simplification.

Fruit, vegetables, grain, grass, trees, all spring from the soil. They are rooted in it and fed by it in part. They are also fed by rain, air and sunlight. All are inter-related. These products of the earth are at one remove from the micro-organisms, insects, animals and man himself. Here again the inter-relationship between the soil and its dependents is astounding, for the soil itself has been partly created by the decomposing bodies of micro-organisms, releasing chemicals that in turn break down rock and help turn it back into soil. As the hierarchy of life advances from the simpler to the more complex forms, so with decomposition is the cycle of growth and decay maintained. Eroded land can be restored by planting a succession of vegetation that rebuilds the soil step by step, until once again it is able to support crops. This is a good example of biological procedure, in that it is intensifying and accelerating natural processes. Chemical methods are often man-made short-cuts, which by over-simplification degrade and ultimately negate the processes of Nature.

Technologists do not yet accept the need to work in harness with Nature's cycle of operations. The second half of the bio-cycle, the phase of decomposition, is considered unprofitable and thus, if possible, ignored. The residues which ought to be returned to the soil are poured into the rivers, or into the air, or on to the ground, often in forms impossible for Nature to digest. They therefore pollute and contaminate the environment. It is truly appalling that agriculture, which of all industries should be a model for working with Nature—by means which enable it to renew its resources indefinitely—should become another polluter of the planet. When the soil is not renewed, it is mined like the minerals which are extracted for industry. These—like coal or oil—do not possess endless reserves, but are finite and will one day run out. Yet agriculture is the basic industry of all, upon which man can with confidence depend, since good husbandry can render its resources infinite. For this reason it is agriculture and not urban industry that should receive priority in Government policy. It follows that farm prices and wages should set the standard by which all other prices and wages are gauged: not vice versa as at present. Our values are upside down.

Pollution by agriculture is accelerating. In the animal factories, manure is not returned to the land but piled up in stinking heaps, the liquid let run into lagoons or diverted into the drains, where it becomes a burden on sewage. A cow's excrement is at least eight times greater than a human being's, so that some of the large animal units are the equivalent of small towns. Thus we not only waste a vast mass of invaluable material, but also create a totally unnecessary source of pollution and expense to the community. Town-bred man regards excreta as a disgusting nuisance, but the countryman knows that it plays an essential part in the bio-cycle, to be returned whence it came. Some farmers however are so infected with the virus of industrialised husbandry that they are reduced to saying that dung has no value: otherwise instead of being a residue, it would be retained by the animal as a nutrient. This in itself is a ludicrous statement, quite apart from the fact that organisms will excrete rather than absorb many elements in excess of their requirements. As most animals today are given an unbalanced diet, their excreta will contain much that is of value, together with chemical residues derived from methods by which their food has been grown and processed. This is why bio-philosophers talk of 'drug-addicted' farming.

Agro-industry spreads destruction in ever-widening ecological circles. For example, the separation of animals from the land, to which they have been tied by immemorial associations and to which they have become naturally adapted, leads to monocultural cereal cropping. A high proportion of barley is grown for 'barley beef', and the grain is also fed in large quantities to the broiler and battery units which total millions of birds. No crop has ever taken up so great a percentage of land as barley does today. In order to grow it and other cereals, miles of hedges are removed, trees uprooted, and whole territories transformed. Should these crops become unprofitable, barley in particular—and there are signs of it happening already—will the landscape be restored? Who will pay for the restoration?

A wise government would establish grazing grants in place of fertiliser subsidies, and withhold assistance from all farmers who separate land from livestock. Grass is our most important crop, because it is the best soil creator and conserver, but it needs animals to make it profitable. To relate stock to soil is to conserve the best in both, and through rotations to reach the right sequence in that relationship. Conservation is the essence of good husbandry—the direct antithesis of penitentiary stock-raising and dustbowl monocropping—and it is common sense. That it also conserves natural beauty is of the highest importance, for a beautiful and living landscape refreshes the spirit, and stimulates many feelings and thoughts which lie dormant but suppressed in the urbanised life of today. Good husbandry therefore benefits human ecology, which man ignores to his spiritual cost.

Soil

To understand soil is to grasp the essentials of organic farming. Sir George Stapledon wrote:

> The soil is like no other material used in industry: it is a material pulsating with life, but easily prone to sickness and easy to destroy totally. Active soil capable of promoting healthy plant growth is a strictly limited commodity on our planet. To realise this fully is a first essential to a deep appreciation of the true significance of agriculture. Not only is soil limited in quantity, but to maintain it at the highest possible pitch of fruitfulness demands an inborn sense of duty and unremitting vigilance. The chief care of the worthy farmer is to husband his vital resources in terms of soil particles, humus and animal and vegetable residues. Always he is on guard not to exploit his raw materials in response to rising markets for particular commodities.[5]

This was written in 1946. In the twenty-four years since that date, the sentences that succeed this same quotation have been proved only too true.

> Unfortunately the trend of recent decades has not been to encourage thriftiness and husbandship among farmers: it has been rather to ridicule those virtues—so widely divorced from fundamentals had the mind of the dominant town dweller become. Food, tobacco, beer, all products of the soil, had to be cheap, no matter where or how the parent crops were grown, no matter at all if the very character of the farmer was destroyed.

Prophetic words from one of England's greatest agricultural thinkers and teachers. Stapledon stressed again and again that soil was not to be compared to a machine. He compared it rather to the tree of life.

Hundreds of books[6] have been written about the soil: its origins, structure, and multitudinous population, visible and invisible. It is an inexhaustible subject of infinite wonder, in which the bare recital of statistics astound: for instance, that over a thousand million arthropods[7] may be present in a single acre of grassland. Soil study is the necessary preliminary to good husbandry, and there are even those who assert that 'the soil makes the climate'.

A Frenchman, Maxime Guillaume, who has devoted many years of his life to the regeneration of soils in Africa, has written a book of this very title, *Le Sol fait le Climat*.[8] In his view, the state of the soil and the way it is managed are essential factors in determining the action of wind and water. Bad husbandry can actually unbalance the climate, and by a boomerang effect a whole region can be degraded into a desert. Guillaume gives numerous examples from his own experience, as do other writers of authority, such as Richard St. Barbe Baker (founder of The Men of the Trees), and Anne Francé-Harrar, many of whose studies are based on the work of her husband, Professor George Harrar, the biologist, renowned for his research into the breeding of hybrid cereals in Mexico. Professor Geoffrey Dimbleby, head of the Department of the Human Environment at London University, has also pointed out that as the fertility of an area declines, the farmers adapt themselves to the lower level by altering their crop and stock husbandry until at last, around the Mediterranean, they have been left with nothing but eroded hills and voracious goats.

Del Pelo Pardi, the Italian agriculturalist, has written:

> Fertile and productive soil must contain air: this is essential so that the roots of the plant and the microbe population may breathe. . . . The soil of a rough pasture is formed of crumbs of perfect size; the herbage as it dies down withers and decomposes on the ground; the decomposing plants do much more however than manufacture the substance which in turn assures a true crumb structure, since they also yield various nutritive elements; and these add to the productive power of the soil—that is, they are the true fertilisers. Most important, they encourage useful microbes to multiply. So we see that, in relation to soil, life perpetually renews itself through its own residues.[9]

This is the key to the value of farmyard manure, which is a combination of animal and plant residues. Its cementing substances assist in forming soil crumbs of the right size; its nutritive qualities enrich the soil with food for crops; and its population of microbes transform essential elements for plant use. In a raw state however it can do harm if applied to the land, and needs first to be turned into compost. Composting prevents putrefaction which is anaerobic, and encourages decomposition which is aerobic, a process not yet fully understood but which involves the activity of oxygen; but we do know that it operates naturally in the top soil of fertile land, and that it breaks down the excreta of grazing animals without letting it putrefy. Likewise composting manure from housed cattle requires the dung first to be mixed with straw or other litter, and then stacked according to a regular routine—which nowadays can be mechanised. Mature compost looks like damp tobacco, dark and crumbly, and must be spread *over* the land, not *in* it. Assimilation by the soil takes time, and ploughing in inhibits the process of digestion. When a field is re-ploughed, one sometimes sees straw with a whiteish mould: which means that putrefaction, not decomposition, is taking place. New methods are however now being devised for ageing slurries in tanks to bring about decomposition without putrefaction; but more research is needed so that farm practice dovetails into the natural bio-cycle.

A healthy soil, thriving with microbes and worms, must also be well drained. Microbes create a sponge-like lattice of fine spaces in the soil, which circulates the water horizontally; worms make long vertical channels through the subsoil for water to drain downwards, when in excess. Increasing use of heavy machinery—itself an economic shortcut to saving labour—is a common source of damage to soil structure, since by destroying the complex of air and water passages it attacks organic activity. Good natural drainage is essential to fertility.

The Soil Association

Since healthy soil performs so many important functions, it follows that to treat it as some inert substance, rather than a living entity—even though plants may be fed with artificial fertilisers—leads to infertility and erosion. This has been demonstrated by the Soil Association on land at New Bells Farm, Haughley, in Suffolk. The experiment was started in the 1930s under the direction of Lady Eve Balfour, who divided the holding into three sections—organic, mixed and stockless. The organic section received no fertilisers or sprays, but relied entirely on composted manure from stock for its fertility. The mixed section received both compost and fertilisers; while the stockless section was laid down to monocultural cereal growing by conventional methods. The mixed and organic sections—each of approximately seventy-five acres carrying both crops and stock—were organised on a ten-year rotation, which included four years of temporary grass and an occasional crop of lucerne, and regular folding by sheep, poultry and dairy cattle. The system was formalised in 1947, since which date two ten-year rotations have been completed: so that it is reasonable to assume that the soil has had time to adjust itself to the treatment. Soil samples taken in 1970 by N.A.A.S. show that the organic section has the best structure and the stockless the worst, being lumpy, doughy and intractable. The mixed section has a high percentage of good crumbly particles, but is not entirely free of lumps. The stockless section will none the less yield average crops of cereals, if well fertilised with artificials.

On another Soil Association farm, where the previous owner had grown grain for fourteen successive years, barley was sown without fertiliser and the crop could barely be seen for weeds. Yet when strips on the organic section were left unmanured, the crop was little different to that of the previous year; even on the mixed section, the absence of fertilisers had small effect on yield for one season. This shows that the fields which had never been grassed, grazed, or spread with composted manure, had reached a stage where they had to rely on fertilisers alone for fertility. They were hooked.

Addiction to fertilisers leads to other troubles, of which 'run-off' is a striking example. The phrase means what it says. Excess fertiliser not assimilated by plants literally runs off into the ditches and thence into the rivers. Run-off alone, but particularly when joined with sewage and detergent wastes, leads to serious contamination. Eutrophication occurs: which means that vegetation is so overfed that it makes too heavy a demand upon the oxygen content of the water. The fish and other living organisms, including the vegetation itself, begin to suffocate and die—to the extent that the self-cleansing properties of the river are over-burdened and overcome. The water is rendered lifeless.

There is no need to seek further examples of the consequences of bad husbandry. In agriculture, as in industry, waste—in whatever form—will have to be recycled or reintegrated into the productive process, or otherwise absorbed, if the whole community is not to suffer. This will require a complete reversal of the present trend in farm practice. Factory farming—which is an economic formula—will in the interests of posterity have to be replaced by a return to good husbandry; but whether this will happen in time to save posterity remains to be seen. Perhaps economics may yet provide the answer, in that the new synthetic foods seem likely to drive factory farm products out of the market. Your 'knitted steak' made from a by-product of the oil industry, or 'mock milk' extracted from greenstuff, will be cheaper than barley-fed beef, or the lactic product of intensive dairy herds. You will probably not notice much difference in taste. The choice for the customer will then lie between the synthetic and the organic. Synthetic food will provide the basic rations, so long as its raw materials last. Otherwise one can imagine a situation in which farming again becomes a craft, yielding quality food for the discerning, who will be prepared to pay the extra price.

At the present time only a small minority can earn their livelihood from all-out organic farming. Most organically minded farmers find it impossible to avoid a restricted use of artificials and sprays. This is no criticism of organics, but of our society which allows economic forces to impose quick-return methods on farming, hostile alike to soil and health. Yet there are a few encouraging signs. N.A.A.S. (A.D.A.S.) has now set up county groups to study and advise on conservation in agriculture; one can only hope that concern for hedges and trees will not camouflage a lack of concern for the conservation of the soil itself. Even the ancillary agricultural industries are diversifying their products, nervous lest there may be a drop in the sales of inorganic aids and antibiotics—whatever their advertisements and public pronouncements may tell us. The transition from orthodox to organic farming can no more be done overnight than a drug addict or dypsomaniac can be taken off drugs or alcohol at once. The transition will involve a gradual return to well-tried systems, using all modern aids that are not deleterious to soil, plant, animal and man, in order to offset the damage done in the past. As it spreads, the organic answer will create a tradition that all farmers can modify in their own way, in the interests of good husbandry and the conservation of the environment.

Notes

Introduction

1. Quoted in *Prophet of the New Age* by Robert Waller, Faber, 1962.
2. *Human Ecology*, edited by Robert Waller, Faber, 1964, p. 50.
3. E.g. *The Farm and the Village*, Faber, 1969, and several other books.
4. *Akenfield: Portrait of an English Village* by Ronald Blythe, Allen Lane, 1969.
5. *The Living Soil*, Faber, 1943.
6. E.g. *The Way of the Land*, Faber, 1942.
7. E.g. *Country Planning*, O.U.P., 1944.

Part One

1. An outstanding example was that of Jack O'Newbury, nickname of John Winchcombe, a prosperous clothier of that town, who in 1513 sent a hundred men at his own expense to fight the Scots at Flodden. The men arrived too late for action—but no matter.
2. For example, the order that all corpses should be buried in woollen shrouds.
3. Googe's book seems to have signalled a spate of farming manuals, several of positive and practical value, in the seventeenth century. They included works by Leonard Mascall on cattle, Sir Hugh Plat on manuring and sowing, Gervase Markham on a variety of subjects (not always his own work), John Gerard on herbs, Rowland Vaughan on meadow drowning, Charles Butler and John Levett on bees. Later came Gabriel Plattes, who took out a patent for a corn drill; Walter Blith, pioneer of field drainage; and John Worlidge, another prolific author and inventor.
4. Some six million acres of open arable and common grazing land were redistributed and fenced during the sixty years of George III's reign alone, 1760–1820.
5. William Cobbett, *Political Register*, 1835.
6. Two years later, in 1836, the ancient and anomalous custom of paying tithe in kind was replaced by a money rent based on the average price of corn over seven years. This was an ecclesiastical tax harking back to the time when the parson was indeed the 'persona', or only literate and educated man in the community—priest, teacher and welfare officer in one—who had to be supported by a special contribution.
7. In my own family papers, I found the following note, probably written by my great-aunt Hilary about the year 1835, when living in Petersfield: 'A bad Charity— nothing but green faggots to be had—coals much better—Buriton people like coals very much—manage very well without grates. Papa wrote a little plan of a coal concern— giving £5 8s. to make 6 ton, if the farmers will give carriage from Emsworth.'
8. See *The Reclamation of Exmoor Forest* by C. S. Orwin and Roger Sellick, David and Charles, 1970.
9. From *Villages of the White Horse* by Alfred Williams, Duckworth, 1913. See also *Alfred Williams* by Leonard Clark, David and Charles, 1969.

10. The three letters were reprinted in full in *The Toilers of the Field*, Longman, 1892.

11. From 'The Country Sunday', one of Jefferies' last essays published in *Field and Hedgerow*, Longman, 1889.

12. From *Sharpen the Sickle* by Reg. Groves, Porcupine Press, 1949.

13. For a discerning account of this period, see *History of British Agriculture 1846–1914* by Christabel S. Orwin and Edith H. Whetham, Longman, 1964.

14. Sibella Charlotte Norman, who married my grandfather Harry Bonham-Carter in 1862, was a bridesmaid at the wedding. The event was reported in the local press in more than ordinarily fulsome language.

15. Father of Sibella, see above.

16. *Lord Wantage V.C., K.C.B.*, A Memoir by his wife, Smith, Elder, 1907. *Estate Villages* by M. A. Havinden, with contributions by D. S. Thornton and P. D. Wood, Lund Humphries for the University of Reading, 1966.

17. The Rochdale Equitable Pioneers founded their co-operative organisation in 1844. See the several histories of the Co-operative Movement.

18. See Part Two.

19. My principal authority for this and following paragraphs is *Forestry in the English Landscape* by Roger Miles, Faber, 1967.

20. *Silva, or a Discourse of Forest Trees and the Propagation of Timber in His Majesty's Dominions* by John Evelyn; Address to the Royal Society, 1662.

21. Miles, op. cit., p. 42.

22. Ibid.

23. Ibid., pp. 48–49.

24. Ibid., p. 49.

25. Ibid., pp. 49–50.

26. German forestry expert, prominent in British forestry. At one time he held the post of Inspector-General of Forests in India.

27. Miles, op. cit., p. 50.

28. See p. 69.

29. *The Wheelwright's Shop* by George Sturt, C.U.P., 1948; a classic autobiography of the period 1884–91, tells the story of the decline of one trade in inimitable fashion.

30. Sharp was not of course single-handed in his work. Intelligent interest in folklore had long preceded him. Folk songs were being collected and published in the 1880s and 1890s by the Rev. Sabine Baring Gould, Lucy Broadwood and Frank Kidson; while the Folk Song Society was founded in 1899. Sharp however is generally acknowledged as the principal rescuer of the folk dance, and as the founder of the English Folk Dance Society in 1911. The two societies were amalgamated in 1932.

31. Similar rescue work has of course been done in Wales, Scotland and Ireland. As however this is a book about the English countryside, I have preferred to choose English examples and illustrations. See *Folk Music of Britain . . . And Beyond*, by Frank Howes, Methuen, 1969.

32. *English Farming, Past and Present* by Lord Ernle, sixth edition, Heinemann and Frank Cass, 1961, pp. 512–13.

33. Orwin and Whetham, op. cit., p. 341: quoting *Agriculture and Economic Progress* by E. M. Ojala, O.U.P., 1952, p. 66.

34. Ibid., p. 342: quoting from the analysis made by F. D. Taylor in *Farm Economist*, vol. viii, no. 4 (1955). See also *Agricultural Output of Great Britain*, 1912, H.M.S.O., Cmd. 6277, pp. 17–20.

35. Ernle, op. cit., pp. 524–6.

36. Orwin and Whetham, op. cit., chapter 13.

37. Ibid. p. 373 et seq., and Ernle, op. cit., p. 440 et seq., are the main sources for the paragraphs on agricultural education and research.

38. For example in *The Journal of Agricultural Science*, started in 1905 by a group of Cambridge agriculturalists in association with Hall.

39. *English Farming, Past and Present*—see Bibliography. Prothero (Lord Ernle) was President of the Board of Agriculture 1916–19.

40. As distinct from the wartime measures, 1917–20, which proved only temporary.

41. For example in his *The Farm and the Village, The Pattern and the Plough*, and other books, published by Faber.

42. *Agriculture* (History of the Second World War) by Keith A. H. Murray, H.M.S.O. and Longmans, 1955, p. 11: quoting Sir Thomas Middleton.

43. First published by Faber in 1932.

44. Despite wartime rent control apparently.

45. Sheep bought in for fattening.

46. Folding means moving sheep by means of hurdles over, say, a field of roots, so that the crop is eaten off, and the ground improved by dunging and treading.

47. Street, op. cit., p. 210.

48. Ibid., pp. 222–4.

49. Ibid., pp. 231–2.

50. Ibid., pp. 227–8.

51. Williams and Norgate, 1926.

52. I.e. the Transport and General Workers Union.

53. Robertson Scott, from Chapter II.

54. The whole of this section is based upon Murray, op. cit., and *Principles for British Agricultural Policy*, edited by H. T. Williams, O.U.P., 1960.

55. Ernle, Table II of Appendix VI, gives the following figures:

	1921	1931
Bailiffs, Foremen, Shepherds, Foresters, Mechanics, etc.	55,426	46,783
Agricultural Labourers	549,329	466,686
	604,755	513,469

56. Radio was also becoming popular and influential among country-people.

57. *Problems of Rural Life* by C. S. Orwin, C.U.P., 1945, p. 93.

58. Ibid., p. 97.

59. Statutory smallholdings were first made available by the Act of 1892.

60. See *Departmental Committee of Inquiry into Statutory Smallholdings, First Report*, H.M.S.O., 1966, Cmnd. 2936. The *Second Report*, published in 1967, Cmnd. 3303, deals principally with the Land Settlement Association. See also pp. 168–9.

61. All information based on literature supplied by the Land Settlement Association, and on the *Second Report* quoted above.

62. Miles, op. cit., pp. 83–84.

63. *Post-War Forest Policy*, H.M.S.O., 1943, Cmnd. 6447; and *Post-War Forest Policy: Private Woodlands*, H.M.S.O., 1944, Cmnd. 6500.

64. Miles, op. cit., p. 87.

65. Ibid.

66. Quotation and substance of this paragraph from ibid., pp. 88–89.

Part Two: A

1. *In a Liberal Tradition* by Victor Bonham-Carter, Constable, 1960, p. 9.

2. Exact statistics seem impossible to obtain. In his *Derelict Britain*, Pelican, 1969, John Barr quotes 127,000 acres as the official total for derelict land for England, Wales and Scotland in 1968, but he suggests 250,000 acres as being nearer the mark.

3. *Man and Environment* by Robert Arvill, Pelican, 1969, p. 8.

4. *The Universal Dictionary of the English Language*, edited by Henry Cecil Wyld, Routledge and Kegan Paul, 1961.

5. Thanks to the growing awareness of conservation among sportsmen, and the educational activities of organisations such as the British Field Sports Society.

6. *The Vanishing Wild Life of Britain* by Brian Vesey-FitzGerald, MacGibbon and Kee, 1969. Collecting is still a source of danger, but much less than in the past.

7. Ibid., p. 100.

8. *A Handbook for Naturalists*, edited by Winwood Reade and R. M. Stuttard, Evans Bros., 1968. I have also drawn on other chapters in this useful book for historical and technical information.

9. 'A Hundred Years of Bird Protection' by Charles Wilson, published in *Birds*, journal of the Royal Society for the Protection of Birds, September–October 1969. It is well known that the writer, W. H. Hudson, also did much to popularise the cause of birds.

10. Reconstituted in 1968.

11. Quotations from the prospectus issued by the Field Studies Council, 9 Devereux Court, Strand, London, W.C.2.

12. Published by Collins in the *New Naturalist* series in 1969. This book has provided me with essential information about conservation and the wider issues of planning. The *New Naturalist* series of books was immensely influential in the cause of conservation.

13. *Report on the Distribution of the Industrial Population*; Chairman, Sir Anderson Montague-Barlow, H.M.S.O., 1940, Cmnd. 6153.

Report on Land Utilisation in Rural Areas; Chairman, Lord Justice Scott, H.M.S.O., 1942, Cmnd. 6378.

Final Report on Compensation and Betterment; Chairman, Lord Justice Uthwatt, H.M.S.O., 1942, Cmnd. 6386.

14. See reference on 114.

15. In July 1945 the Government set up the National Parks Committee, Chairman Sir Arthur Hobhouse, which published its Report in 1947, H.M.S.O., Cmnd. 7121. In the same year a separate sub-committee, also chaired by Sir Arthur, produced *Footpaths and Access to the Countryside*, H.M.S.O., Cmnd. 7207.

16. H.M.S.O., 1947, Cmnd. 7122.

17. W. H. Auden, *The Orators*, Book II, 'Six Odes', IV, Faber, 1966. See comment by Frank McEachran in his *Spells*, para. 466, Blackwell, 1954.

18. *The Making of the English Landscape*, by W. G. Hoskins, Hodder and Stoughton, 1955, p. 162.

19. Ibid., p. 165. Hoskins refers to *The Industrial Revolution in the Eighteenth Century*, by F. J. Mantoux, Jonathan Cape, 1928.

20. See Morris's Manifesto published in 1877, when he founded the Society for the Protection of Ancient Buildings.

21. See p. 49.

22. Quotations from *Commons, Forests and Footpaths* by Lord Eversley, Cassell, 1910, pp. 305–8.

23. This happened in 1969 in respect of a road through Saltram Park, near Plymouth. Information in these paragraphs derives from *The Continuing Purpose* by Robin Fedden, Longmans, 1968, and from National Trust literature. *Note*: The National Trust for Scotland was founded in 1931.

24. Fedden, op. cit., p. 23.

25. Ibid., p. 30 and chapter 12.

26. Ibid., chapter 13.

27. Ibid., p. 54.

28. Lawrence Chubb was another great name in the amenity movement. Secretary of the National Trust 1895–6, and Secretary of the Commons, Footpaths and Open Spaces Preservation Society, 1896–1948. He received a knighthood for his services.

29. Quotation from the original constitution of the Y.H.A.

30. Town Planning Act 1909.

31. The C.P.R.E. was inaugurated in 1926 at a meeting held at the Royal Institute of British Architects, on the initiative of Sir Guy Dawber and Sir Patrick Abercrombie. Its objects were: (a) to organise concerted action to secure the protection of rural scenery and of country and town amenities from disfigurement or injury; (b) to act either directly or through its members as a centre for furnishing or procuring advice and information upon any matters affecting the protection of amenities; (c) to arouse, form and educate public opinion in order to ensure the promotion of these objects. By 1969 the constituent organisations totalled forty-six, and the number of affiliated bodies 192. In 1970 Protection was substituted for Preservation.

32. Miles, op. cit., p. 71.

33. Later Secretary of the Ramblers' Association and recently knighted for his services.

34. His brother, Professor G. M. Trevelyan, Q.M., the eminent historian, also rendered valuable service, as President of the Y.H.A.

35. The Nature Conservancy was set up first as a Research Council, then reconstituted by Royal Charter as a separate legal entity.

36. For example, the Public Health Act 1875 empowered local authorities to frame by-laws applicable to the building of new houses.

37. Appointed in 1937. See Note 13.

38. His two books were: *Tomorrow*, 1898, and *Garden Cities of Tomorrow*, 1902.

39. *Green-Belt Cities* by Sir Frederic J. Osborn; revised edition published by Evelyn, Adams and Mackay, 1969.

40. Modern ideas as to the optimum size of towns exceed Howard's.

Part Two: B

1. The organisation of the Trust is referred to later in the chapter. Leonard and Dorothy Elmhirst were the senior Trustees, as founders and prime movers of the Dartington Hall enterprise. The other two original Trustees were F. A. S. Gwatkin and A. O. Elmhirst. Additional Trustees were appointed during and after the war.

2. See *Rabindranath Tagore, Pioneer in Education* edited by L. K. Elmhirst, John Murray, 1961. Also other published and unpublished material in Dartington Hall Records.

3. The Cosmopolitan Club.

4. For a personal and perceptive appreciation of Dorothy Elmhirst by Sir Julian Huxley, see the *Dartington Hall News* of 19th December, 1969.

5. R. L. Johnson, who succeeded me as Records Officer at Dartington, and C. Eric

McNally, who was responsible for all the binding, incidental printing, and collation of the illustrative material. Mrs Joan Mitchell also typed out the entire history for duplication.

6. The history is entitled *The Enterprise of Dartington Hall, 1925–56: with Supplement 1956–65*. Copies are kept at the Records Office, Dartington.

7. *Dartington Hall* by Victor Bonham-Carter, with an Account of the School by W. B. Curry, Phoenix House, 1958. Republished in paperback by the Exmoor Press, 1970.

8. The same might be said of the 'hippy' phenomenon today, but that is a subject outside the scope of this book.

9. For a comprehensive account of the origins and historical development of Dartington before the advent of the Elmhirsts, see *Dartington Hall* by Anthony Emery, O.U.P., 1970.

10. An outstanding example was the foundation by Leonard Elmhirst of the International Conference of Agricultural Economists in 1929, and the Institute of Agrarian Affairs in 1941.

11. Weir did much good work for the Society for the Protection of Ancient Buildings, and for private patrons such as Lord Curzon, for whom he undertook the repair of Tattersall and Bodiam Castles.

12. W. E. Hiley was awarded the C.B.E. in 1956, and honoured additionally by two of the principal forestry societies of the country before his death in 1961.

13. Tom Brown had been one of the first pupils at the Forestry School, Forest of Dean. He joined the Forestry Commission, and became a District Officer in Devon and Cornwall under C. O. Hanson, and was given charge of the Eggesford, Halwill and Okehampton State Forests 1919–29. He then worked for Dartington Woodlands 1929–41, when he joined Timber Control, as Chief Inspector of the Devon and Cornwall area. He was awarded M.B.E. in 1953.

14. Two examples must suffice: (1) the International Conference of Craftsmen in Pottery and Textiles, 17th–27th July, 1952; (2) the Summer School of Music, transferred from Bryanston in 1953, and held annually at Dartington since that date.

15. The main Dartington shops and tea-rooms are located at Shinners Bridge, on the Totnes–Plymouth road; with branches opposite the forecourt of the Hall.

16. Dartington Hall Ltd. was formed in 1929, Staverton Builders Ltd. in 1930, Dartington Orchards Ltd. in 1941, and Dartington Woodlands Ltd. in 1947.

17. It is of significance that latterly the preponderance of investment by the Dartington Hall Trust has been with the various Dartington commercial companies. This speaks for itself as evidence of the Trustees' faith in their own enterprises.

18. For example, the Sickness and Benevolence, and Old People's Housing schemes.

19. By means of the School, and later the Adult Education Centre.

20. By means of the Arts Department, now the Dartington College of Arts.

21. By means of the Estate Laboratory, and offices for research in agricultural and forestry economics.

22. Quotation from the first School prospectus, published in 1926.

23. Bonser Report, Dartington Hall Records, made by Dr and Mrs Bonser, of the Teachers College, Columbia University, in the summer of 1928.

24. Dorothy Elmhirst told me, not long before she died, that the curriculum worked out for the early Dartington Hall School was 'pretty thin'.

25. Curry had been senior science master at Bedales School, Petersfield, and before 1931 headmaster of Oak Lane Country Day School, Philadelphia.

26. Curry's principal works were *The School*, John Lane, 1934; *Education for Sanity*, Heinemann, 1947; and the chapter relating to the School in *Dartington Hall* by Victor Bonham-Carter, Exmoor Press, 1970. See also *The Independent Progressive School*, edited by Hubert Child, Hutchinson, 1962; and an article in the *Weekend Telegraph* of 22nd April, 1966 by Edward Blishen.

Part Three

1. Information from the Conservation Society, and reports by the General Register Office published by H.M.S.O.

2. 'Land and Human Populations' by Sir Joseph Hutchinson, C.M.G., Sc.D., F.R.S., Drapers' Professor of Agriculture, University of Cambridge. Published in *Advancement of Science*, Vol. 23 (September 1966).

3. *The Optimum Population for Britain*, edited by L. R. Taylor, published for the Institute of Biology by the Academic Press, 1970. The Introduction by the editor gives a masterly summary of information and opinions expressed at the Symposium.

4. The concept was developed in *The African Husbandman* by William Allan, Oliver and Boyd, 1965.

5. Source as for Note 2.

6. Includes deer forest in Scotland.

7. Already exempt from rates on agricultural land and buildings, farmers were soon absolved from planning control on most of their buildings as well.

8. For example, schemes for water supplies, land drainage, new buildings, etc.

9. For example, ploughing up old pasture, lime and fertiliser subsidies, etc.

10. After 1951 the system was modified to the extent that, generally, the Government paid the difference between the market price and the guaranteed price: in other words, a deficiency payment system which with certain qualifications was still in force in 1970. For recent changes, see the Postscript, p. 207.

11. In 1970 a further reorganisation was announced, whereby all existing scientific and technical services were to be incorporated into a new service, known as the Agricultural Development and Advisory Service (A.D.A.S.), to start in March 1971.

12. Faced by a growing commitment on deficiency payments whenever over-production occurred, the Government countered by tying the guaranteed price to a 'standard quantity' or quota for a particular commodity, everything in excess to take its chance on the market. On the other hand it promised not to reduce guarantees by more than a fixed percentage in any one year or series of years; and it co-ordinated these measures with international agreements aimed at limiting food imports from abroad.

13. Two main methods have come under investigation. One is to store liquid or semi-liquid manure, and return it to the land by pipeline or tanker-spreader. The other is to reduce the quantity of effluent by microbiological action in a lagoon or oxidation ditch, and spread the indigestible solids over the land in the ordinary way.

14. Quoted from 'Maximum Profit—Not Maximum Output' by H. G. C. Sexton, in *Country Life* of 2nd July, 1970.

15. Buying groups exist independently of marketing groups. When both functions are combined, they approach more nearly to the farmers' 'co-op', but on a selective and compulsory basis.

16. In 1962 the National Farmers' Union set up the Agricultural Central Trading Co. Ltd. (A.C.T.) to help co-ordinate the groups. In the same year the Government formed the Agricultural Marketing and Development Committee (A.M.D.E.C.) for 'promoting the business efficiency of local producers' marketing organisations, and

assisting the formation of new ones'. Some of the functions of this body were taken over by the Central Council for Agricultural and Horticultural Co-operation, following the passage of the Agriculture Act 1967, which offers financial assistance for co-operative production and marketing. A.M.D.E.C. was dissolved in 1971.

17. In 1970 the Agricultural Mortgage Corporation was lending money to farmers at 10¾ per cent.

18. *The Structure of Agriculture*, H.M.S.O., 1966.

19. *The Agricultural Significance of the Hills* by B. R. Davidson and G. P. Wibberley; Report No. 3, Wye College, November 1956.

20. The special forms of assistance were extended in 1951 and 1956 to livestock-rearing farms 'down the hill', while the scale of grants has latterly been increased.

21. The Rural Development Board set up for Wales was abolished in 1970. Local feeling was hostile. Criteria for amalgamation were considered unrealistic and harsh, likewise the measures for integration with other forms of land use. This was a tactical failure. On the other hand the Rural Development Board for the North Pennines seemed better based and handled, but this too was abolished in 1971.

22. The critical measurement adopted was not one of acreage, but of 'standard man days', each of eight hours' work by an adult male under average working conditions.

23. The criterion of 'standard man days' was an important element in the N.A.A.S. assessment.

24. *Farming in Britain Today* by J. G. S. and Frances Donaldson, in association with Derek Barber, Allen Lane, The Penguin Press, 1969, p. 128.

25. About 200,000 holdings of an average size of sixteen acres, according to the Government Survey of 1966.

26. 8600 full-time, 6800 part-time. See *Departmental Committee of Inquiry into Statutory Smallholdings*, H.M.S.O., 1966–7.

27. Donaldson, op. cit., p. 128.

28. In 1971 it was stated on behalf of agriculture that three per cent of the working population of the country was manning an industry with a turnover exceeding £2000 million a year – more than steel or motor cars.

29. Paul Cheshire of Reading University, writing in *The Sunday Times* of 8th February, 1970.

30. I am deliberately omitting any reference to the impact upon food prices and home agriculture, should Britain join the Common Market. At the time of writing there is no certainty of this taking place, but see Postscript.

31. Architectural Press, 1967, pp. 103–8, for this and the next two quotations.

32. The total value of agricultural exports in 1969 was £400 million.

33. Milk heated to ultra-high temperatures and packed in aseptic cartons.

34. Weller, op. cit., p. 159.

35. See the Agricultural Land Classification Reports, first published in 1965. These show how cropping is affected by physical factors.

36. Latest edition published by Longmans, 1962.

37. *The Changing Use of Land in Britain* by Robin H. Best and J. T. Coppock, Faber, 1962.

38. Geoffrey Sinclair, Head of Field Survey, under Miss Coleman, writes: 'Most agricultural and urban mapping was done by volunteers, but grant-aid was necessary to secure the completion in England and Wales of the field work and the vegetation mapping. Publication is on the 2½-inch scale. A Fringe/Scape analysis is also under way for the production of special maps at 1:400,000. On the basis of land-use data, Wild-

scape, Farmscape and Townscape are defined. Where none of these clearly characterises the landscape, fringes are indicated. Recognition and ₊napping of these fringes have great planning significance. The largest project is a Wildscape Atlas which will replace the orthodox land-use sheets in upland areas. This is designed to show all vegetation types by species and habitat types in addition to all woodland areas. Scale, 1:100,000.'

39. Weller, op. cit., pp. 165–6.

40. Ibid., p. 169.

41. Contributed to *The Optimum Population for Britain*. See Note 3.

42. Miles, op. cit., p. 100.

43. Ibid.

44. 1,800,000 acres of plantation under Commission ownership, 1,200,000 acres in management schemes on private estates.

45. One of the most cogent statements directed against softwood forestry is entitled *The Future of Industrial Cellulose: Unlimited or End in Sight?* by H. C. Dawkins of the Commonwealth Forestry Institute, Oxford. The essentials of his thesis were first presented to the High Wycombe branch of the Institute of Wood Science in February 1967. In this paper the author suggested that 'fine timber will indeed be the *only* possible direct material product of forestry in the not-so-distant future, because cellulose will cease to be either practicable or economic as a bulk raw material for industry. . . . The primary purpose of a forest might be its scenic value, its water or wildlife, its pheasants, its shelter and environment, its concealment of mine workings or all of these, and from it we will aim to obtain the best possible yield of woods, mainly in due course the ornamental or artistic, without jeopardising its principal objectives and assisting thereby to pay for them.'

46. *Forestry, Agriculture and Marginal Land*, A Report by the Natural Resources (Technical) Committee, H.M.S.O., 1957.

47. This was one of the aims of the Rural Development Boards envisaged in the Agriculture Act 1967, but which ran into trouble and have since been abolished.

48. Quoted from *Timber, Your Growing Investment*. Text by H. L. Edlin, Forestry Commission Booklet No. 23, H.M.S.O., 1969.

49. A powerful critic is Professor Geoffrey Dimbleby, head of the Department of Human Environment at the University of London, who is strongly opposed for instance to the operations of the Forestry Commission in the New Forest.

50. No comparable machinery exists for consultation outside National Parks, Areas of Outstanding Natural Beauty (A.O.N.B.s), or land controlled by the Rural Development Boards. There is intermittent pressure e.g. by organisations such as the Ramblers' Association, to bring forestry under planning and ensure complete control by statutory means. See the quotation from Miles, op. cit., p. 95.

51. Miles, op. cit., p. 95.

52. *Forestry in the Landscape* by Sylvia Crowe, Forestry Commission Booklet No. 18, H.M.S.O., 1966.

53. Proceedings of Association of River Authorities Conference, May 1969.

54. These are nett figures, based on statistics from the Water Resources Board, after allowing for re-use. See 'Planning our future water resources', by L. E. Taylor, published in *Chemistry and Industry*, 1970, pp. 668–73.

55. River Authorities were earlier known as Catchment Boards (1930), and River Boards (1945). There are separate organisations for Scotland and N. Ireland.

56. Quoted from his address to the National Conference of the Council for the

Protection of Rural England (C.P.R.E.), held at Exeter University in September 1969.

57. Robert Arvill in *Man and Environment*, Pelican Original, 1969, p. 69.

58. Inaugurated by the Mineral Workings Act 1951.

59. Quoted from the Lower Swansea Valley Project Report.

60. Government aid of up to seventy-five per cent of the cost of reclamation is also available for National Parks and A.O.N.B.s; but these are not places where dereliction occurs on any scale. Grant-aid is also applicable to afforestation.

61. *Derelict Britain*, by John Barr, Pelican Original, 1969, p. 206.

62. Formerly known as the Conservation Corps.

63. Farming, forestry, gardening, estate work, water management, local extractive industries (other than mass mining operations), etc.

64. Many people of course travel much farther for daily employment, but I suggest five to ten miles as the optimum radius. If regular journeys are too long, or otherwise too burdensome for the person concerned, he or she will ultimately decide to seek a new home nearer work.

65. Quality goods, not amenable to mass production, offer obvious scope. In addition a number of country firms are under contract manufacturing small parts and components which large urban enterprises do not wish to bother with, and find it better business to farm out. See Note 66.

66. Much valuable research into the problems of small industry in the countryside has been carried out by Miss K. S. Woods. See particularly her *Development of Country Towns in the South-West Midlands during the 1960s*, published by the Oxford Agricultural Economics Research Institute in August 1968.

67. See *People and the Countryside* by H. E. Bracey, Routledge and Kegan Paul, 1970, pp. 52–56.

68. The Redcliffe-Maud Report 1969 for the reform of local government, being based on population, was particularly urban-biassed. It is too early to comment upon the Government's proposals, issued in February 1971.

69. So far as I know this procedure is not yet in force, but it is implied in certain provisions incorporated in The Countryside Act 1968, arising out of the Exmoor controversy, as related in the text.

70. The best account is now available in *The Vegetation of Exmoor* by Geoffrey Sinclair, Exmoor Press, 1970.

71. First published in *The Architect's Journal* of 20th June, 1965, and reprinted in the Civic Trust Survey, *The Challenge of Leisure*.

72. The Nature Conservancy is a component of the National Environment Research Council (N.E.R.C.).

73. 'Broadly speaking Nature Reserves are established primarily for their high scientific interest or because they are ideally suited for the teaching of field biology or for a combination of these reasons.' S.P.N.R. Conservation Liaison Committee Technical Publication No. 2, p. 8.

74. In 1970 only 0·6 per cent of all land in the U.K. was in Nature Reserves.

75. A useful guide to procedure is *Definitive Maps of Public Paths* by Mary McArevey, Commons, Open Spaces and Footpaths Preservation Society, 1970.

76. The National Parks Commission was renamed The Countryside Commission, and re-constituted with wider powers under the Countryside Act 1968.

77. Committee for Environmental Conservation (CoEnCo) was formed in November 1969. Its purpose is 'harness the local and specialised expertise of voluntary bodies, by providing an organisation at national level which will enable them to speak to the

Government on matters of general principle affecting the environment'. In a sense CoEnCo is the voluntary counterpart of the statutory National Environment Research Council (N.E.R.C.).

Postscript

1. Horticulture is likely to benefit most from the imposition of levies.

2. E.g. the dissolution of A.M.D.E.C. (see Note 16, Part Three) and the replacement of N.A.A.S by A.D.A.S. (see Note 11) in early 1971.

3. H.M.S.O., 1971.

Appendix

1. *The Living Soil* by Lady Eve Balfour, Faber, 1943.

2. *The Living Rocks* by Harry Walters, Classic Publications, 1967.

3. Hydroponics is a system of raising plants in salt solutions, without soil.

4. Published in *The Soil Association Journal*, July 1970.

5. *Human Ecology* by Sir George Stapledon, edited by Robert Waller, Soil Association, 1968, p. 55 et seq.

6. Notably *The World of the Soil* by Sir John Russell, Fontana, 1961.

7. Arthropods, i.e. segmented creatures such as woodlice, spiders, centipedes and other insects.

8. *Le Sol fait le Climat* by Maxime Guillaume, Editions Vie et Action, 1970.

9. Quoted from 'Soils, Manures and Artificial Fertilisers' by Tommaso Del Pelo Pardi, published in *The Soil Association Journal*, April 1965.

Background Bibliography

All sources of information are recorded in the Notes; but the following list is recommended as a guide to general reading.

Part One
ERNIE, LORD, *English Farming, Past and Present*, Heinemann and Frank Cass, 1961.
HOWES, FRANK, *Folk Music of Britain . . . And Beyond*, Methuen, 1969.
MILES, ROGER O., *Forestry in the English Landscape*, Faber, 1967.
MURRAY, KEITH A., *Agriculture* (History of the Second World War), H.M.S.O. and Longmans, 1955.
ORWIN, CHRISTABEL S. and WHETHAM, EDITH H., *History of British Agriculture, 1846–1914*, Longmans, 1964.
TROW-SMITH, ROBERT, *Society and the Land*, Cresset Press, 1953.

Part Two—A
HOSKINS, W. G., *The Making of the English Landscape*, Hodder and Stoughton, 1955.
The New Naturalist Series, published by Collins, and particularly
STAMP, SIR DUDLEY, *Nature Conservation in Britain*, Collins, 1969.
OSBORN, SIR FREDERIC J., *Green-Belt Cities*, Evelyn, Adams and Mackay, 1969.
READE, WINWOOD and STUTTARD, R. M., *A Handbook for Naturalists*, Evans Bros., 1968.

Part Two—B
BONHAM-CARTER, VICTOR and CURRY, W. B., *Dartington Hall*, The Exmoor Press, 1970.
EMERY, ANTHONY, *Dartington Hall*, O.U.P., 1970.

Part Three
ARVILL, ROBERT, *Man and Environment*, Pelican, 1969.
BARR, JOHN, *Derelict Britain*, Pelican, 1969.
BEST, ROBIN H. and COPPOCK, J. T., *The Changing Use of Land in Britain*, Faber, 1962.
BRACEY, H. E., *People and the Countryside*, Routledge and Kegan Paul, 1970.
DONALDSON, J. G. S. and F., and BARBER, D., *Farming in Britain Today*, Allen Lane, The Penguin Press, 1969.
FAIRBROTHER, NAN, *New Lives, New Landscapes*, Architectural Press, 1970.
MILES, ROGER O., *Forestry in the English Landscape*, Faber, 1967.
PATMORE, J. ALLAN, *Land and Leisure*, David and Charles, 1970.
TAYLOR, L. E., editor, *The Optimum Population for Britain*, Academic Press, 1970.
WELLER, JOHN, *Modern Agriculture and Rural Planning*, Architectural Press, 1967.

Appendix
STAPLEDON, SIR GEORGE, *Human Ecology*, edited by Robert Waller, Faber, 1964.

Index

This Index is divided for convenience into General Subjects and Personalities.

GENERAL SUBJECTS

PERSONALITIES